THE
FATEFUL
LIGHTNING

THE FATEFUL LIGHTNING

CIVIL WAR
EYEWITNESS REPORTS

Compiled and Edited by

Harold Elk Straubing

Paragon House Publishers

New York

First paperback edition, 1987
Published by
Paragon House Publishers
2 Hammarskjöld Plaza
New York, New York 10017

Library of Congress Cataloging-in-Publication Data

The fateful lightning.

Originally published under title: Civil War
eyewitness reports.
Includes index.
1. United States—History—Civil War,
1861-1865—Personal narratives. I. Straubing,
Harold Elk, 1918–
E601.C52 1987   973.7′8   87-1744
ISBN 0-913729-64-7 (pbk.)

For my wife, Helen, who saw me through World War II and my daughter, Michelle, who saw me through the war between the states.

Contents

Preface

The span of the curious who find the Civil War a fascinating panorama covers historians and scholars to the itinerant tourist looking for some place of interest to visit. Some of the scenes of battle remain untouched, untrampled except for the people who carry maps and cameras. Other sites are not that fortunate. Gettysburg hosts 1.5 million people a year, has a newly built tower that stands 307 feet tall with an observation deck so that visitors can view the area where 43,000 men were killed.

Part of the fascination with the period is derived from the fact that this was a war fought in our own backyard. Our troops didn't run off to the beaches of Europe, the deserts of Africa, the islands of the South Pacific, isolated portions of Asia, or the Middle East. In a handful of states, 2.3 million men were involved in a fight to the death. On one side, the Federal forces had the factories, the ships, and the railroads. The Confederacy had the superior generals, a united front, and the greatest will to do battle.

So the Civil War in the United States has become a giant board game. The generals/admirals can be charted dashing into battle with their troops/sailors gallantly following close behind. The brutality of the war is also well known. It was a war where commanding officers on horseback, along with foot soldiers, died in the heat of the fighting. Admiral and common sailor, alike, fell in the midst of naval engagements. Civilians suffered incredible hardships. This was the period that ended wooden battleships, and introduced the twentieth-century navy.

Weaponry was becoming more sophisticated, and the ability to kill and maim far exceeded the medical care afforded the wounded. The basic weapon used by both sides as the war progressed was the Springfield rifle, 1861 model. An expert rifleman could get off two shots in a minute. The ammunition was a paper cartridge that contained powder and ball. The infantryman tore it open with his teeth, poured the powder down the barrel, and jammed in the bullet with his thumb. Then, with the aid of his ramrod, he would force the bullet down. He placed the ramrod back in its tube, pulled back the hammer, put a percussion cap on the nipple under the hammer; now the rifle was ready for firing. The bullet was the minie ball, a conical lead slug about one-half inch in diameter and weighing about an ounce. When it hit a man, the ball smashed bones making amputations necessary. Intestinal wounds, because of the tearing action, were almost always fatal. From the various cannons, ugly injuries were caused by grape shot and shrapnel. First aid stations were set up close to the fighting, but antiseptics were unknown. The wounded that survived the initial attack suffered infection and gangrene as dirty fingers probed wounds; bandages were made of old uniforms, and rags were applied to the torn flesh. Final statistics revealed that between battlefield losses and prisoner of war camps, one out of every four soldiers died during the war.

When hostilities began, the United States Army had 115 trained medical officers. At the start of mobilization twenty-seven of them resigned. Three entered private practice and twenty-four went to the Confederacy. By the end of the war, the medical corps for the Union alone numbered in excess of ten thousand men. Edwin Stanton, Secretary of War under Lincoln, turned down all pleas for an ambulance service. Field commanders had to evacuate the wounded in whatever manner was available. Some moved by trains, others by boat. It took some convincing, but General McClellan finally gave permission to form an ambulance corps that first saw service at the Battle of Antietam in September 1862.

I first began to wonder about the individuals swept up in the Civil War, regardless of rank, during World War II when I marched and hiked through the hills of Virginia and Pennsylvania as an army recruit, covering the same trails that the soldiers in blue and those in grey uniforms had trod less than eighty years before. I was bitten by the progeny of insects that tasted those who wore both uniforms; chiggers have no respect for any flag. I began to wonder about the average soldier and sailor in the Civil War. What did he feel, experience, as the generals and their adjutants sat in their headquarters mapping strategies and deciding what would be "acceptable losses" among the troops. What were the generals and admirals thinking, saying? What did the people on the home front encounter when they went shopping for food and clothing? There was no rationing, and in most instances there was no longer any product. What happened to slaves as they became free? What kind of treatment was afforded the American Indian as Federal troops moved West?

Here is a kaleidescope of events of that amazing period covering different phases of the Civil War in the United States from the homefront to the front lines. Here is history carved from the heart of America by Americans who lived during the most trying of times. Smell the gunpowder, and endure the deprivation. Experience the maturing of the United States when it happened, by the people who made it happen.

This book presents what many people feel is the real birth of our nation, and it is written by the people who suffered through the pain and the agony.

MEN AT WAR

THE ARMY

Ball's Bluff and
the Union High Command

A reconnaissance blunder set off a battle that ended in a Federal disaster. The scouts had been deceived or were mistaken. They relayed the information that only a handful of Confederate troops were stationed in Leesburg. Based on this information, all arrangements were made to proceed with the attack. Because of the topography and the lack of adequate transportation, what should have been an easy Union victory became an abysmal defeat.

Colonel Baker, an inept military commander, and ex-United States Senator from Oregon, led an ill-fated charge that not only killed many of his men but took his life as well. It was a minor battle, as battles go, but since an ex-senator lost his life, a congressional investigation questioned the leadership of the army. McClellan, fighting for his chance to take complete charge, indirectly placed the blame on General Winfield Scott, General-in-Chief of the Army. Of course Scott knew nothing about the skirmish at Ball's Bluff, but he was in command of the army and accepted the responsibility.

A month later General Scott resigned, and Major General McClellan moved into his job. It was a little battle that cost 350 lives, with 500 men taken prisoner, but because of the Battle of Ball's Bluff, the destiny of the war took a new direction.

The following excerpt is taken from *The Civil War in Song & Story* by Frank Moore (P. F. Collier, 1865).

The history of the battle of Ball's Bluff has never been pub-

3

lished. No event of the war since the assault upon Fort Sumter created a like sensation; and the cause of the disaster, the name of the persons culpable, or the plans and purposes of the officers who ordered the movement, have not officially or certainly been made known. The report of General Stone, in command, was not satisfactory to the country, and Congress called upon the War Department for the facts. Major-General McClellan, who, it was known, ordered the movement, refused to furnish the facts. The insulted Congress repeated its demand, and received a second time the same answer.

A joint committee of both Houses of Congress was appointed to inquire into the "conduct of the present war," especially, as was remarked in the debate, "as regards the battle of Ball's Bluff."

That Committee has as yet made no report*. General Stone, by order of the President, was arrested and imprisoned upon several charges involving disloyalty, and "for misconduct at the battle of Ball's Bluff."

After a confinement of six months he was discharged without trial, and the cherished expectations of the public for the facts so long withheld were again disappointed.

Ball's Buff, so called from Mr. Ball, a farmer living in the vicinity, is a bold embankment, of one hundred feet elevation, on the Virginia shore of the Potomac, three miles from Leesburg northwesterly, and an equal distance from Edwards' Ferry in a southern direction. Poolsville, Md., lies opposite, five miles, and by the road running easterly, Washington is distant thirty-four miles. From the river's edge to the summit, the Bluff is covered with trees and bushes, which, joining with the woods on either side, enclose above, in the form of a half circle, an open natural clearing of seven acres. In the middle of the Potomac, in front of the Bluff, lies Harrison's Island, a fertile strip of land two hundred yards wide and four miles long.

---

*This paper was written in July, 1862. The report of the War Committee, published in March, 1863, corroborates all its statements. The late restoration of Gen. Stone to active duty is a vindication and acquittal of misconduct charged upon him, and places the responsibility upon another.

At a distance of half a mile north of the Bluff is Smoot's Mill, situated upon a gentle slope of the bank, and near to it a road leads from the river, by an easy ascent to the Leesburg turnpike, which, running southerly to Drainesville, passes near to Edwards' Ferry. On the day of the battle General McCall, with twenty-four thousand men, was in that turnpike, nine miles from Ball's Bluff, and General Gorman, with fourteen hundred men was at Edwards' Ferry on the Virginia side. The whole distance from Ball's Bluff to the Maryland side of the Potomac, across Harrison's Island, is not six hundred yards.

On Sunday night, Oct. 20, 1861, in obedience to orders of General Stone, Colonel Devens of the Fifteenth Mass. Volunteers, proceeded with three hundred men, from camp at Poolsville to a point opposite Ball's Bluff and Harrison's Island, and in three small boats crossed to the Virginia shore, arriving at the summit just before daylight. The landing-place was soft and mucky, and the ascent winding and difficult. At the same time four companies of the First Minnesota Volunteers crossed the river at Edwards' Ferry. No enemy was encountered at either place, and his pickets had not been seen for two days. Whatever knowledge of the topography of our country our forces possessed had been acquired by distant observation from Maryland, and no guide accompanied them.

At daybreak Colonel Devens led his troops over the open field, and through the woods towards and within one mile of Leesburg, where, in scattered small numbers he descried rebels, and after exchanging several volleys with them at long range, fell back to the woods. Here being attacked, he repulsed the enemy with small loss on both sides, and then retired to the Bluff, where he was joined by the remainder of his regiment, and by Colonel Lee with one hundred men of the Twentieth Mass. Volunteers, making in all seven hundred and twenty Federal troops across the river. The day was fair.

At the same time, eight o'clock, A.M., Colonel Baker arrived from his camp near Poolsville on the Maryland side, opposite where he found the first battalion of the California regiment, six hundred and eighty officers and men, Lieutenant-Colonel Wistar commanding. He was informed of an order from General Stone, then at Edwards' Ferry, that in the event of heavy firing in front, the California Battalion should cross and reinforce Colonel Devens. Upon inquiring as to the means of transportation, and learning that they consisted of two frail scows, each capable of carrying twenty-five men, and the river deep and rapid, Colonel Baker rode in haste to Edwards' Ferry that he might have better assurance of an order so extraordinary.

Meanwhile several dead and wounded arrived from the Bluff, where firing was growing more frequent, and three companies of the California regiment crossed to Harrison's Island. Colonel Baker returned from Edwards' Ferry at eleven o'clock, bearing a written order from General Stone to reinforce or retire Colonel Devens, "in his discretion."

The returned wounded reported the enemy in force, pressing Colonel Devens. How could seven hundred men be safely retired in two small boats under the fire of a bloodthirsty and superior enemy? Shall they be left to their fate, or will he reinforce them and share their peril? Colonel Baker was not long in determining upon his course of duty.

A larger scow, discovered in the canal running parallel to the river, was with great labor dragged across the tow-path and launched in the channel. Placing Captain Ritman in charge of the transportation of the troops, and directing that they should cross as rapidly as possible, with his staff composed of Assistant Adjutant-General Harvey and Captain Young, Brigade Quartermaster, Colonel Baker embarked for the Island, where, on the western side, he found three hundred men awaiting their chance to go over to the Virginia shore. Impressed with the grave responsibility of his position, Colonel Baker was silently remarking the two small boats plying with their heavy freight of reinforcements, when his attention was called to an officer of one of the Massachusetts regiments standing on the Virginia shore, who cried out, "We can see three regiments of the enemy coming down from Leesburg."

Colonel Baker responded, "All right; be of good cheer— there will be more for us to whip"—and immediately crossed the river. On reaching the summit, and assuming command, he found the Massachusetts troops drawn up on the right of the field in good order, quietly awaiting a nearer attack of the enemy, who, though silent, with the exception of occasional shots, were known to be in large force in the woods in the front and on the right. It was three o'clock before all of the California battalion had crossed and climbed the Bluff, which, joined to two companies of the Tammany regiment, made with the Massachusetts troops, our whole force seventeen hundred.

An order was received from General Stone advising Colonel Baker that the enemy was four thousand strong, and that he might count upon General Gorman coming to his reinforcement from Edwards' Ferry, on the left. He decided, therefore, not to advance, but await the arrival of the promised aid, formed his line of battle by placing Colonel Devens and his command on the right at the border of the woods, resting upon and making a right angle with the centre, composed of two companies of Twentieth Mass. and two companies of the Tammany regiment; the California battalion forming the left and touching the woods bounding the plateau to the south.

The ground, sloping from a point distant thirty yards from the edge of the cliff, afforded a fair cover for men lying upon their faces, from the increasing fire of the enemy in the woods. At three o'clock Colonel Coggswell of the Tammany regiment arrived upon the field, and being received by Colonel Baker with much enthusiasm, was placed in command of the artillery, consisting of one six-pounder and two mountain howitzers, then in charge of Lieutenant Bramhall, of the Ninth New York State Militia. The pieces were drawn into the open field, twenty yards in advance of the centre of the line of battle.

Colonel Baker, with his staff on foot,—there were no mounted officers on the field,—traversed several times the whole line of forces under his command, addressing pleasant words to officers and men, and setting them an example of coolness, courage, and confidence. From the Maryland shore frequent shells came flying over the river and bluff, bursting harmlessly far in the rear of the enemy, who seemed patiently to defer his attack until we crossed in greater numbers.

At precisely four o'clock loud yells proceeded a flashing line of fire in the woods, and the report of a thousand rifles announced the opening of the engagement with part of the enemy, several of whom had climbed into the trees, that they might have a better aim at our recumbent men. For nearly an hour showers of bullets and buck-shot continued to pour upon our devoted line; but considering the nearness of the enemy, the casualties were not very great. On our part the cannon alone for the first half hour responded with thundering voice, clearly telling General Stone and the Union forces at Edwards' Ferry of the hot engagement near them; and flying farther, reached the ears of General McCall and his division, which by order of Major-General McClellan, was returning to its camp at Drainesville. Six thousand troops had, during the afternoon, assembled at the crossing place opposite the bluff, but by reason of the small means of transportation, were obliged to remain there regarding in helplessness and rage the unequal contest. A rope had been stretched across the channel to the island, which aided much in the passage of the boats; but from the Virginia side there was no rope, and the solitary leaky scow was poled over and back slowly.

By five o'clock nearly two thousand men had ascended to the bluff, and engaged in most part in returning the fire of the enemy. Notwithstanding the discouraging aspect of matters, our troops generally exhibited good feeling, determined courage, and obedience to command. The wounded and some dead were carried by their comrades down the hill, who, after placing them in the boat, returned to the field. The enemy was several times driven back with great loss by discharges of the cannon, which after the artillery men had been killed or wounded, was loaded and fired by Colonel Coggswell, Lieutenant Bramhall, and other officers. A volley of musketry from the thick forest on the left attracted our attention, and Colonel Baker, thinking it came from the expected and promised reinforcement from Edwards' Ferry, ordered a company of the California men to advance cautiously, and discover if they were friends or foes.

The officer commanding the company, having called out, "Who are you?" received for answer, "Confederates!" and another volley following immediately, many of our men were killed and wounded. Colonel Baker fell dead, struck with three balls. Five or six rebels ran from the woods towards his body, lying ten yards in advance of the line of battle, when Captain Bieral, of the California regiment, with a dozen of his men, dashed forward, and driving the others back, rescued the corpse and sword, which were immediately carried from the field by Captain Young, who had but a moment before been ordered by Colonel Baker to go to General Stone, and report the state of the engagement, and ask for reinforcements.

At the same time Lieutenant Colonel Wistar and Lieutenant Bramhill, being severely wounded, were helped down the hill, and with Colonel Baker's body, safely reached the island. At the last discharge of the cannon it recoiled even to the edge of the cliff, and falling over, was inextricably lost in the rock and jungle. Later the two howitzers, which had not been fired during the engagement, were thrown over the bank, and they with the cannon were afterwards recovered by the enemy.

By seniority Colonel Coggswell assumed command, and regarding the battle as hopelessly lost, and there being no retreat by the river, he determined to fight his way to Edwards' Ferry. By his order the Fifteenth Massachusetts moved across the field from the right to the left of the line, where the two companies of the Tammany regiment had already moved. While making the proper arrangements for retreat, a rebel officer misled our troops by approaching them and giving a command to charge upon a large body of the enemy who now occupied our late position on the right. Rushing forward en masse, our men received a destructive fire, and the line being broken, general confusion ensued for a few moments. Re-forming in line, several volleys were exchanged with the enemy, who were now near, in sight, in front, with considerable loss on both sides; but night coming on, and no one knowing the road to Edwards' Ferry, Colonel Coggswell abandoned his plan of retreat to that point, and gave an order to fall back to the river's bank, below the Bluff, leaving two companies above to hold the enemy in check. At this moment, the only boat in the channel was seen to go down, overloaded with wounded and fugitives; and thus disappeared the only means of escape, except by swimming. The enemy soon occupied the heights, and poured down a fatal fire upon the crowded mass below. Three times bodies of our men climbed to the summit, and after delivering their fire, returned to their helpless comrades below. Throwing their arms and clothing into the river, many swam for the island, while others, aided by the increasing darkness, crept along the bank above and below the

Bluff, and on logs, and in a small skiff which by good fortune was found, escaped.

There was no formal surrender, but a sullen submission to adverse fate. The colors, heavily weighted with stones, were cast into the stream.

At eight o'clock all firing and noise had ceased, save the moans of the wounded, and the shrieks of the drowning in their vain attempts to swim to the island. At midnight twenty-two-commissioned officers and seven hundred and ten men were prisoners of war, on their march to Leesburg.

Never was a conquered army less subdued in spirit. Astounded, bewildered, indignant, there was no feeling of shame, for never did soldiers conduct themselves with more courage. Each man felt that something had gone wrong. "Some one had blundered," or maybe worse, and silently marching under the rebel guard, each sought in his own mind, or in whispering voices of his companions, for an explanation of the disaster.

The enemy's force engaged is not known, but is stated in the report of Colonel Evans, who commanded them, at twenty-six hundred. It is believed that there were full four thousand. His loss was not less than four hundred, mostly killed. On our side the casualties cannot be precisely stated, as many were missing whose death by drowning or killed on the field could not be ascertained. The total loss was one hundred and fifty killed, two hundred wounded, and seven hundred and ten taken prisoners.

Such is the narrative of the affair at Ball's Bluff, as told by those who were engaged in it, but had no part in its planning, and are still ignorant of its purpose. As stated, all attempts to discover the object of sending across the Potomac at that point a small force, while Generals McCall and Smith, with over twenty thousand men, were already on the Virginia side, within nine miles of Leesburg, have not been successful. In vain is the inquiry repeated, "Why was Ball's Bluff chosen as a crossing-place, while, at a distance of one half mile above it, the land slopes to the river bank, and an easy ascent and open country would have placed our force on equal footing with the enemy? Why was not transportation provided in advance, adequate for a successful withdrawal of Colonel Devens and Lee and their commands or for throwing over a large force for their support?

The movement was not unpremeditated, and there was no want of boats or material for pontoons and bridges in the vicinity of Harrison's Island. An army of ten thousand men had been lying idle at Poolsville for months, expecting at some time to cross the river. The canal leading to Washington offered excellent facilities for furnishing the necessary means for crossing, and three frail scows, made of inch plank, and one skiff, were all that our army found there on the day of the battle.

Why were not the promised reinforcements sent to our aid from Edwards' Ferry? During the engagement fourteen hundred troops, under the command of General Gorman, awaited on the Virginia shore, at Edwards' Ferry, an order to march to our aid; and in his report General Gorman says, that the moment Colonel Baker fell, General Stone sent an order for them to throw up intrenchments! There was no enemy between Edwards' Ferry and the battle field, and we may fairly suppose that one hundred men coming up and attacking them on their flank would have changed the fortunes of that day.

That night General McClellan, at Washington, having learned of the disastrous result of the expedition he had ordered, dispatched an order to General Banks, at Darnstown, Md., twelve miles from Ball's Bluff, to march his division to the Potomac, at the same points, which during the day had been occupied by eight thousand of our troops, vainly demanding transportation to their commands over the river! Generals McCall and Smith, at Drainesville, Va., received no orders. Two days afterwards all of the Federal forces returned to their respective camps; and thus concluded the affair of Ball's Bluff.

Diary of a Conscientious Objector

As the war wore on, volunteers needed to fill out the ranks became scarce. Wounded and crippled veterans began flooding home, dulling the edge of patriotism. Conscription acts were required to refill the ranks, and the Confederacy passed a strong law including all able-bodied men between the ages of eighteen and thirty-five. The only exception was an owner or overseer of twenty or more slaves. The Union's draft act had too many loopholes. Each state was responsible for a quota that was broken down into congressional districts. If there were enough volunteers from the district, there was no need for conscripting any·one. If an individual was drafted, upon the payment of three hundred dollars, he would be exempt, but he would be subject to the next draft call. If he found a substitute to take his place, he would have a permanent exemption.

Brokers set up businesses and for a fee they would find a substitute. They offered money to alcoholics, tramps, the feebleminded, etc. It was a type of soldier that proved to be of very little use to the army. Other states offered bounty to any man who would enlist. These men received as much as one thousand dollars to join the armed forces. Many would promptly desert and show up in another state, enlisting to receive another bounty.

The army was much concerned with the quality of recruits it was receiving, and so when men who had religious objections to the war were brought into the armed forces, they were promptly lumped with the other malcontents the draft had produced. The following diary excerpts of a conscientious objector illustrate to what lengths the army went to make "soldiers" of draftees who were snatched out of their homes and friendly environments and tossed into the cold, hard world of war. These excerpts are taken from *The Civil War Diary of Cyrus Pringle* (Pendle Hill Pamphlet 122, printed by Sowers Printing Co., Lebanon, Pennsylvania, June 1962.). A Quaker, Pringle was drafted into the Union forces on July 13, 1863, at Burlington, Vermont.

Brattleboro. 26th, 8th month, 1863. Twenty-five or thirty caged lions roam lazily to and fro through this building hour after hour through the day. On every side without, sentries pace their slow beat, bearing loaded muskets. Men are ranging through the grounds, or hanging in synods about the doors of the different buildings, apparently without a purpose. Aimless is military life, except betimes its aid is deadly. Idle life blends with violent death-struggles till the man is unmade a man; and henceforth there is little of manhood about him. Of a man he is made a soldier, which is a man-destroying machine in two senses—a thing for the prosecuting or repelling an invasion like the block of stone in the fortress or the plate of iron on the side of the *Monitor*. They are alike. I have tried in vain to define a difference, and I see only this. The iron-clad with its gun is a bigger soldier; the more formidable in attack, the less liable to destruction in a given time; the block the most capable of resistance, both are equally obedient to officers. Or the more perfect is the soldier, the more nearly he approaches these in this respect.

Three times a day we are marched out to the mess houses for our rations. In our hands we carry a tin plate, whereon we bring back a piece of bread (sour and tough most likely), and a cup. Morning and noon a piece of meat, antique betimes, bears company with the bread. They who wish it receive in their cups two sorts of decoctions: in the morning burnt bread, or peas perhaps, steeped in water with some saccharine substance added (I dare not affirm it to be sugar). At night steeped tea extended by some other herbs probably and its pungency and acridity assuaged by the saccharine principle aforementioned. On this we have so far subsisted and, save some nauseating, comfortably. As we go out and return, on right and left and in front and rear go bayonets. Some substitutes heretofore have escaped and we are not to be neglected in our attendants. Hard beds are healthy, but I query cannot the result be defeated by the *degree?* Our mattresses are boards. Only the slight elasticity of our thin blankets breaks the fall of our flesh and bones thereon. Oh! now I praise the discipline I have received from uncarpeted floors through warm summer nights of my boyhood.

The building resounds with petty talk; jokes and laughter and swearing. Something more than that. Many of the caged lions are engaged with cards, and money changes hands freely. Some of the caged lions read, and some sleep, and so the weary day goes by.

L. M. M. and I addressed the following letter to Governor Holbrook and hired a corporal to forward it to him.

Brattleboro, Vt., 26th, 8th month, 1863.

Frederick Holbrook,
      Governor of Vermont:—

We, the undersigned members of the Society of Friends, beg leave to represent to thee, that we were lately drafted in the 3rd Dist. of Vermont, have been forced into the army and reached the camp near this town yesterday.

That in the language of the elders of our New York Yearly Meeting, "We love our country and acknowledge with gratitude to our Heavenly Father the many blessings we have been favoured with under the government; and can feel no sympathy with any who seek its overthrow."

But that, true to well-known principles of our Society, we cannot violate our religious convictions either by complying with military requisitions or by the equivalents of this compliance—the furnishing of a substitute or payment of commutation money. That, therefore, we are brought into suffering and exposed to insult and contempt from those who have us in charge, as well as to the penalties of insubordination, though liberty of conscience is granted us by the Constitution of Vermont as well as that of the United States.

Therefore, we beg of thee as Governor of our State any assistance thou may be able to render, should it be no more than the influence of thy position in our behalf.

Truly Thy Friend,

Cyrus G. Pringle.

P.S.—We are informed we are to be sent to the vicinity of Boston tomorrow.

27th—On board train to Boston. The long afternoon of yesterday passed slowly away. The morning passed by, the time of our stay in Brattleboro, and we neither saw nor heard anything of our Governor. We suppose he could not or would not help us. So as we go down to our trial we have no arm to lean upon among all men; but why dost thou complain, oh, my Soul? Seek thou that faith that will prove a buckler to thy breast, and gain for thee the protection of an arm mightier than the arms of all men.

Camp Vermont: Long Island, Boston Harbor, 28th.—In the early morning damp and cool we marched down off the heights of Brattleboro to take train for this place. Once in the car the dashing young cavalry officer, who had us in charge, gave notice he had placed men through the cars, with loaded revolvers, who had orders to shoot any person attempting to escape, or jump from the window, and that anyone would be shot if he even put his head out of the window. Down the beautiful valley of Connecticut, all through its broad intervales, heavy with its crops of corn or tobacco, or shaven smooth by the summer harvest; over the hard and stony counties of northern Massachusetts, through its suburbs and under the shadow of Bunker Hill Monument we came into the City of Boston, "the Hub of the Universe." Out through street after street we were marched double guarded to the wharves, where we took a small steamer for the island some six miles out in the harbor. A circumstance connected with this march is worth mentioning for its singularity:

at the head of this company, like convicts (and feeling very much like such), through the City of Boston walked, with heavy hearts and down-cast eyes, two Quakers.

Here on this dry and pleasant island in the midst of the beautiful Massachusetts Bay, we have the liberty of the camp, the privilege of air and sunshine, and hay beds to sleep upon. So we went to bed last night with somewhat of gladness elevating our depressed spirits.

Here are many troops gathering daily from all the New England States except Connecticut and Rhode Island. Their white tents are dotting the green slopes and hill-tops of the island and spreading wider and wider. This is the flow of military tide here just now. The ebb went out to sea in the shape of a great shipload just as we came in, and another load will be sent before many days. All is war here. We are surrounded by the pomp and circumstance of war, and enveloped in the cloud thereof. The cloud settles down over the minds and souls of all; they cannot see beyond, nor do they try; but with the clearer eye of Christian faith I try to look beyond all this error unto Truth and Holiness immaculate: and thanks to our Father, I am favored with glimpses that are sweet consolation amid this darkness.

This is one gratification: the men with us give us their sympathy. They seem to look upon us tenderly and pitifully, and their expressions of kind wishes are warm. Although we are relieved from duty and from drill, and may lie in our tents during rain and at night, we have heard of no complaint. This is the more worthy of note as there are so few in our little (Vermont) camp. Each man comes on guard half the days. It would probably be otherwise were their hearts in the service; but I have yet to find the man in any of these camps or at any service who does not wish himself at home. Substitutes say if they knew all they know now before leaving home they would not have enlisted; and they have been but a week from their homes and have endured no hardships. Yesterday L. M. M. and I appeared before the Captain commanding this camp with a statement of our cases. He listened to us respectfully and promised to refer us to the General commanding here, General Devens; and in the meantime released us from duty. In a short time afterward he passed us in our tent, asking our names. We have not heard from him, but do not drill or stand guard; so, we suppose, his release was confirmed. At that interview a young lieutenant sneeringly told us he thought we had better throw away our scruples and fight in the service of the country; and as we told the Captain we could not accept pay, he laughed mockingly, and said he would not stay here for $13.00 per month. He gets more than a hundred, I suppose.

How beautiful seems the world on this glorious morning here by the seaside! Eastward and toward the sun, fair green isles with outlines of pure beauty are scattered over the blue bay. Along the far line of the mainland white hamlets and towns glisten in the morning sun; countless tiny waves dance in the wind that comes off shore and sparkle sunward like myriads of gems. Up the fair vault, flecked by scarcely a cloud, rolls the sun in glory. Though fair be the earth, it has come to be tainted and marred by him who was meant to be its crowning glory. Behind me on this island are crowded vile and wicked men, the murmur of whose ribaldry riseth continually like the smoke and fumes of a lower world. Oh! Father of Mercies forgive the hard heartlessness and blindness and scarlet sins of my fellows, my brothers.

In Guard House. 31st—Yesterday morning L. M. M. and I were called upon to do fatigue duty. The day before we were asked to do some cleaning about camp and to bring water. We wished to be obliging, to appear willing to bear a hand toward that which would promote our own and our fellows' health and convenience; but as we worked we did not feel easy. Suspecting we had been assigned to such work, the more we discussed in our minds the subject, the more clearly the right way seemed open to us; and we separately came to the judgment that we must not conform to this requirement. So when the sergeant bade us "Police the streets," we asked him if he had received instructions with regard to us, and he replied we had been assigned to "Fatigue Duty." L. M. M. answered him that we could not obey. He left us immediately for the Major (Jarvis of Weathersfield, Vt.). He came back and ordered us to the Major's tent. The latter met us outside and inquired concerning the complaint he had heard of us. Upon our statement of our position, he apparently undertook to argue our whimsies, as he probably looked upon our principles, out of our heads. We replied to his points as we had ability; but he soon turned to bullying us rather than arguing with us, and would hardly let us proceed with a whole sentence. "I make some pretension to religion myself," he said, and quoted the Old Testament freely in support of war. Our terms were, submission or the guard-house. We replied we could not obey.

This island was formerly occupied by a company, who carried on the large farm it comprises and opened a great hotel as a summer resort.

The subjects of all misdemeanors, grave and small, are here confined. Those who have deserted or attempted it; those who have insulted officers and those guilty of theft, fighting, drunkenness, etc. In *most*, as in the camps, there are traces yet of manhood and of the Divine Spark, but some are abandoned, dissolute. There are many here among the substitutes who were actors in the late New York riots. They show unmistakably the characteristics and sentiments of those rioters, and especially hatred to the blacks drafted and about camp, and exhibit this in foul and profane jeers heaped upon these unoffending men at every opportunity. In justice to the blacks I must say they are superior to the whites in all their behavior.

31st P.M.—Several of us were a little time ago called out one by one to answer inquiries with regard to our offenses. We replied we could not comply with military requisitions. P. D. being last, was asked if he would die first, and replied promptly but mildly, *Yes*.

Here we are in prison in our own land for no crimes, no offense to God nor man; nay, more: we are here for obeying the commands of the Son of God and the influences of his Holy Spirit. I must look for patience in this dark day. I am troubled too much and excited and perplexed.

1st, 9th month—Oh, the horrors of the past night—I never before experienced such *sensations* and fears; and never did I feel so clearly that I had nothing but the hand of our Father to shield me from evil. Last night we three lay down together on the floor of a lower room of which we had taken possession. The others were above. We had but one blanket between us and the floor, and one over us. The other one we had lent to a wretched deserter who had skulked into our room for *relief*, being without anything of his own. We had during the day gained the respect of the fellows, and they seemed disposed to let us occupy our room in peace. I cannot say in quiet, for these caged beasts are restless, and the resonant boards of this old building speak of bedlam. The thin board partitions, the light door fastened only by a pine stick thrust into a wooden loop on the casing, seemed small protection in case of assault; but we lay down to sleep in quiet trust. But we had scarcely fallen asleep before we were awakened by the demoniac howlings and yellings of a man just brought into the next room, and allowed the liberty of the whole house. He was drunk, and further seemed to be laboring under delirium tremens. He crashed about furiously, and all the more after the guard tramped heavily in and bound him with handcuffs, and chain and ball. Again and again they left, only to return to quiet him by threats or by crushing him down to the floor and gagging him. In a couple of hours he became quiet and we got considerable sleep.

In the morning the fellow came into our room apologizing for the intrusion. He appeared a smart, fine-looking man, restless and uneasy. P. D. has a way of disposing of intruders that is quite effectual. I have not entirely disposed of some misgivings with respect to the legitimacy of his use of the means, so he commenced reading aloud in the Bible. The fellow was impatient and noisy, but he soon settled down on the floor beside him. As he listened and talked with us the recollections of his father's house and his innocent childhood were awakened. He was the child of pious parents, taught in Sabbath School and under pure home influences till thirteen. Then he was drawn into bad company, soon after leaving home for the sea; and, since then, has served in the army and navy,—in the army in Wilson's and Hawkins' (brigades). His was the old story of the total subjection of moral power and thralldom to evil habits and associates. He would get drunk, whenever it was in his power. It

was wrong; but he could not help it. Though he was awakened
and recollected his parents looking long and in vain for his
return, he soon returned to camp, to his wallowing in the mire,
and I fear to his path to certain perdition.

    3rd—A Massachusetts major, the officer of the day, in his
inspection of the guard-house came into our room today. We
were lying on the floor engaged in reading and writing. He was
apparently surprised at this and inquired the name of our books;
and finding the Bible and Thomas Kempis' *Imitation of Christ*,
observed that they were good books. I cannot say if he knew we
were Friends, but he asked us why we were in here.
    Like all officers he proceeded to reason with us, and to
advise us to serve, presenting no comfort if we still persisted in
our course. He informed us of a young Friend, Edward W. Holway of Sandwich, Mass., having been yesterday under punishment in the camp by his orders, who was today doing service
about camp. He said he was not going to put his Quaker in the
guardhouse, but was going to bring him to work by punishment.
We were filled with deep sympathy for him and desired to cheer
him by kind words as well as by the knowledge of our similar
situation. We obtained permission of the Major to write him a
letter open to his inspection. "You may be sure," said E. W. H.
to us at W. (Washington.), "the Major did not allow it to leave
his hands."
    This forenoon the Lieutenant of the Day came in and acted
the same part, though he was not so cool, and left expressing
the hope, if we would not serve our country like men; that God
would curse us. Oh, the trials from these officers! One after
another comes in to relieve himself upon us. Finding us firm
and not lacking in words, they usually fly into a passion and
end by bullying us. How can we reason with such men? They
are utterly unable to comprehend the pure Christianity and spir-
ituality of our principles. They have long stiffened their necks
in their own strength. They have stopped their ears to the voice
of the Spirit, and hardened their hearts to his influences. They
see no duty higher than that to country. What shall we receive
at their hands?

This Major tells us we will not be tried here. Then we are to be sent into the field, and there who will deliver us but God? Ah, I have nursed in my heart a hope that I may be spared to return home. Must I cast it out and have no desire but to do the will of my Master. It were better, even so. O, Lord, Thy will be done. Grant I may make it my chief delight and render true submission thereto.

Yesterday a little service was required of our dear L. M. M., but he insisted he could not comply. A sergeant and two privates were engaged. They coaxed and threatened him by turns, and with a determination not to be baffled took him out to perform it. Though guns were loaded he still stood firm and was soon brought back. We are happy here in guardhouse—too happy, too much at ease. We should see more of the Comforter—feel more strength—if the trial were fiercer; but this is well. This is a trial of patience.

13th—Last night we received a letter from Henry Dickinson, stating that the President, though sympathizing with those in our situation, felt bound by the Conscription Act, and felt liberty, in view of his oath to execute the laws, to do no more than detail us from active service to hospital duty, or to the charge of the colored refugees. For more than a week have we lain here, refusing to engage in hospital service; shall we retrace the steps of the past week? Or shall we go South as overseers of the blacks on the confiscated estates of the rebels, to act under military commanders and to report to such? What would become of our testimony and our determination to preserve ourselves clear of the guilt of this war?

P.S. We have written back to Henry Dickinson that we cannot purchase life at cost of peace of soul.

Camp Near Culpeper. 25th—My distress is too great for words; but I must overcome my disinclination to write, or this record will remain unfinished. So, with aching head and heart, I proceed.

Yesterday morning we were aroused early for breakfast and

for preparation for starting. After marching out of the barracks, we were first taken to the armory, where each man received a gun and its equipments and a piece of tent. We stood in line, waiting for our turn with apprehensions of coming trouble. Though we had felt free to keep with those among whom we had been placed, we could not consent to carry a gun, even though we did not intend to use it; and, from our previous experience, we knew it would go harder with us, if we took the first step in the wrong direction, though it might seem an unimportant one, and an easy and not very wrong way to avoid difficulty. So we felt decided we must decline receiving the guns. In the hurry and bustle of equipping a detachment of soldiers, one attempting to explain a position and the grounds therefore so peculiar to ours to junior, petty officers, possessing liberally the characteristics of these: pride, vanity, conceit, and an arbitrary spirit, impatience, profanity, and contempt for holy things, must needs find the opportunity a very unfavorable one.

We succeeded in giving these young officers a slight idea of what we were; and endeavored to answer their questions of why we did not pay our commutation, and avail ourselves of that provision made expressly for such; of why we had come as far as that place, etc. We realized then the unpleasant results of that practice, that had been employed with us by the successive officers into whose hands we had fallen, of shirking any responsibility, and of passing us on to the next officer above.

A council was soon holden to decide what to do with us. One proposed to place us under arrest, a sentiment we rather hoped might prevail, as it might prevent our being sent on to the front; but another, in some spite and impatience, insisted, as it was their duty to supply a gun to every man and forward him, that the guns should be put upon us, and we be made to carry them. Accordingly the equipment was buckled about us, and the straps of guns being loosened, they were thrust over our heads and hung upon our shoulders. In this way we were urged forward through the streets of Alexandria; and, having been put upon a long train of dirt cars, were started for Culpeper. We came over a long stretch of desolated and deserted country, through battlefields of previous summers, and through many camps now lively with the work of this present campaign.

Seeing, for the first time, a country made dreary by the war-blight, a country once adorned with groves and green pastures and meadows and fields of waving grain, and happy with a thousand homes, now laid with the ground, one realizes as he can in no other way something of the ruin that lies in the trail of war. But upon these fields of Virginia, once so fair, there rests a two-fold blight, first that of slavery, now that of war. When one contrasts the face of this country with the smiling hillsides and vales of New England, he sees stamped upon it in characters so marked, none but a blind man can fail to read, the great irrefutable arguments against slavery and against war, too; and must be filled with loathing for these twin relics of barbarism, so awful in the potency of their consequences that they can change even the face of the country.

Through the heat of this long ride, we felt our total lack of water and the meagreness of our supply of food. Our thirst became so oppressive as we were marched here from Culpeper, some four miles with scarcely a halt to rest, under our heavy loads, and through the heat and deep dust of the road, that we drank water and dipped in the brooks as we passed, though it was discolored with the soap the soldiers had used in washing. The guns interfered with our walking, and slipping down, dragged with painful weight upon our shoulders. Poor P. D. fell out from exhaustion and did not come in till we had been some little time at the camp. We were taken to the 4th Vermont regiment and soon apportioned to companies. Though we waited upon the officer commanding the company in which we were placed, and endeavored to explain our situation, we were required immediately after to be present at inspection of arms. We declined, but an attempt was made to force us to obedience, first, by the officers of the company, then, by those of the regiment; but, failing to exact obedience of us, we were ordered by the colonel to be tied, and, if we made outcry, to be gagged also, and to be kept so till he gave orders for our release. After two or three hours we were relieved and left under guard, lying down on the ground in the open air, and covering ourselves with our blankets, we soon feel asleep from exhaustion, and fatigue of the day.

This morning the officers told us we must yield. We must

obey and serve. We were threatened great severities and even death. We seem perfectly at the mercy of the military power, and more, in the hands of the inferior officers who, from their being removed from Washington, feel less restraint from those Regulations of the Army, which are for the protection of privates from personal abuse.

26th—Yesterday my mind was much agitated: doubts and fears and forebodings seized me. I was alone, seeking a resting-place and finding none. It seemed as if God had forsaken me in this dark hour; and the Tempter whispered, that after all I might be only the victim of a delusion. My prayers for faith and strength seemed all in vain.

But this morning I enjoy peace, and feel as though I could face anything. Though I am as a lamb in the shambles, yet do I cry, "Thy will be done," and can indeed say,—

> Passive to His Holy will
> Trust I in my Master still
> Even though he slay me.

I mind me of the anxiety of our dear friends about home, and of their prayers for us.

Oh, praise be to the Lord for the peace and love and resignation that has filled my soul today! Oh, the passing beauty of holiness! There is a holy life that is above fear; it is a close communion with Christ. I pray for this continually but am not free from the shadow and the tempter. There is ever present with us the thought that perhaps we shall serve the Lord the most effectually by our death, and desire, if that be the service He requires of us, that we may be ready and resigned.

3rd, 10th month—Today dawned fair and our Camp is dry again. I was asked to clean the gun I brought, and declining, was tied some two hours upon the ground.

At Washington. 6th—At first, after being informed of our delining to serve in his hospital, Colonel Foster did not appear altered in his kind regard for us. But his spleen soon became evident. At the time we asked for a trial by court-martial, and it was his duty to place us under arrest and proceed with the preferring of his charges against us. For a while he seemed to hesitate and consult his inferior officers, and among them his Chaplain. The result of the conference was our being ordered into our companies, that, separated, and with the force of the officers of a company bearing upon us, we might the more likely be subdued. Yet the Colonel assured L. M. M., interceding in my behalf, when the lieutenant commanding my company threatened force upon me, that he should not allow any personal injury. When we marched next day I was compelled to bear a gun and equipments. My associates were more fortunate, for, being asked if they would carry their guns, declined and saw no more trouble from them. The captain of the company in which P. D. was placed told him he did not believe he was ugly about it, and that he could only put him under arrest and prefer charges against him. He accordingly was taken under guard, where he lay till we left for here.

The next morning the men were busy burnishing their arms. When I looked toward the one I had borne, yellow with rust, I trembled in the weakness of the flesh at the trial I felt impending over me. Before the Colonel was up I knocked at his tent, but was told he was asleep, though, through the opening, I saw him lying gazing at me. Although I felt I should gain no relief from him, I applied again soon after. He admitted me and, lying on his bed, inquired with cold heartlessness what I wanted. I stated to him, that I could never consent to serve, and, being under the war-power, was resigned to suffer instead all the just penalties of the law. I begged of him release from the attempts by violence to compel my obedience and service, and a trial, though likely to be made by those having no sympathy with me, yet probably in a manner conformable to law.

He replied that he had shown us all the favor he should; that he had, now, turned us over to the military power and was going to let that take its course; that is, henceforth we were to be at the mercy of the inferior officers, without appeal to law, justice, or mercy. He said he had placed us in a pleasant position, against which we could have no reasonable objection, and that we had failed to perform our agreement. He wished to deny that our consent was only temporary and conditional. He declared, furthermore, his belief, that a man who would not fight for his country did not deserve to live. I was glad to withdraw from his presence as soon as I could.

I went back to my tent and lay down for a season of retirement endeavoring to gain resignation to any event. I dreaded torture and desired strength of flesh and spirit. My trial soon came. The lieutenant called me out, and pointing to the gun that lay near by, asked if I was going to clean it. I replied to him that I could not comply with military requisitions, and felt resigned to the consequences. "I do not ask about your feelings; I want to know if you are going to clean that gun?" "I cannot do it," was my answer. He went away saying, "Very well," and I crawled into the tent again. Two sergeants soon called for me, and taking me a little aside, bid me lie down on my back, and stretching my limbs apart tied cords to my wrists and ankles and these to four stakes driven in the ground somewhat in the form of an X.

I was very quiet in my mind as I lay there on the ground (soaked) with the rain of the previous day, exposed to the heat of the sun and suffering keenly from the cords binding my wrists and straining my muscles. And, if I dared the presumption, I should say that I caught a glimpse of heavenly pity. I wept, not so much from my own suffering as from sorrow that such things should be in our own country, where Justice and Freedom and Liberty of Conscience have been the annual boast of Fourth-of-July orators so many years. It seemed that our fore-fathers in the faith had wrought and suffered in vain, when the privileges they so dearly bought were so soon set aside. And I was sad, that one endeavoring to follow our dear Master should be so generally regarded as a despicable and stubborn culprit.

After something like an hour had passed, the lieutenant came with his orderly to ask me if I was ready to clean the gun. I replied to the orderly asking the question, that it could but give me pain to be asked or required to do anything I believed wrong. He repeated it to the lieutenant just behind him, who advanced and addressed me. I was favored to improve the opportunity to say to him a few things I wished. He said little; and, when I had finished, he withdrew with the others who had gathered around. About the end of another hour his orderly came and released me.

I arose and sat on the ground. I did not rise to go away. I had not where to go, nothing to do. As I sat there my heart swelled from joy from above. The consolation and sweet fruit of tribulation patiently endured. But I also grieved, that the world was so far gone astray, so cruel and blind. It seemed as if the gospel of Christ had never been preached upon earth, and the beautiful example of his life had been utterly lost sight of.

Some of the men came about me, advising me to yield, and among them one of those who had tied me down, telling me what I had already suffered was nothing to what I must yet suffer unless I yielded; that human flesh could not endure what would be put upon me. I wondered if it could be that they could force me to obedience by torture, and examined myself closely to see if they had advanced as yet one step toward the accomplishment of their purposes. Though weaker in body, I believed I found myself, through divine strength, as firm in my resolution to maintain my allegiance to my Master.

The relaxation of my nerves and muscles after having been so tensely strained left me that afternoon so weak that I could hardly walk or perform any mental exertion.

I had not yet eaten the mean and scanty breakfast I had prepared, when I was ordered to pack my things and report myself at the lieutenant's tent. I was accustomed to such orders and complied, little moved.

The lieutenant received me politely with, "Good morning, Mr. Pringle," and desiring me to be seated, proceeded with the writing with which he was engaged. I sat down in some wonderment and sought to be quiet and prepared for any event.

"You are ordered to report to Washington," said he; "I do not know what it is for." I assured him that neither did I know. We were gathered before the Major's tent for preparation for departure. The regimental officers were there manifesting surprise and chagrin; for they could not but show both, as they looked upon us, whom the day before they were threatening to crush into submission, and attempting also to execute their threats that morning, standing out of their power and under orders from one superior to their Major Commanding E. M. As the bird uncaged, so were our hearts that morning. Short and uncertain at first were the flights of Hope. As the slave many times before us, leaving his yoke behind him, turned from the plantations of Virginia and set his face toward the far North, so we from out a grasp as close and as abundant in suffering and severity, and from without the line of bayonets that had so many weeks surrounded us, turned our backs upon the camp of the 4th Vermont and took our way over the turnpike that ran through the tented fields of Culpeper.

At the War Office we were soon admitted to an audience with the Adjutant General, Colonel Townsend, whom we found to be a very fine man, mild and kind. He referred our cases to the Secretary of War, Stanton, by whom we were ordered to report for service to Surgeon General Hammond. Here we met Isaac Newton, Commissioner of Agriculture, waiting for our arrival, and James Austin of Nantucket, expecting his son, Charles L. Austin, and Edward W. Holway of Sandwich, Mass., conscripted Friends like ourselves, and ordered here from the 22nd Massachusetts.

We understand it is through the influence of Isaac Newton that Friends have been able to approach the heads of Government in our behalf and to prevail with them to so great an extent. He explained to us the circumstance in which we are placed. That the Secretary of War and President sympathized with Friends in their present suffering, and would grant them full release, but that they felt themselves bound by their oaths that they would execute the laws, to carry out to its full extent the Conscription Act. That there appeared but one door of relief open—that was to parole us and allow us to go home, but subject to their call again ostensibly, though this they neither wished nor proposed to do. That the fact of Friends in the Army and refusing service had attracted public attention so that it was not expedient to parole us at present. That, therefore, we were to be sent to one of the hospitals for a short time, where it was hoped and expressly requested that we would consent to remain quiet and acquiesce, if possible, in whatever might be required of us. That our work there would be quite free from objection, being for the direct relief of the sick; and that there we would release none for active service in the field, as the nurses were hired civilians.

These requirements being so much less objectionable than we had feared, we felt relief, and consented to them. I. N. went with us himself to the Surgeon General's office, where he procured peculiar favours for us; that we should be sent to a hospital in the city, where he could see us often; and that orders should be given that nothing should interfere with our comfort, or our enjoyment of our consciences.

Thence we were sent to Medical Purveyor Abbot, who assigned us to the best hospital in the city, the Douglas Hospital.

The next day after our coming here I. N. and James Austin came to add to our number E. W. H. and C. L. A., so now there are five of us instead of three. We are pleasantly situated in a room by ourselves in the upper or fourth story, and are enjoying our advantages of good quarters and tolerable food as no one can except he has been deprived of them.

8th—Today we have a pass to go out to see the city.

9th—We all went, thinking to do the whole city in a day, but before the time of our passes expired, we were glad to drag ourselves back to the rest and quiet of D. H. During the day we called upon our friend I. N. in the Patent Office. When he came to see us on the 7th, he stated he had called upon the President that afternoon to request him to release us and let us go home to our friends. The President promised to consider it over night. Accordingly yesterday morning, as I. N. told us, he waited upon him again. He found there a woman in the greatest distress. Her son, only a boy of fifteen years and four months, having been enticed into the Army, had deserted and been sentenced to be shot the next day. As the clerks were telling her, the President was in the War Office and could not be seen, nor did they think he could attend to her case that day. I. N. found her almost wild with grief. "Do not despair, my good woman," said he, "I guess the President can be seen after a bit." He soon presented her case to the President, who exclaimed at once, "That must not be, I must look into that case, before they shoot that boy"; and telegraphed at once to have the order suspended.

I. N. judged it was not a fit time to urge our case. We feel we can afford to wait, that a life may be saved. But we long for release. We do not feel easy to remain here.

11th—Today we attended meeting held in the house of a Friend, Asa Arnold, living near here. There were about four persons besides ourselves. E. W. H. and C. L. A. showed their copy of the charges about to have been preferred against them in court-martial before they left their regiment, to a lawyer who attended the meeting. He laughed at the Specification of Mutiny, declaring such a charge could not have been lawfully sustained against them.

The experiences of our new friends were similar to ours, except they fell among officers who usually showed them favor and rejoiced with them in their release.

13th—L. M. M. had quite an adventure yesterday. He being fireman with another was in the furnace room among three or four others, when the officer of the day, one of the surgeons, passed around on inspection. "Stand up," he ordered them, wishing to be saluted. The others arose; but by no means L. The order was repeated for his benefit, but he sat with his cap on, telling the surgeon he had supposed he was excused from such things as he was one of the Friends.

Thereat the officer flew at him, exclaiming he would take the Quaker out of him. He snatched off his cap and seizing him by the collar tried to raise him to his feet; but finding his strength insufficient and that L. was not to be frightened, he changed his purpose in his wrath and calling for the corporal of the guard had him taken to the guard-house. This was about eleven A.M. and he lay there till about six P.M., when the surgeon in charge, arriving home and hearing of it, ordered the officer of the day to go and take him out, telling him never to put another man into the guard-house while he was in charge here without consulting him. The manner of his release was very satisfactory to us, and we waited for this rather than effect it by our own efforts. We are all getting uneasy about remaining here, and if our release do not come soon, we feel we must intercede with the authorities, even if the alternative be imprisonment.

The privations I have endured since leaving home, the great tax upon my nervous strength, and my mind as well, since I have had charge of our extensive correspondence, are beginning to tell upon my health and I long for rest.

20th—We begin to feel we shall have to decline service as heretofore, unless our position is changed. I shall not say but we submit too much in not declining at once, but it has seemed most prudent at least to make suit with Government rather than provoke the hostility of their subalterns. We were ordered here with little understanding of the true state of things as they really exist here; and were advised by Friends to come and make no objections, being assured it was but for a very brief time and only a matter of form. It might not have been wrong; but as we find we do too much fill the places of soldiers (L. M. M.'s fellow fireman has just left for the field, and I am to take his place, for instance), and are clearly doing military service, we are continually oppressed by a sense of guilt, that makes our struggles earnest.

21st—I. N. has not called yet; our situation is becoming intolerable. I query if patience is justified under the circumstances. My distress of mind may be enhanced by my feeble condition of health, for today I am confined to my bed, almost too weak to get downstairs. This is owing to exposure after being heated over the furnaces.

26th—Though a week has gone by, and my cold has left me, I find I am no better, and that I am reduced very low in strength and flesh by the sickness and pain I am experiencing. Yet I still

persist in going below once a day. The food I am able to get is
not such as is proper.

5th, 11th month—I spend most of my time on my bed, much of
it alone. And very precious to me is the nearness I am favored
to attain unto the Master. Notwithstanding my situation and
state, I am happy in the enjoyment of His consolations. Lately
my confidence has been strong, and I think I begin to feel that
our patience is soon to be rewarded with relief; insomuch that
a little while ago, when dear P. D. was almost overcome with
sorrow, I felt bold to comfort him with my assurance of my belief,
that it would not be long so. My mind is too weak to allow of
my reading much; and, though I enjoy the company of my companions a part of the time, especially in the evening, I am much
alone; which affords me abundant time for meditation and waiting upon God. The fruits of this are sweet, and a recompense
for affliction.

6th—Last evening E. W. H. saw I. N. particularly on my behalf,
I suppose. He left at once for the President. This morning he
called to inform us of his interview at the White House. The
President was moved to sympathy in my behalf, when I. N. gave
him a letter from one of our Friends in New York. After its
perusal he exclaimed to our friend, "I want you to go and tell
Stanton that it is my wish all those young men be sent home at
once." He was on his way to the Secretary this morning as he
called.

Later—I. N. has just called again informing us in joy that
we are free. At the War Office he was urging the Secretary to
consent to our paroles, when the President entered. "It is my
urgent wish," said he. The Secretary yielded; the order was
given, and we were released. What we had waited for so many
weeks was accomplished in a few moments by a Providential
ordering of circumstances.

7th—I. N. came again last evening bringing our paroles. The

preliminary arrangements are being made, and we are to start this afternoon for New York.

Note. Rising from my sick-bed to undertake this journey, which lasted through the night, its fatigues overcame me, and upon my arrival in New York I was seized with delirium from which I only recovered after many weeks, through the mercy and favor of Him, who in all this trial had been our guide and strength and comfort.

The contents of the diary are confirmed by the minutes of the Representative Meeting in New York. Cyrus Pringle's companions mentioned in the diary were Lindley M. Macomber (L. M. M.) and Peter Dakin (P. D.) from Vermont, as well as Edward W. Holway (E. W. H.) of Sandwich, Mass., and Charles L. Austin (C. L. A.) of Nantucket.

Henry Dickinson (H. D.) mentioned in the diary was a member and representative of the Representative Meeting and William Wood (W. W.) was its clerk. Most of the other initials follow prior mention, including D. H. (Douglas Hospital) and I. N. (Isaac Newton).

Battle of Shiloh

The Federal forces were on the march, and General Grant was anxious to capture Corinth, Mississippi, an important rail junction and the gateway to the Mississippi valley. Corinth was under the protection of General Johnston who commanded 41,000 troops. General Grant was confident that his 43,000 men could take the city. General Halleck was cautious and asked Grant to wait for reinforcements. General Wallace would join him with five thousand men and General Buell would join him with 22,000 more. This would assure victory.

Johnston was aware that Grant had bivouacked twenty miles north of Corinth at Pittsburg Landing in Tennessee waiting for additional troops. Johnston was also aware that he could never stand up under so great a force that was being amassed, and he decided to attack before the reinforcements arrived. The Rebel army was made up almost wholly of green troops, who had never seen battle and were completely undisciplined. They thought war was one huge game and all of them looked forward to the "fun" of battle. On the twenty-mile march to Pittsburg Landing, General Johnston found that his troops resembled a mob more than an army. The short distance took them three days, and while they had been cautioned that they were very near to the enemy and silence was mandatory, they kept shooting off their rifles to "test" them, and took occasional shots at rabbits and running deer. They cheered everytime an officer passed their ranks, and more than one Confederate officer worried about the success of this mission.

General Grant's army contained a great many green troops, too. General Prentiss's brigades had been organized only eleven days before and still hadn't been issued any ammunition. Grant requested his officers that the men not be asked to dig in, because if they thought a battle was imminent, many would desert, others would be too frightened to follow orders.

It was under these conditions that the Battle of Shiloh began, early in the morning of Sunday, April 6, 1862. General Grant's reinforcements showed up at the very last minute and snatched victory from sure defeat. The battle lasted two days. The Confederacy lost 11,000 men, the Federal forces suffered 13,000 dead, and 3,000 men became prisoners of war.

The misery of the retreat is described by a Rebel eyewitness:

> In this ride I saw more of human agony and woe than I trust I shall ever again be called to behold. The retreating host wound along a narrow and almost impossible road. Here was a long line of wagons loaded with wounded piled in like bags of grain, groaning and cursing; while the mules plunged on in mud and water, the latter sometimes coming into the wagons. Next was a struggling regiment of infantry, pressing on past the train of wagons; then a stretcher, borne upon the shoulders of four men, carrying a wounded officer; then soldiers staggering along, with an arm broken and hanging down or other fearful wounds. To add to the horrors of the scene, the elements of heaven marshaled their forces—a fitting accompaniment of the tempest of human desolation and passion which was raging. A cold drizzling rain commenced about nightfall, and finally turned to pitiless, blinding hail. I passed wagon trains filled with wounded and dying soldiers, without even a blanket to shield them from the driving sleet and hail which fell in stones as large as partridge eggs, until it lay on the ground two inches deep. Some three hundred men died during that awful retreat, and their bodies were thrown out to make room for others who, although wounded, had struggled on through the storm hoping to find shelter, rest, and medical care.

General Halleck increased his forces to 100,000 and in five days marched in to conquer Corinth.

The noise, confusion, and horror of the battle is told by a Union officer in the following account taken from *The Civil War in Song & Story* by Frank Moore (P. F. Collier, 1865).

"On that peaceful Sunday morning of April 6, 1862, the sun was rising with splendor. I had walked out to enjoy the fresh air, and, returning by my friend Lieut. D's tent, I called upon him. Said he, 'H., take a cup of coffee; I have found some milk.' 'Don't care if I do,' said I. 'I always write home on Sunday morning, and like to do it over a good cup of coffee.' 'Yes, I mean to write to my little wife,' said D. 'I expect to resign soon. Don't you want a pair of new shoulder-straps, H. and brand new pair of gauntlets?' I told D. I would take them; and in a moment left his tent, after making him promise to take tea with me.

"But how were things at tea time? D. was mangled and dead, lying by the roadside at the hospital by the Landing, with hundreds of others, and I had passed the most momentous day of my life—had participated in one of the greatest battles, exceeding in fury, courage, waste, stupendousness, and gallantry, the wildest dreams of my youth.

"On the evening of the 5th, the 18th Wisconsin infantry arrived and were assigned to General Prentiss's division, on the front. They cooked their first suppers in the field that night at nine o'clock, and wrapped themselves in their blankets, to be awakened by the roar of battle, and receive, thus early, their bloody baptism. Before they had been on the field one day, their magnificent corps was decimated, most of the officers killed.

"I saw an intelligent looking man with his whole diaphragm torn off. He holding nearly all of his viscera with both hands and arms.

"On going to the field the second day, our regiment strode on in line over wounded, dying, and dead. My office detaching me from the lines, I had an opportunity to notice incidents about the field. The regiment halted amidst a gory, ghastly scene. I heard a voice calling, "Ho, friend! ho! for God's sake, come here.'

I went to a gory pile of dead human forms in every kind of stiff contortion; I saw one arm raised, beckoning me. I found there a rebel, covered with clotted blood, pillowing his head on the dead body of a comrade. Both were red from head to foot. The dead man's brains had gushed out in a reddish and grayish mass over his face. The live one had lain across him all that horrible, long night in the storm. The first thing he said to me was, 'Give me some water. Send me a surgeon—won't you! Oh God! What made you come down here to fight us? We never would have come up there.' And then he affectionately put one arm over the form, and laid his bloody face against the cold, clammy, bloody face of his dead friend.

"I filled his canteen nearly—reserving some for myself—knowing I might be in the same sad condition. I told him we had no surgeon in our regiment, and that we would have to suffer, if wounded, the same as he; that other regiments were coming, and to call on them for surgeon; that they were humane.

"'Forward! shouted the Colonel; and 'Forward' was repeated by the officers. I left him.

"The above recalls to mind one of the hardest principles in warfare—where your sympathy and humanity are appealed to, and from sense of expediency, you are forbidden to exercise it. After our regiment had been nearly annihilated, and were compelled to retreat under a galling fire, a boy was supporting his dying brother on one arm, and trying to drag him from the field and the advancing foe. He looked at me imploringly, and said, 'Captain, help him—*wont* you? Do, Captain; he'll live.' I said, 'He's shot through the head; don't you see? and can't live—he's dying now.' 'Oh, no, he aint, Captain. Don't leave me.' I was forced to reply: 'The rebels wont hurt him. Lay him down and come, or both you and I will be lost.' The rush of bullets and the yells of the approaching demons hurried me away—leaving the young soldier over his dying brother.

"Nearly every rebel's face turned black immediately after death. Union men's faces retained the natural pallor two or three days.

"I ate my dinner on Monday within six paces of a rebel in four pieces. Both legs were blown off. His pelvis was the third piece, and his head and chest were the fourth piece. Those four pieces occupied a space of twelve feet square. I saw five dead rebels in a row, with their heads knocked off by a round shot. Myself and other amateur anatomists, when the regiment was resting temporarily on arms, would leave to examine the internal structure of man. We would examine brains, heart, stomach, layers of muscles, structure of bones, etc. for there was every form of mutilation.

"At home I used to wince at the sight of a wound or of a corpse; but here, in one day, I learned to be among the scenes I am describing without emotion. My friend, Adjutant ———, and myself, on the second night, looking in the dark for a place to lie down, he said, 'Let's lie down here. Here's some fellows sleeping.' We slept in quiet until dawn revealed that we had passed a night among sprawling, stiffened, ghastly corpses.

"I saw one of our dead soldiers with his mouth crammed full of cartridges until the cheeks were bulged out. Several protruded from his mouth. This was done by the rebels.

"On the third day most of our time was employed in burying the dead. Shallow pits were dug, which would soon fill with water. Into these we threw our comrades with a heavy splash, or a dump against solid bottom. Many a hopeful, promising youth thus indecently ended his career.

"Some of our boys were disposed to kick the secesh into these pits. One fell in with a heavy dump on his face. The more humane proposed to turn him over. 'Oh, that'll do,' said a Union Missourian, 'for when he scratches, he'll scratch nearer to hell.' This is a hard story, I know, but I want you to see real war.

"I stood in one place in the woods near the spot of the engagement of the 57th Illinois, and counted eighty-one dead rebels. There I saw one tree, seven inches in diameter, with thirty-one bullet holes. Such had been death's storm. Near the scenes of the last of the fighting, where the rebels precipitately retreated, I saw one grave containing one hundred and thirty-seven dead rebels, and one side of it another grave containing forty-one dead Federals. Several other trenches were in view from that spot.

"One dead and uniformed officer lay covered with a little housing of rails. On it was a fly-leaf of a memorandum-book with the pencil writing: 'Federals, respect my father's corpse.'

Many of our boys wanted to cut off his buttons and gold cord; but our Colonel had the body religiously guarded.

"Many of our regiments were paid off just previously to the battle, and our dead comrades were robbed of hundreds of thousands of dollars. The rebels were surprised and abashed at the apparent wealth of our army. They attired themselves in our uniforms, and rifled from officers' trunks tens of thousands of dollars worth of fine clothing, toilet articles, and interesting souvenirs of every man's trunk. They made themselves stupid and drunk over our fine victuals and wines. They seem to have gone mad with the lust of plunder.

"To show how complete and successful was the advance of the enemy, their advance guard lay in the woods on the 5th, witnessing our parades and reviews. One of our returned paroled prisoners, a mule driver, who was captured two days before the battle, has told me that he was taken through their whole army, which was camped three miles from ours, the night before the attack.

"A resident here told me that on the retreat of the rebel army from Shiloh, it was utterly routed and demoralized.

"Two women, laundresses in the 16th Wisconsin, running to the rear when the attack was commenced, were killed.

"My poor friend Carson, the scout, after having fought and worked, and slaved from the beginning of the war, unrequited, comparatively, and after having passed hundreds of hair-breadth escapes, and through this wild battle was killed by almost the last shot. A round shot took off his whole face and tore part of his head. Poor Carson! We all remember your patriotism, your courage, your devotion. We will cheer, all we can, the bereaved and dear ones you have left."

The Indian during the Civil War

At the beginning of the war, all the great Indian tribes had been driven west of the Mississippi, into what was known as Indian territory, a small area hedged in on all sides by territories which had already become states of the Republic, or would soon be such. In Minnesota, Iowa, Oregon, and in the Territories, Indians existed but were restricted to certain reservations. The policy pursued regarded the permanent interest of the white man alone, while it bestowed temporary indulgence upon the red man. It was unfortunate that the patronage which the government bestowed upon the Indians was frequently dispensed through agents who took many opportunities to defraud the supposed beneficiaries. Perhaps President Lincoln's disinterest in the affairs of the Indians dated back to his participation in the Black Hawk war of 1832 when he held the rank of Captain. His job was to help push the Indians across the Mississippi.

The summer of 1862 found twelve hundred Sioux Indians in revolt. In August they attacked settlements of whites and began a series of massacres unrivalled at that time for brutality and horror. The loss of life was estimated at eight hundred and the property damage at more than three million dollars. News was leaked by the Federal government that the massacres were instigated by Confederate emissaries.

But General Nelson A. Miles has another story to tell in his *Personal Recollections and Observations* (The Werner Co., 1896).

Urgent need of practically withdrawing the troops from the

frontier, forced the government by the exigencies of the Civil War and the continuance of that contest for four years, gave the Indians encouragement as well as opportunity to acquire firearms and munitions of war which they would not otherwise have been able to obtain. The disastrous results were soon felt all along the frontier, especially in the Northwest, where occurred what is known as the "Minnesota Massacre of 1862," and in the Southwest, particularly in Arizona and New Mexico; and it became speedily apparent that whatever the pressure at the front, large bodies of volunteer troops must be located and maintained in the Indian country, sufficient to overawe the hostile tribes and keep them in subjection.

The Indian uprising in Minnesota in the year 1862, like many others, was that of a people quiet and semicivilized, to avenge real or imaginary wrongs. They suddenly rose and fell upon the unprotected settlements and destroyed upward of a thousand people—men, women and children. As speedily as possible a large force of troops was thrown against the hostiles, under the command of General Sibley, who conducted an energetic and successful campaign, resulting in the subjugation of such portions of the Sioux Indians as did not escape across the border into Canadian territory.

The following extract from "Heard's History of the Sioux War" will exhibit some of the causes leading to that outbreak. The council referred to in the extract was held in November 1852, and was of great importance, as bearing upon subsequent events.

"The room was crowded with Indians and white men when Red Iron was brought in guarded by soldiers. He was about forty years old, tall and athletic; about six feet in his moccasins, with a large, well-developed head, quiline nose, thin compressed lips, and physiognomy beaming with intelligence and resolution. He was clad in the half-military, half Indian costume of the Dakota chiefs. He was seated in the councilroom without greeting or salutation from any one. In a few minutes the governor, turning to the chief in the midst of a breathless silence, by the aid of an interpreter opened the council.

"Governor Ramsey asked: 'What excuse have you for not coming to the council when I sent for you?'

"The chief rose to his feet with native grace and dignity, his blanket falling from his shoulders, and purposely dropping the pipe of peace he stood erect before the governor with his arms folded, and his right hand pressed on the sheath of his scalping knife. With firm voice he replied:

'I started to come, but your braves drove me back.'

"*Governor Ramsey:* 'What excuse have you for not coming the second time I sent for you?'

"*Red Iron:* 'No other excuse than I have given you.'

"*Governor Ramsey:* 'At the treaty I thought you a good man, but since you have acted badly. I am disposed to break you. I do break you.'

"*Red Iron:* 'You break me! My people made me a chief. My people love me. I will still be their chief. I have done nothing wrong.'

"*Governor Ramsey:* 'Why did you get your braves together and march around here for the purpose of intimidating other chiefs, and prevent their coming to the council?'

"*Red Iron:* 'I did not get my braves together, they got together themselves to prevent boys going to council to be made chiefs to sign papers, and to prevent single chiefs going to council at night, to be bribed to sign papers, for money we never got. We have heard how the Medewakantons were served at Mendota; that by secret councils you got their names on paper, and took away their money. We don't want to be served so. My braves wanted to come to council in the daytime, when the sun shines, and we want no councils in the dark. We want all our people to go to council together, so that we can all know what is done.'

"*Governor Ramsey:* 'Why did you attempt to come to council with your braves, when I had forbidden your braves coming to council?'

"*Red Iron:* 'You invited the chiefs only, and would not let the braves come too. This is not the way we have been treated before, and this is not according to our customs; for among Dakotas, chiefs and braves go to council together. When you first sent for us there were two or three chiefs here, and we wanted to wait till the rest would come, that we might all be in council

together and know what was done, and so that we might all
understand the papers and know what we are signing. When we
signed the treaty the traders threw a blanket over our faces and
darkened our eyes, and made us sign papers which we did not
understand and which were not explained or read to us. We
want our Great Father at Washington to know what has been
done.'

"Governor Ramsey: Your Great Father has sent me to represent him, and what I say is what he says. He wants you to pay
your old debts in accordance with the paper you signed when
the treaty was made, and to leave that money in my hands to
pay these debts. If you refuse to do this I will take the money
back.'

"Red Iron: 'You can take the money back. We sold our land
to you, and you promised to pay us. If you don't give us the
money I will be glad, and all our people will be glad, for we
will have our land back if you don't give us the money. That
paper was not interpreted or explained to us. We are told it gives
about 300 boxes ($300,000) of our money to some of the traders.
We don't think we owe them so much. We want to pay all our
debts. We want our Great Father to send three good men here to
tell us how much we do owe, and whatever they say we will
pay; and that's what all these braves say. Our chiefs and all our
people say this.'

All the Indians present responded, 'Ho! ho!'

"Governor Ramsey: 'That can't be done. You owe more than
your money will pay, and I am ready now to pay your annuity,
and no more; and when you are ready to receive it the agent
will pay you.'

"Red Iron: 'We will receive our annuity, but we will sign
no papers for anything else. The snow is on the ground, and we
have been waiting a long time to get our money. We are poor;
you have plenty. Your fires are warm. Your tepees keep out the
cold. We have nothing to eat. We have been waiting a long time
for our moneys. Our hunting season is past. A great many of our
people are sick for being hungry. We may die because you won't
pay us. We may die, but if we do we will leave our bones on the
ground, that our Great Father may see where his Dakota children
died. We are very poor. We have sold our hunting grounds and

the graves of our fathers. We have sold our own graves. We have no place to bury our dead, and you will not pay us the money for our lands.'

"The council was broken up, and Red Iron was sent to the guardhouse, where he was kept till the next day. Between thirty and forty of the braves of Red Iron's band were present during this arraignment before the governor. When he was led away they departed in sullen silence, headed by Lean Bear, to a spot a quarter of a mile from the council house, where they uttered a succession of yells; the gathering signal of the Dakotas. Ere the echoes died away Indians were hurrying from their tepees toward them, prepared for battle. They proceeded to the eminence near the camp, where mouldered the bones of many warriors. It was the memorable battle ground where their ancestors had fought, in a conflict like Waterloo, the warlike Sacs and Foxes, thereby preserving their lands and nationality. Upon this field stood two hundred resolute warriors ready to do battle for their hereditary chief. Lean Bear, the principal brave of Red Iron's band, was a large, resolute man, about thirty-five years of age, and had great influence in his nation.

"Here, on their old battle ground, Lean Bear recounted the brave deeds of Red Iron, the long list of wrongs inflicted on the Indians by the white men, and proposed to the braves that they should make a general attack on the whites. By the influence of some of the half breeds, and of white men who were known to be friendly to them, Lean Bear was induced to abandon his scheme, and finally the tribe, being starving, consented to give up their lands and accept the sum of money offered to them.

"Over $55,000 of this treaty money paid for debts of the Indians went to one Hugh Tyler, a stranger in the country, 'for getting the treaty through the Senate, and for necessary disbursements in securing the assent of the chiefs.'

"Five years later another trader, under the pretence that he was going to get back for them some of this stolen money, obtained their signatures to vouchers by means of which he cheated them out of $12,000 more. At this same time he obtained a payment of $4,500 for goods he said they had stolen from him. Another man was allowed a claim of $5,000 for horses he said they had stolen from him.

"In 1858 the chiefs were taken to Washington, and agreed to the treaties for the cession of all their reservations north of the Minnesota River, under which, as ratified by the Senate, they were to have $166,000; but of this amount they never received one penny till four years afterward, when $15,000 in goods were sent to the Lower Sioux, and these were deducted out of what was due them under former treaties."

The Red Iron mentioned here was a man of great sagacity and of the highest personal character. He opposed with all his influence, and at the risk of his life, the outbreak of 1862, but the current against him was too strong.

The Sand Creek massacre is perhaps the foulest and most unjustifiable crime in the annals of America. It was planned by and executed under the personal direction of J. M. Chivington, Colonel of the First Colorado Cavalry, on the 27th of November, 1864, at a point in Colorado about forty miles from Fort Lyon. The details of the massacre are too revolting to be enumerated and I dismiss the matter with the statement, for the benefit of those who would care to look into the details, that three letters from Helen Hunt Jackson appeared in the New York Tribune, January 31, February 22, and February 28, 1880, reviewing the official testimony and presenting such facts therefrom that could be printed. But for that horrible butchery it is a fair presumption that all the subsequent wars with the Cheyennes and Arapahoes and their kindred tribes might possibly have been averted. In the official report of the Indian Peace Commission of 1868, alluded to the Sand Creek massacre, or the Chivington massacre as it is more generally known, the statement is deliberately made that: "It scarcely has its parallel in the records of Indian barbarity. Fleeing women, holding up their hands and praying for mercy, were shot down; infants were killed and scalped in derision; men were tortured and mutilated in a manner that would put to shame the savages of interior Africa. No one will be astonished that a war ensued, which cost the government $30,000,000, and carried conflagration and death into the border settlements. During the spring and summer of 1865 no less than 8,000 troops were withdrawn from the effective forces engaged against the rebellion to meet this Indian war." A line of military posts from the Platte River northwest to the Upper Big Horn and Yellowstone became necessary, and this in its turn aggravated the Indian disaffection, since it pierced their hunting grounds and disarranged their hunting plans.

The following letter received from Major General Dodge, in reply to my inquiry, gives so clear an exposition of the situation of affairs at the time referred to when the writer was in command of the Department of Kansas and the Territories, that I present it entire.

No. 1 Broadway, New York
July 19th, 1895

Gen. Nelson A. Miles,
Governor's Island, New York.

Dear Sir:

My recollections of the Indian Campaign of 1865–6, without having the records before me, are as follows:

The general plan was to move four columns so as to strike all the Indians at once, and to follow them winter and summer until we caught them or they surrendered.

I had had a good deal of experience in the Indian country and had set forth my views to Gen. Grant, and in an answer to a despatch from him had stated that I could make an Indian Campaign in the winter; and in the winter of 1864–5, I made a short Indian Campaign, opening all the routes that had been closed up between the Missouri River, Denver, New Mexico, Fort Laramie, etc., and this brought on a general movement in 1865.

The column that moved against the Southern Cheyennes and Arapahoes was under the command of Maj. Gen. John B. Sanborn. One of his detachments overtook a body of Indians somewhere near the Arkansas. They were under George Bent. He defeated them and brought about a temporary peace with those tribes. I suppose his success and his views in this matter were the reasons for his being placed upon the Peace Commission afterward. The interference by the Southern Commission virtually defeated all my plans against the Comanches and Apaches and we suffered for it later on.

In this battle George Bent was killed. The two Bent boys, Charles and George, I had captured in the South, in Northern Arkansas. I knew their father, Col. Bent, well, and when they surrendered to me I paroled them and sent them to their home in Colorado. They did not stay there long before one of them went at the head of the Southern Cheyennes, and of the Indians organized on the Arkansas and South; and Charles was at the head of the Northern Cheyennes, Arapahoes and Sioux. Both of these boys had been educated in some Catholic Institution in St. Louis; I think it was called "The Brothers College."

Column No. 2 was commanded by Col. Nelson Cole. He moved from Omaha up to Loup Fork to its head and crossed to the Niobrara River, and there divided his column, one division passing up the South Fork of the Cheyenne River under Lt. Col. Walker, with 500 pack mules and no train. This column was to follow the divide of the Black Hills and the western base, while Cole himself moved up the eastern base with his command, both joining at the Belle Fourche fork of the Cheyenne; after which they were to proceed and join me at Powder River, and so on. Col. Cole's columns fought several times and did good work.

Column No. 3 started from Sioux City and was simply an escort of one regiment to the Sawyer's Military Road Service. This column moved to and up the Niobrara to the Cheyenne, then up the Cheyenne to the vicinity of Pumpkin Buttes; which is almost east of the old Fort Reno Crossing of Powder River, where Charles Bent, with the Northern Cheyennes and a part of the Sioux, corralled them; and Sawyer, who had charge of the entire outfit, commenced parleying with them, and lost several of his men.

When the officer in command, who I think was Capt. Walford of the United States Troops, assumed command, corralled his train and fortified his position and got word to me, I immediately, by forced marches of my cavalry, undertook to capture Bent, at the same time, relieving Sawyer; but Bent got wind of the movements by his runners, and got away before they reached him. I then sent Sawyer through, under charge of one of my officers, on the route we had made to the Yellowstone River, namely: Fetterman Reno Crossing of the Powder River, thence across to the foot of the Big Horn Mountains by what was afterwards Fort McKinstry, and so on by the road now well known and traveled that we established to Montana.

Column No. 4 started from Salt Lake, under Gen. P. E. Conner, marched by way of the South Pass and Wind River, crossing the spurs of the Big Horn Mountains, and surprised and captured the Northern Cheyennes and Sioux on Tongue River. In this battle they captured all the camp equipage, some 800 ponies, etc. I sent to Conner, before the battle, a battalion of Pawnees who engaged in the fight. They killed and scalped some squaws and children and caused considerable unfriendly comment.

I myself moved by way of the Smoky Hill fork of the Republican across to Julesberg, to Fort Laramie, to where Fort Fetterman now is, and thence across to the Powder River and Big Horn. All the Indians in that country kept ahead of me until nearly all the Northern bands were concentrated between the Powder River and the Yellowstone. We captured and wiped out one band of Sioux who had been down on the Laramie Plains and had captured a portion of a company of Michigan volunteers who were escorting a supply train, and had burnt and butchered them. I got word of it, and knowing their trails, sent some cavalry, with two companies of Pawnees under Maj. North, to where they crossed Salt Creek; and those troops took this band in as they came north to join Bent.

The chief of the Indian party, an old Sioux, when he saw he was caught, walked out and harangued Maj. North, of the Pawnees, who spoke their language, and told him he was ready to die as he had been down on the Plains, and was full up to here of white men, putting his hand to his mouth. These troops wiped out this whole band. From them they captured the property taken from the Michigan Company, among which was one blank book in which the Indians described in their own picture language the whole trip and what they had done, showing the burning of the Michigan soldiers tied to the wheels of the wagons. The book was a curiosity and sent it forward to the War Department.

After the battle of Tongue River, as I was following up the Sioux and other bands who were over in front of Cole and who were not in the fight with Connor, I received orders from Gen.

Pope and Gen. Grant to return immediately to Fort Laramie, to send out runners to the Indians and bring them in there and conclude a peace with them. I protested, stating that within sixty days more I would be able to kill or capture all the Indians that were hostile, as they were nearly worn out and in front of me. I had then followed them steadily for six months or more, and they were becoming used up daily. Grant answered that he understood, but that was President Johnson's order, that the policy of the Government had changed, and there was no remedy but to promptly do the best that I could to gather the hostiles in at once. This order I promptly complied with; but my leaving the chase so abruptly and returning to Laramie, etc., the Indians did not understand, and I was unable to make a peace treaty that I would recommend. My troops in passing over and around the Black Hills, north of the North Platte, panned out considerable gold. There were several Californians and other miners in those regiments, and I knew any treaty that did not give us the country south of the Belle Fourche fork of the Cheyenne would not be of any use to us, as the troops, as soon as I disbanded them, would pour over into that portion of the Black Hills regardless of any treaty.

I therefore, endeavored to so make the line that the Indians should stay north of the Belle Fourche fork of the Cheyenne River. But the Indians insisted upon the North Platte as the line. They finally proposed to accept the South fork of the Cheyenne, but I would not accept this, so I declared a truce with them, simply agreeing for the winter that they should remain north of the Platte, and if they behaved themselves they would not be molested and if they did not, I would make a winter campaign again. They promised to comply with my demands, and I reported the facts and my reasons to my superiors.

Finally the Sherman-Harney Peace Commission was formed, who made the treaty that allowed them to come to the South fork of the Cheyenne. But as soon as my soldiers were disbanded they carried home the news of their discoveries in the Black Hills, and especially to California, and prospectors from that country and from Colorado and other points went to all the streams north of the Platte and violated the treaty. Our Government seemed unable to induce them to comply with the terms of the treaty. This brought first complaints, then protests, and finally the Sitting Bull war, and we who were building the U. P. Railway suffered from their depredations, stealing, killing, etc., from 1866 on.

I wrote Gen. Sherman strongly both before and after I left the service, as to the result of a treaty giving this line which the Indians demanded, and as I knew the country better than any one else, and the determination of the Indians, I would not agree to it. Gen. Pope and others did not agree with me. They believed they could conquer the Indian by kindness and that the line the Indians demanded could be protected against white people crossing it, although I had opened right through that territory a military wagon road, a short and excellent route from the Missouri to all points in Montana, and my troops were loaded with stories of mines of silver, gold and coal existing all over that country.

In one snowstorm on the Powder River we lost nearly or quite one thousand head of cavalry horses which had been weakened by long marches and poor feed. We also abandoned on Powder River about one hundred empty army wagons, remounting the cavalry on mules and on the 800 ponies Connor had captured; thus putting the cavalry in the fall of 1865 right on the Yellowstone, finely mounted and really fresh; and between the Yellowstone and Missouri, if the balance of the Indians had crossed the Yellowstone, we would have caught the last band that stuck together.

After the battle of Tongue River the Arapahoes that were not captured, scattered and made their way home; so did many of the Sioux, but the Cheyennes and part of the Sioux stuck together and came in at Fort Laramie.

In the campaign I selected the general positions for the following military posts, not the exact sites: Near the Big Horn River at the foot of the Big Horn Mountains, afterwards called McKinstry; at the crossing of the Powder River; the location at Fort Sanders on the Laramie Plains; also at the U. P. crossing of the North Platte, afterwards called Fort Steele; Fort Dodge on the Arkansas; also a post on the Smoky Hill fork of the Republican; I think it was afterwards called Sheridan, and others. I sent troops to occupy them in the spring of 1866.

I write you thus fully, in general, so as to enable you, if you are following these matters up, to form a thorough idea of the campaign and the general details as I understand them. Of course I have written this without going into the records fully, but you will find that they carry out these views pretty generally.

I am, very truly yours,
G. M. Dodge

P.S. General Grant intended to send me 12,000 men, but so many were mustered out that I had all told about 5,000. As fast as they arrived the governors of States would get orders for their muster out."

The results of the recall of General Dodge from the Powder River were a series of disasters of which the greatest was the Fetterman massacre of December 21, 1866, near Fort Phil Kearney, in which eighty-two officers and soldiers lost their lives, none of the command being left alive to tell the story.

The troops having been recalled and scattered in posts, the Indians, some of them, were enticed to Laramie to make a treaty, while others continued on the war path, cutting off detachments and emigrant trains, just as if peace had not been declared.

The Army Arrives
at the Chickahominy River

Confederate soldiers had strong feelings of patriotism, and a fervor to do battle. Young men in their teens hastened to answer the call to the colors. Fourteen-year-old James Dinkins found himself in the Seven Days battle that began at Savage Station and ended with the Federal forces in retreat after the battle at Malvern Hill.

General Lee was defending Richmond as General McClellan advanced on the city. In the battle that ensued the Union casualties were reported at fifteen thousand, Confederate losses just under twenty thousand. It was almost a certain victory for the Union forces, and they would have marched into Richmond, but that McClellan, against the advice of his generals, refused to risk any more Federal troops and pulled back his forces. Richmond was saved, and the Union licked its wounds.

In his story of the Seven Days battle, Private Dinkins refers to himself as the "Little Confederate." This excerpt is taken from *The Personal Recollections and Experiences in the Confederate Army* by James Dinkins (Robert Clarke, 1897).

The Army of Northern Virginia was now on the south side of Chickahominy, busily engaged digging ditches and throwing up breast-works. General McClellan crossed a large body of his army, and began to fortify his position on our right. General Johnston determined to prevent it, and moved General A. P.

Hill's division to the attack, which brought on the battle of Seven Pines (Fair Oaks), one of the most stubbornly contested battles for the time it lasted during the war. Griffith's brigade occupied a ravine on Mrs. Price's farm, being held in reserve. The horrors of the battle could well be understood by the great number of wounded that were hurried to the rear. We expected every moment to be called on, but we did not move until after night. About ten o'clock we moved to the front, passing over the dead and wounded of both armies. Our troops had driven the enemy from its works, and far beyond, leaving its dead and wounded in our hands. Griffith's brigade stood on picket all night, amid the groans of the wounded and dying, and among thousands of the dead. We were cautioned to keep very quiet, the enemy were but a few yards from us, and would open fire if they discovered us.

Captain Bostwick, of Company "H," Eighteenth Mississippi, known as the Hamer Rifles from Yazoo county, was a very large and fleshy man. He owned a body-servant named Tom, who was ordinarily very faithful and generally on hand, but the surroundings just now were not congenial to any of us, to say nothing of Tom. Captain Bostwick was a fearless man, who knew no danger, but wanted to obey orders. He was hungry, and began in a low tone to call, "Tom! Tom! TOM!" Tom did not answer, but the Yanks did. We were lying down in a thicket of small pines, which were riddled in a few minutes. It seemed as if they had a million men, and the way we clung to the ground would have been credible to a lot of flounders. We remained quiet for an hour or so, and when daylight came the enemy had recrossed the Chickahominy. In this battle General Johnston was severely wounded. He was carried to Richmond and placed in the Ballard Hotel, where he lay between life and death for some weeks. At this time peerless Robert E. Lee was assigned to the command of the Army of Northern Virginia. Griffith's brigade was returned to the ravine on Mrs. Price's farm, through which ran the Chickahominy river, and here we remained several days watching the enemy. Each day our artillery would take position and shell the enemy, who responded in good shape. It finally reached the point when the latter would fire on a single man who exposed himself. During all this time our wagons and servants were far in the rear. We had not seen Uncle Freeman for two weeks, and we wondered what had become of him. He finally turned up, however, one afternoon, just as the sun was disappearing behind the woods. Uncle Freeman had been in Richmond doing odd jobs to make money, with which to buy something to eat for our mess. He reached the left of the line, and stood gazing at the Yankee camps across the river. He had a blue bucket of molasses on his head, and a sack of baker's bread and bologna sausage in his hand. Uncle Freeman had curiosity like other people, and against the advice of several men he walked up to the crown of the hill and watched the enemy. He had been there probably three minutes when about twenty guns opened on him. The shells tore up the ground and threw dirt fifty feet high. But when the dust cleared away Uncle Freeman was gone. We afterward learned he was in Richmond, nine miles away, for supper. What became of his supplies we never knew, but the circumstance made a Christian of Uncle Freeman. He held prayer-meeting every night in camp after that for a month, and would force the other negroes in the regiment to attend. He said, "I gwine ter bless de Lord all the balance of my life, for sparing me on that occasion." Uncle Freeman, until the day of his death, would tell about how the Yankees blowed him plumb to Richmond. We asked him what became of the molasses. He said, "Gord er mighty knows. I aynt seed em sence."

William Blake, a warm friend of the Little Confederate, was detailed by Colonel Griffin as courier for the regiment. He was called "Billie Blake," and was a pet of the entire regiment. Billy was exceedingly handsome, and up to this time managed to keep himself well dressed. He and the Little Confederate were about the same age. They were very successful foragers, and generally knew what was going on. By some means, Billy got hold of a box of paper collars, the first they ever heard of. He divided them with his friend, and they agreed when one was soiled it should be given to Uncle Freeman to wash. They each gave Uncle Freeman some soiled clothes and two paper collars, requesting him to have them ready that afternoon. Soon Uncle Freeman had the things in a kettle boiling. When he was ready to take them out, which he proceeded to do with a stick, he could not find the collars. He knew he had put them in the kettle together with other things, and could not account for their absence. The two boys were sitting at the root of a large tree, watching and listening to Uncle Freeman. He said, "Hi, here! What dun 'come of dem nice white collars?" He raked the bottom of the kettle again and again, but found no collars. He then emptied the water and found a few fragments of paper. He said, "My God! Dis is mighty curious. I put dem collars in that kettle sure, and I been standing here all the time." The boys heard him talking, so Billy said to him, "Uncle Freeman, hurry up! Bud and I want to go." Uncle Freeman walked over to the boys with a few scraps of paper in his hand. He said, "Mars Billy, did you give me any white collars to wash?" "Yes." said Billy. "We gave you two, and we would like to have them right away. We are going to town." Uncle Freeman was greatly troubled. He could not explain the loss, so Billy told him he must pay for them, and that each one was worth a dollar. Billy collected two dollars from him, and arranged with another friend, Jim Finley, to tell Uncle Freeman they were paper, and, of course could not be washed. Well, now, maybe Uncle Freeman didn't rear and charge! It was a long time before Billy Blake could get any more clothes washed by Uncle Freeman. He talked about it for several weeks, saying, "Nobody but a Yankee would er made collars out of paper to 'ceive folks." Of course, the two dollars were returned to Uncle Freeman many times over.

Billy Blake was a gallant soldier, as brave as Forrest. He was desperately wounded at Gettysburg, and lay on the field a day and night without attention. He was finally picked up, but with little hope that he would recover. The Federal surgeons amputated one of his legs near the hip, but Billy still lives, and is a prominent citizen of New Orleans, where he is surrounded by a lovely family and a large circle of friends. He and the Little Confederate are still devoted friends.

Uncle Freeman was faithful and true to the last, and his honesty was unimpeachable. He was my friend as well as my servant, and, negro though he was, I drop a sad but willing tear to his memory, and as a tribute to his loyalty.

The seven days' battles of Richmond will be a study for future military leaders. A writer in the Boston Transcript wrote, "McClellan was the greatest general developed on either side, and while he was not always successful, he never suffered defeat." This statement will not be sustained by a single man who served in the "Army of the Potomac" during the seven days' battles. General McClellan was not only defeated at Richmond, but he was routed. Nor is this fact a disparagement of him as a great commander. On the contrary, we believe he was the only general at that time who could have saved the Union Army. The attack of General Lee's army was irresistible. No troops on earth, with the arms then in use, could have withstood his charges. It has been thirty-three years since those great battles were fought, but the scenes and incidents which our Little Confederate witnessed on those occasions are as fresh in his mind as when they occurred, and his opinion of what took place has been confirmed again and again by subsequent experience and study.

Stonewall Jackson, with his command, was in the Shenandoah Valley confronting a superior force. General Lee's plan provided that he should move with great dispatch to the rear of McClellan's right flank. The attack was made on Thursday afternoon. The enemy's right flank was doubled back on his right center, having been driven from his works at every point where an attack was made. It was hoped that Jackson would reach his rear on Friday, but he did not. On Saturday, the battle of "Gains' Mill" was fought. Griffith's brigade was held in reserve. We watched Cobb's Georgia brigade move forward through the Chickahominy swamp under a deadly fire from what was known as the "Wild Cat Battery." This fort, from which the big guns were shelling Cobb's men, was casemated with railroad iron, which had ten to fifteen feet of earth thrown on top. In front of this, and also of the breast-works on either side, all the timber had been cut down, falling in the directions of our lines. All the small branches of the trees had bayonets stuck on them, and it was impossible for Cobb's men to make much headway, but in spite of the obstructions, these brave Georgians pushed on. We watched them with great admiration, and saw them finally climb over the enemy's works. The enemy, however was reinforced, and very soon drove the Georgians back, yet the gallant fellows reformed and captured the fort the second time, but were driven back again. Night closed the battle. Griffith's brigade

moved forward, and remained in line of battle all night. It was
understood we would renew the attack in the morning. Two
men, Bateman Brown and William Howd were detailed from
Company "C" Eighteenth Mississippi regiment, with instructions to crawl as near the enemy's works as possible, and report
the first movement of any attempt to retreat. We heard that in
case he moved, we would attack and hold him. Brown and Howd
returned about two o'clock Sunday morning with the information, but we did not advance. It was said because General Magruder, our division commander, failed to carry out his
instructions. About sunrise we moved forward, and soon had
possession of the enemy's works without firing a gun. As we
stood in the fort and ditches, we wondered what it all meant.
Suddenly the enemy's batteries, a mile off, began shelling our
line. We formed on both sides of the York River Railroad. There
were evidences of great confusion in the enemy's ranks. All
kinds of army and camp stuff were scattered in every direction,
cooking utensils, medical, commissary and quartermaster supplies, and hundreds of other things. It was intensely hot, and to
prevent our men from getting water, medicines were thrown in
the wells and springs.

While waiting the order to advance, a wicket shell struck
the railroad section house just in our front and exploded, a piece
of which we distinctly saw pass over our heads. In falling it
struck General Griffith on the thigh, tearing the flesh down to
his knee, while he was sitting on his horse near the fort just in
our rear. He was removed to Richmond, where he died that
night. His death was a great grief as well as a great loss. He was
a man of much promise, and while he had already distinguished
himself, would certainly have won still greater distinction had
he lived.

Colonel William Barksdale of the Thirteenth Mississippi,
the senior colonel of the brigade, assumed command. We moved
forward, overtook the enemy about two miles distant, and immediately brought on the battle of Savage Station (the enemy
called it Peach Orchard), where only two regiments of Barksdale's brigade were engaged, the Thirteenth and Twenty-first
Mississippi, but several other brigades were in it, and all together made a very hot fight. The battle was carried into the

night, a terrific rain followed, and next morning the ground was covered with pools of water. Several thousand Federal soldiers lay dead and wounded on the field and in the adjacent woods. Our little Confederate had lost his shoes in the mud of the Chickahominy bottom the day before, and asked a friend (Fort Saunders) to accompany him among the dead, and see if they could find a pair to fit. They examined several pairs, and finally Saunders said, "Here is a good pair of boots, but they are so wet I can not pull them off." He told the little Confederate, "Hold on to one arm while I pull at the boot," and while thus engaged the Yankee's leg came off. A shell had nearly torn it off before, but we had not observed it. When Saunders fell backward with the leg, the Little Confederate said, "I do not want any shoes," and starting away passed a man he supposed to be dead, who had a splendid haversack which the little fellow fancied he wanted. He thought it would be no harm to take the haversack, and stooped down to do so. As he pulled at it, the Yankee opened his eyes and asked for water, saying, "There is a spoon in my haversack." The Little Confederate took the spoon and gave him water from a pool near by. The man died after drinking the third spoonful. The Little Confederate did not disturb the haversack, but he kept the spoon and has it yet. It is a very large tablespoon, engraved "H. E. C.," and was manufactured by Butler & Mc-Carthy. He advertised it in the Detroit Free Press for a year, but never elicited an inquiry or response of any kind. He used the spoon through the balance of the war, but wore the end off parching corn.

On looking over the battle field, we found evidence of great confusion and defeat. The enemy threw away their guns and every thing else which would impede their flight, but the guns were nearly all bent or broken. They had placed them between two saplings as they ran and bent the barrels. Prior to this time we had very few rifles. Nothing but old muzzle-loading, smoothbore muskets. It will, therefore, be easily understood at what disadvantage we fought at long range. The only thing we could do was to "charge 'em," and get within smooth-bore distance. Up to this time our men had driven the enemy from every point of attack. We remained in the Savage Station neighborhood Monday while the cavalry were trying to locate them. During

Sunday night after the battle, "Stonewall Jackson" reached our line, but too late to cut off the enemy's retreat. Our inability to hold him in position on the Chickahominy enabled him to escape before General Jackson could arrive.

Monday afternoon General D. H. Hill found the enemy in what is known as White-Oak Swamp, trying to reach his gunboats on the James River. General Hill attacked him with great vigor, driving him two miles, but lost a number of his men. It was a hard fought battle, and thousands of Federal dead lay on the field. Proper credit has never been given General Hill for this engagement. He fought an army three or four times his strength, and drove them so long as daylight lasted. Barksdale's brigade reached the battlefield about eleven o'clock at night and stood picket until morning. It was a terrible march, the night as dark as Erebus. As we worked our way through the woods we stumbled on the dead and wounded at every step, and the wounded would often cry out in their intense suffering. All night we could hear them begging for water, and occasionally one would beg to be killed and relieved of his suffering. Up to this time our Little Confederate had never seen such horrible sights, and had never been very badly frightened, but he now realized very forcibly that war was terrible, and his chances of ever seeing home again were largely against him. When morning came the enemy had retreated. Again our command moved slowly back into the road leading from Richmond to "Turkey Bend" on the James River. We had nothing to eat since Saturday except green apples, the troops were tired and sleepy. Barksdale's brigade halted in the main road, and the Eighteenth Mississippi regiment stood at a point where it forks with another. There was a large oak tree in the fork, on which three sign boards were nailed. One pointing to Richmond, one to Turkey Bend, and the other to some place now forgotten. We were silently waiting and not a sound was heard. The men had no information about the enemy. President Davis, General Lee, General Jackson and a few others galloped up to the point where we were, and in a moment General Huger came up. Mr. Davis was dressed in citizen's clothes. I remember he wore a Panama hat, and I thought him the grandest looking man I had ever seen. General Lee inquired of General Huger, "Do you occupy Malvern Hill?" General Huger answered, "No, the enemy has obstructed the road by throwing large trees across it. I could not reach Malvern Hill with my artillery." General Lee remarked, "You should have done so with your infantry. Move at once."

But it was too late. McClellan's army was strongly posted on Malvern Hill at the time the conversation occurred. Malvern Hill was the key to the situation, and both commanders knew it. Had General Lee's orders been carried out, the Army of the Potomac would have been prisoners the following day.

Soon after the conversation between General Lee and Huger, every thing was headed toward Malvern Hill. The enemy's gun-boats were shelling the woods at every point in our front. Barksdale's brigade reached a position in front of the enemy's lines, screened from view somewhat by small pine trees. We lay down and waited for the command to move forward. Large shells from the gun-boats and from land batteries, also, were tearing and literally smashing everything in reach. The Camden Rifles, a company of the Eighteenth Mississippi, lay under a large oak tree. A ten inch shell struck it about ten feet above the ground, cutting off the entire top. This fell on the Camden Rifles, killing several men and creating a worse panic than if ten times the number had been killed by bullets. Very soon the battle opened. The enemy was massed on all sides of Malvern Hill, his artillery planted, so as to command the country for miles. One line stood above the other on the steep hill. It was a terrible occasion. Brigade after brigade was sent against his lines, and were slaughtered. It was one of the hottest battles ever fought up to that time. It was impossible to reach the top of the hill, and yet the charge was renewed time and again. Barksdale's brigade lost a great many good men. Captain E. G. Henry, of Company "C," Eighteenth Mississippi, was wounded in the leg, about one hundred yards from the enemy's lines, and bled to death before assistance reached him. He was a patriot in the highest sense, a man who regarded duty above all considerations. A great many others were killed, but I remember the universal sorrow at the death of Green B. Crane, a young man of faultless character. He graduated at the University of Mississippi at the breaking out of the war, and gave promise of a brilliant future. He was brave as Caesar, determined as Jackson, and gentle as Ruth. He was liberal, chivalrous and companionable. What more could be said of him? The Little Confederate and Green Crane were school mates and he remembers him with deep and tender affection. The horrors of the battle of Malvern Hill can never be known, and hardly even imagined by those who were not there. While the enemy retreated during the night, our army was badly crippled, but remained on the field. We had retained our position, but at a tremendous sacrifice. What the result would have been had General Lee's orders been carried out must forever remain unknown.

The Spy System

McClellan was a cautious general in that he hated to make a decision to move troops without having information on the strength of the enemy he was about to face. The General eventually placed a great deal of importance on the intelligence gathered by Allan Pinkerton, one of the famous private detectives of the day, who had a flair for organization.

Pinkerton's men would gather details of Confederate troop movements, train schedules, and such minor information as how many men were on sick call, how many large cooking kettles there were in the camps, etc. The master detective would take all this material and produce voluminous reports projecting the figures to cast light on a particular area. The details were so minute that McClellan spent hours studying them, and based many decisions on the data received. And most of the time, the information and the projections were incorrect!

There were other spies employed, many of them women, some in the theater who used travelling plays to move freely behind the lines; others dressed in uniform to conceal their sex, and slipped through the lines.

Charles Anderson Dana was forty-four years old when his appointment as Assistant Secretary of War brought him behind the scenes during one of the most crucial periods in the Civil War. When Secretary Stanton called him to Washington, Dana had been involved for nearly fifteen years in the management of the New York Tribune, a newspaper that played an important part in solidifying Northern sentiment. The following is culled from his memoirs, first published in the *North American Review* in August, 1891, and collected as *Recollections of the Civil War* (D. Appleton & Co., 1898).

After Early's invaders had retired and quiet was restored, I went to Mr. Stanton for new orders. As there was no probability of an immediate change in the situation before Petersburg, the Secretary did not think it necessary for me to go back to Grant, but preferred that I remain in the department, helping with the routine work.

Much of my time at this period was spent investigating charges against defaulting contractors and dishonest agents, and in ordering arrests of persons suspected of disloyalty to the government. I assisted, too, in supervising spies who were going back and forth between the lines. Among these I remember one, a sort of peddler—whose name I will call Morse—who travelled between Washington and Richmond. When he went down it was in the character of a man who had entirely hoodwinked the Washington authorities, and who, in spite of them, or by some corruption or other, always brought with him into the Confederate lines something that the people wanted—dresses for the ladies or some little luxury that they couldn't get otherwise. The things that he took with him were always supervised by our agents before he went away. When he came back he brought us in exchange a lot of valuable information. He was doubtless a spy on both sides; but as we got a great deal of information, which could be had in no other way, about the strength of the Confederate armies, and the preparations and the movements of the enemy, we allowed the thing to go on. The man really did good service for us that summer, and, as we were frequently able to verify by other means the important information he brought, we had a great deal of confidence in him.

Early in October, 1864, he came back from Richmond, and, as usual, went to Baltimore to get his outfit for the return trip. When he presented himself again in Washington, the chief detective of the War Department, Colonel Baker, examined his goods carefully, but this time he found that Morse had many things that we could not allow him to take. Among his stuff were uniforms and other military goods, and all this, of course, was altogether too contraband to be passed. We had all his bills, telling where he bought these things in Baltimore. They amounted to perhaps twenty-five thousand dollars or more. So we confiscated the contraband goods, and put Morse in prison.

But the merchants in Baltimore were partners in his guilt, and Secretary Stanton declared he would arrest every one of them and put them in prison until the affair could be straightened up. He turned the matter over to me then, as he was going to Fort Monroe for a few days. I immediately sent Assistant-Adjutant-General Lawrence to Baltimore with orders to see that all persons implicated were arrested. Lawrence telegraphed me, on October 16th that the case would involve the arrest of two hundred citizens. I reported to the Secretary, but he was determined to go ahead. The next morning ninety-seven of the leading citizens of Baltimore were arrested, brought to Washington, and confined in Old Capitol Prison, principally in solitary cells. There was great satisfaction among the Union people of the town, but great indignation among Southern sympathizers. Presently a deputation from Baltimore came over to see President Lincoln. It was an outrage, they said; the gentlemen arrested were most respectable merchants and faultless citizens, and they demanded that they all be set instantly at liberty and damages paid them. Mr. Lincoln sent the deputation over to the War Department and Mr. Stanton, who had returned by this time, sent for me. "All Baltimore is coming here," he said. "Sit down and hear the discussion."

They came in, the bank presidents and boss merchants of Baltimore—there must have been at least fifty million dollars represented in the deputation—and sat down around the fire in the Secretary's office. Presently they began to make their speeches, detailing the circumstances and the wickedness of this outrage. There was no ground for it, they said, no justification. After half a dozen of them had spoken, Mr. Stanton asked one after another if he had anything more to say, and they all said no. Then Mr. Stanton began, and delivered one of the most eloquent speeches that I ever heard. He described the beginning of the war, for which, he said, there was no justification; being beaten in an election was no reason for destroying the Government. Then he went on to the fact that half a million of our young men had been laid in untimely graves by this conspiracy of the slave interest. He outlined the whole conspiracy in the most solemn and impressive terms, and then he depicted the offense that this man Morse, aided by these several merchants had committed. "Gentlemen," he said, "if you would like to examine the bills of what he was taking to the enemy, here they are."

When Stanton had finished, these gentlemen, without answering a word, got up and one by one went away. That was the only speech I ever listened to that cleared out the entire audience.

Early in the winter of 1863–'64 a curious thing happened in the secret service of the War Department. Some time in the February or March before, a slender and prepossessing young fellow, between twenty-two and twenty-six apparently, had applied at the War Department for employment as a spy within the Confederate lines.

The main body of the Army of Northern Virginia was then lying at Gordonsville, and the headquarters of the Army of the Potomac were at Culpeper Courthouse. General Grant had not yet come from the West to take command of the momentous campaign which afterward opened with his movement into the Wilderness on the 5th of May.

The young man who sought this terrible service was well dressed and intelligent, and professed to be animated by motives purely patriotic. He was a clerk in one of the departments. All that he asked was that he should have a horse and an order which would carry him safely through the Federal lines, and in return, he undertook to bring information from General Lee's army and from the Government of the Confederacy in Richmond. He understood perfectly the perilous nature of the enterprise he proposed.

Finding that the applicant bore a good character in the office where he was employed, it was determined to accept his proposal. He was furnished with a horse, an order that would pass him through the Union lines, and also, I believe, with a moderate sum of money, and then he departed. Two or three weeks later he reported at the War Department. He had been in Gordonsville and Richmond, had obtained the confidence of the Confederate authorities, and was the bearer of a letter from Mr.

Jefferson Davis to Mr. Clement C. Clay, the agent of the Confederate Government in Canada, then known to be stationed at St. Catherine's, not far from Niagara Falls. Mr. Clay had as his official associate Jacob Thompson, of Mississippi, who had been Secretary of the Interior in the Cabinet of President Buchanan, and, like Mr. Clay, had been serving the Confederate Government since its organization.

The letter from Mr. Davis the young man exhibited, but only the outside of the envelope was examined. The address was in the handwriting of the Confederate chief, and the statement of our young adventurer that it was merely a letter of recommendation advising Messrs. Clay and Thompson that they might repose confidence in the bearer, since he was ardently devoted to the Confederate cause and anxious to serve the great purpose that it had in view, appeared entirely probable; so the young man was allowed to proceed to Niagara Falls and Canada. He made some general report upon the condition of the rebel army at Gordonsville, but it was of no particular value, except that in its more interesting features it agreed with our information from other sources.

Our spy was not long in returning from St. Catherine's with a dispatch which was also allowed to pass unopened, upon his assurance that it contained nothing of importance. In this way he went back and forward from Richmond to St. Catherine's once or twice. We supplied him with money to a limited extent, and also with one or two more horses. He said that he got some money from the Confederates, but had not thought it prudent to accept from them anything more than very small sums, since his professed zeal for the Confederate cause forbade his receiving anything for his traveling expenses beyond what was absolutely necessary.

During the summer of 1864 the activity of Grant's campaign, and the fighting which prevailed all along the line, somewhat impeded our young man's expeditions, but did not stop them. All his subsequent dispatches, however, whether coming from Richmond or from Canada, were regularly brought to the War Department, and were opened, and in every case a copy of them was kept. As it was necessary to break the seals and destroy the envelopes in opening them, there was some difficulty in sending them forward in what should appear to be the original wrappers. Coming from Canada, the paper employed was English, and there was a good deal of trouble in procuring paper of the same appearance. I remember also that one important dispatch, which was sealed with Mr. Clay's seal, had to be delayed somewhat while we had an imitation seal engraved. But these delays were easily accounted for at Richmond by the pretense that they had been caused by accidents upon the road and by the necessity of avoiding the Federal pickets. At any rate, the confidence of the Confederates in our agent and in theirs never seemed to be shaken by any of these occurrences.

Finally our dispatch bearer reported one day at the War Department with a document which, he said, was of extraordinary consequence. It was found to contain an account for setting fire to New York and Chicago by means of clock-work machines that were to be placed in several of the large hotels and places of amusement—particularly in Barnum's Museum in New York—and to be set off simultaneously, so that the fire department in each place would be unable to attend to the great number of calls that would be made upon it on account of these Confederate conflagrations in so many different quarters, and thus these cities might be greatly damaged, or even destroyed.

This dispatch was duly sealed up again and way taken to Richmond, and a confidential officer was at once sent to New York to warn General Dix, who was in command there, of the Confederate project. The general was very unwilling to believe that any such design could be seriously entertained, and Mr. John A. Kennedy, then superintendent of police, was equally incredulous. But the Secretary of War was peremptory in his orders, and when the day of the incendiary attempt arrived both the military and the police made every preparation to prevent the threatened catastrophe. The officer who went from Washington was lodged in the St. Nicholas Hotel, one of the large establishments that were to be set on fire, and while he was washing his hands in the evening, preparatory to going to dinner, a fire began burning in the room next to his. It was promptly put out and was found to be caused by a clock-work apparatus which had been left in that room by a lodger who had departed some hours before. Other fires likewise occurred. In every instance these fires were extinguished without much damage and without exciting any considerable public attention, thanks to the precautions that had been taken in consequence of the warning derived from Mr. Clay's dispatch to Mr. Benjamin in Richmond. The plan of setting fire to Chicago proved even more abortive; I do not remember that any report of actual burning was received from there.

Later in the fall, after the military operations had substantially terminated for the season, a dispatch was brought from Canada, signed by Mr. Clay, and addressed to Mr. Benjamin, as Secretary of State in the Confederate Government, conveying the information that a new and really formidable military expedition against northern Vermont—particularly against Burlington, if I am not mistaken—had been organized and fitted out in Canada, and would make its attack as soon as practicable. This was after the well-known attempt upon St. Albans and Lake Champlain, on October 19, 1864, and promised to be much more injurious. The dispatch reached Washington one Sunday morning, and was brought to the War Department as usual, but its importance in the eyes of the Confederate agents had led to its being prepared for transportation with uncommon care. It was placed between two thicknesses of the pair of re-enforced cavalry trousers which the messenger wore, and sewed up so that when he was mounted it was held between his thigh, and the saddle.

Having been carefully ripped out and opened, it was immediately carried to Mr. Stanton, who was confined to his house by a cold. He read it. "This is serious," he said. "Go over to the White House and ask the President to come here." Mr. Lincoln was found dressing to go to church, and he was soon driven to Mr. Stanton's house. After discussing the subject in every aspect, and considering thoroughly the probability that to keep the dispatch would put an end to communications by this channel, they determined that it must be kept. The conclusive reason for this step was that it established beyond question the fact that the Confederates, while sheltering themselves behind the British Government in Canada, had organized and fitted out a military expedition against the United States. But while the dispatch afforded evidence that could not be gainsaid, the mere possession of it was not sufficient. It must be found in the possession of the Confederate dispatch bearer, and the circumstances attending its capture must be established in such a manner that the British Foreign Office would not be able to dispute the genuineness of the document. "We must have this paper for Seward," said Mr. Lincoln. "As for the young man, get him out of the scrape if you can."

Accordingly, the paper was taken back to the War Department and sewed up again in the trousers whence it had been taken three hours before. The bearer was instructed to start at dusk on the road which he usually took in passing through the lines, to be at a certain tavern outside of Alexandria at nine o'clock in the evening, and to stop there to water his horse. Then information was sent through Major-General Augur, commandant of Washington and the surrounding region, to Colonel Henry H. Wells, then provost marshal general of the defenses south of the Potomac, stationed at Alexandria, directing him to be at this tavern at nine o'clock in the evening, and to arrest a Confederate dispatch bearer, concerning whom authentic information had been received at the War Department, and whose description was furnished for his (Wells's) guidance. He was to do the messenger no injury, but to make sure of his person and of all papers that he might have upon him, and to bring him under a sufficient guard directly to the War Department. And General Augur was directed to be present there, in order to assist in the examination of the prisoner, and to verify any dispatches that might be found.

Just before midnight a carriage drove up to the door of the War Department with a soldier on the box and two soldiers on the front seat within, while the back seat was occupied by Colonel Wells and the prisoner. Of course, no one but the two or three who had been in the secret was aware that this gentleman had walked quietly out of the War Department only a few hours previously, and that the paper which was the cause of the entire ceremony had been sewed up in his clothes just before his departure. Colonel Wells reported that, while the prisoner had offered no resistance, he was very violent and outrageous in his language, and that he boasted fiercely of his devotion to the Confederacy and his detestation of the Union. During the examination which now followed he said nothing except to answer a few questions, but his bearing—patient, scornful, undaunted—was that of an incomparable actor. If Mr. Clay and Mr. Benjamin had been present, they would have been more than ever certain that he was one of their noblest young men. His hat, boots, and other articles of his clothing were taken off one by one. The hat and boots were first searched, and finally the dispatch was found in his trousers and taken out. Its nature and the method of its capture were stated in a memorandum which was drawn up on the spot and signed by General Augur and Colonel Wells and one or two other officers who were there for the purpose, and then the dispatch bearer himself was sent off to the Old Capitol Prison.

The dispatch with the documents of verification was handed over to Mr. Seward for use in London, and a day or two afterward the warden of the Old Capitol Prison was directed to give the dispatch bearer an opportunity of escaping, with a proper show of attempted prevention. One afternoon the spy walked into my office. "Ah!" said I, "you have run away."

"Yes, sir," he answered.

"Did they shoot at you?"

"They did, and didn't hit me; but I didn't think that would answer the purpose. So I shot myself through the arm."

He showed me the wound. It was through the fleshy part of the forearm, and due care had been taken not to break any bones. A more deliberate and less dangerous wound could not be, and yet it did not look trivial.

He was ordered to get away to Canada as promptly as possible, so that he might explain the loss of his dispatch before it should become known there by any other means. An advertisement offering two thousand dollars for his recapture was at once inserted in the New York Herald, the Pittsburgh Journal, and the Chicago Tribune. No one ever appeared to claim the reward, but in about a week the escaped prisoner returned from Canada with new dispatches that had been entrusted to him. They contained nothing of importance, however. The wound in his arm had borne testimony in his favor, and the fact that he had hurried through to St. Catherine's without having it dressed was thought to afford conclusive evidence of his fidelity to the Confederate cause.

The war was ended soon after this adventure, and as his services had been of very great value, a new place, with the assurance of lasting employment, was found for the young man in one of the bureaus of the War Department. He did not remain there very long, however, and I don't know what became of him. He was one of the cleverest creatures I ever saw. His style of patriotic lying was sublime; it amounted to genius.

Free Negroes, Contrabands, and Slaves

President Lincoln knew he had to broaden the base of the war and to discourage European trade with the Confederacy. He was ready to make slavery an issue. Britain and France could hardly risk trading with the South which practiced and was fighting for the right to continue the barbarous rite of slavery. Lincoln had long been repelled by the practice of slavery and he readied his Emancipation Proclamation early in 1862. He wanted to announce this new and important policy after an impressive military victory—and that was slow in coming. Seward pointed out that if the Emancipation was declared after a series of Union defeats it would be more like a cry for help than a statement of stern policy.

Antietam gave Lincoln the military action he had been looking for. The North looked upon it as a victory, and he issued his Proclamation in September. It declared freedom for all slaves in those areas where the Federal Government had no authority, but it allowed slavery to continue in slave states which remained under Federal control! Some doubted the legality of the document. The end result was confusion and chaos.

It soon became the personal and professional headache for General William E. Doster, Provost Marshal of Washington, whose memoirs were published as *Lincoln and Episodes of the Civil War* (G. P. Putnam, 1915).

After the Gordian knot, as to the disposition of slaves who

were abandoned by the masters on the advance of the Union
armies, had been cut by the decision of General Butler, accepted
by General Halleck, classifying the slaves with abandoned rebel
cattle and corn, and as such liable to be held and used by the
Union forces, the provost marshal general of the Army of the
Potomac forwarded great numbers of them to Washington for
disposal.

It did not follow, however, that the disposal of them here
was an easy task. General Butler's logic did well enough with
negroes captured on the advance, but that was the smallest part.
How to deal with those who abandoned their masters instead of
being abandoned by them? And it followed by no means because
the runaway said so, that his master was disloyal or even outside
the Union lines. In addition, they were entirely unused to freedom, and were like so many children asking us to take care of,
rear them, teach them, and support them until they knew how
to manage themselves. The free colored negroes at Washington
hated them as rivals. The slaves despised them for being runa-
ways.

Washington, Baltimore, and Alexandria were still slave cities and the Fugitive Slave Law was in full force. The three cities
each still had its slave pen, surrounded by gangs of professional
kidnappers, who found in the contrabands an inexhaustible field
for the exercise of their inhuman trade and for filling the Washington City jail. Warrants were daily issued by the commissioners, under the Fugitive Slave Law, which enabled the slave-
owners of Maryland, or the District of Columbia to send deputy
United States marshals into the midst of a Union regiment or
contraband quarter, to secure for himself the property in any
negro who had escaped from Virginia, and for the pure legal
expenses.

There came to our relief the Act of Congress of July 17,
1862:

> That all slaves of persons who shall hereafter be
> engaged in rebellion against the Government of the
> United States, or who shall in any way give aid or com-
> fort thereto, escaping from such persons and taking ref-
> uge within the lines of the army, and all slaves captured

from such persons or deserted by them and coming under the control of the Government of the United States, and all slaves of such persons found on, or being within, any place occupied by rebel forces and afterwards occupied by the forces of the United States, shall be deemed captives of war, and shall be forever free of their servitude, and not again held as slaves.

Sec. X. That no slaves escaping into any State, Territory, or the District of Columbia, from any other State, shall be delivered up, or in any way impeded or hindered of his liberty, except for crime or some offense against the laws, unless the person claiming said fugitives shall first make oath that the person to whom the labor or service of each fugitive is alleged to be due is his lawful owner, and has not borne arms aginst the United States in the present rebellion, nor in any way given aid and comfort thereto. And no person engaged in the military or naval service of the United States shall, under any pretense whatever, assume to decide on the validity of the claim of any person, or surrender up any such person to the claimant on pain of being dismissed from the service.

To retain the grip the military police had on their people, and comply with the law, the following measures were taken:

Each contraband, on his arrival, was examined by the detectives in relation to the loyalty and residence of his master, and was furnished with a paper signed by General Wadsworth, entitling him to the protection of the military authorities of the United States. He was sent under guard to what was then called Duff Green's Row (later Carrol Prison) next door to the Old Capitol Prison, and guarded by a detachment of the Old Capitol Guard. The house was divided into many small rooms. The contrabands were lodged and under the superintendent of the Old Capitol and were supplied with rations and fuel. For clothing, I turned over to them the stolen second-hand blankets and uniforms recovered in the hands of citizens. The men were divided into squads of twenty under white non-commissioned officers, and made subject to requisitions for laborers in the medical and

quartermaster's bureaus, and received as wages from fifty cents
to one dollar per day.

The quarters now became densely crowded. Efforts were
made to secure them employment in families. But as they were
farm hands, nobody cared to have them. Shortly afterward the
smallpox broke out among them. The sick were kept here, the
house turned into a hospital, and the whole removed to the
barracks, about a mile north of Washington, formerly occupied
by McClellan's bodyguard. A permanent guard was necessary.
The smallpox broke out among them again. I offered to relieve
the lieutenant in charge and ordered him to move his men to a
distance from the contagion. He thought it his duty however to
stand by them in trouble, caught the malady, and died. During
the winter I turned a lot of goods confiscated at Leonardstown
into $2,000, and bought them cheap bedding and clothing at
Philadelphia. As fast as we could get the contrabands employment we shipped them North and made room for others. In spite
of the utmost precautions, the slave-catchers—principally two
named Wise and Allen, succeeded frequently in running these
freemen into the Washington Pen.

One evening, the chief laundress of the Harewood Hospital,
Rachel Sutherland, a contraband who came within our lines at
Aquia Creek, and had General Wadsworth's military protection
on her person, was surprised at the unaccustomed absence of
her husband, Sandy Sutherland, employed at the Patent Office
Hospital. She suspected foul play, and requested Dr. Johnson,
the surgeon in charge of Harewood, to go with her to the city
jail. When there, she was told she could come in, but as soon
as she had passed the door was consigned to a cell. Her three
young children were left at the hospital and the mother's distress was extreme. Dr. Johnson turned to me and indignantly
demanded redress. A little investigation proved that this noto-
rious pair, Wise and Allen, had run her husband into jail although he had also a military protection on his person.

I sent down a lieutenant and ten men with orders to release
the negroes, peaceably if they could, forcibly, if they must.

The jail guards refused to deliver them, but the lieutenant
marched his men inside and, resistance being useless, the fugitives were given up, the mother restored to her children and

the husband placed under the bayonets of the United States at the Patent Office. Next day I caught the kidnappers and gave them six week's solitary confinement in the old Capitol. When released they returned to the business. This dispute was referred to President Lincoln, who refused to interfere.

On another occasion the jail officers were not so easily frightened.

Complaint having been made to Wadsworth, in the evening, that the contraband quarters had been invaded and a Virginia negro taken to the jail, the general ordered a lieutenant to go down and release him. The deputy, Phillips, refused and sent for Bradley, his attorney, to advise him what course to pursue. Bradley came and advised him not to give up his negro.

Meanwhile Lamon returned and ordered off the lieutenant. The lieutenant made a charge and captured Phillips and Bradley, and Lamon captured one private soldier and quickly locked the door. There was no use trying to force the door at that hour, and besides he had no instructions to proceed to violence. So he took Messrs. Bradley and Phillips to the Central Guard House where they stayed overnight. Early in the morning, Lamon summoned a *posse comitatus* in the name of the United States to release his deputy and his faithful counselor. One man responded. The rest had no fancy for charging on a house full of soldiers. So the two remained in confinement. Meanwhile I came to the headquarters and Wadsworth, somewhat chagrined at the excess of his orders and failure, directed me to go down and set matters to rights. I accordingly took down a battalion of infantry and waited for the marshal. Diplomatic negotiations ensued. I demanded my soldier and my negro—together with the keys to every cell, and stated that after that I would be willing to talk about the deputy and the counselor. The marshal refused to give up the keys. Meanwhile, McDougal, Senator from California arrived and began an oration on the sacredness of the Constitution of the United States as embodied in the person of the marshal. To cut matters short I took possession by force, released the soldier and the contraband, and found a number of others in like situation with military protections hidden away in cells. There was a general delivery. Then I thought we could afford to be magnanimous and released the deputy and counselor. Lamon hurried to the White House to procure the instant arrest of Wadsworth and myself. Fortunately for all concerned President Lincoln was not at home. I say fortunately for him, for these conflicts were not to his taste—he preferred to let matters decide themselves. Such secret catching of slaves continued, even after the Emancipation Proclamation was issued January 1, 1863, and after slavery had been abolished in the District.

The passage of the Act of Congress provided for the emancipation of slaves, and the payment of the masters in the District of Columbia fell like a stroke of lightning on the slaveholders, and when they had recovered a little, the impulse of most was to run their slaves into Maryland. They seemed to act like a master whose house is burning and carries his furniture from room to room, unable to comprehend the system as doomed and bound to go down. The trouble they had to encounter was getting the negroes off. These knew their right very well and any attempt at force would of course have produced an outcry and would have brought the military down on the heads of the masters. Therefore, there was, all at once, a strange benignity about the bearing of masters toward these people and then gentle persuasion to go on a visit to Baltimore or across the Anacostia or to some country seat beyond the District line. One man had the hardihood to ask me to just do nothing about his slaves. He was going to coax them off and if I didn't interfere would succeed. I declined to be neutral, and saw to it that this class was very well informed of what they had to gain by staying where they were. Thus, masters who were wise hastened to draw their pay and retain their servants for wages. As a rule the people were very much attached and stayed where they were, but the number of rich, free negroes at Washington forbade any general, successful attempt to trick them out of their freedom. I heard some who were run out into Maryland and also that they escaped altogether—leaving the master with nothing.

Colonel Rose's
Escape from Libby Prison

As the war progressed, prisoners of war became a problem for both sides. The Confederacy needed fighting men desperately, and the Union was reluctant to make any trades because they knew the soldiers would soon be turned against them again. But neither side had adequate medical care, food, or housing for the men in their care. Special officers, who were noted for their barbarity, were put in charge of the Prisoner of War camps, which eventually became living hells where men died slowly and painfully from scurvy, diarrhea, malnutrition, typhoid, etc. Some prisoners were shot by their guards for trivial offenses or used for target practice.

The wounded, the recent amputees, and those with running sores soon found themselves covered with maggots, flies, and other insects that lived on their flesh and blood. There were no toilet facilities; drinking water and food were scarce, and any packages coming from the outside containing food, blankets, clothing, or medicine were confiscated by the guards. The men were ridden with vermin, but too weak to remove them.

In the North prisoners froze in winter; other prisoners broiled in the South during summer. There was little or no shelter from the elements. The final score revealed that thirty thousand Union men died in prison, and the Confederates had twenty-six thousand dead.

One of the better prisons was Libby Prison, a converted warehouse in Richmond, Virginia that was for Union officers only. This seeming paradise among prisons had many dissatisfied men whose only thought was of escape. Colonel Frank

Moran relates his experience in the prison and his escape; the source is *Famous Adventures and Prison Escapes of the Civil War* (The Century Co., 1898).

Among all the thrilling incidents in the history of Libby Prison, none exceeds in interest the celebrated tunnel escape which occurred on the night of February 9, 1864. I was one of the 109 Union officers who passed through the tunnel, and one of the ill fated 48 that were retaken. I and two companions— Lt. Charles H. Morgan of the 21st Wisconsin regiment, who has since served several terms in Congress from Missouri, and Lt. William L. Watson of the same company and regiment— when recaptured by the Confederate cavalry were in sight of the Union picket posts. Strange as it may appear, no accurate and complete account has ever been given to the public of this, the most ingenious and daring escape made on either side during the civil war. Twelve of the party of fifteen who dug the tunnel are still living, including their leader.*

Thomas E. Rose, Colonel of the 77th Pennsylvania Volunteers, the engineer and leader in the plot throughout,—now a captain in the 16th United States Infantry, was taken prisoner at the battle of Chickamauga, September 20, 1863. On his way to Richmond he escaped from his guards at Weldon, N.C., but after a day's wandering about the pine forests with a broken foot, was retaken by a detachment of Confederate cavalry and sent to Libby Prison, Richmond, where he arrived October 1, 1863.

Libby Prison fronts on Carey Street, Richmond, and stands upon a hill which descends abruptly to the canal, from which its southern wall is divided only by a street, and having a vacant lot on the east. The building was wholly detached, making it a comparatively easy matter to guard the prison securely with a

---

*This report was first made in 1885.

small force and keep every door and window in full view from without. As an additional measure of safety, prisoners were not allowed on the ground-floor, except that in the daytime they were permitted to use the first floor of the middle section for a cook room. The interior embraced nine large warehouse-rooms, 105 × 45, with eight feet from each floor to ceiling, except the upper floor, which gave more room, owing to the pitch of the gable roof. The abrupt slant of the hill gives the building an additional story on the south side. The whole building really embraces three sections, and these were originally separated by heavy blank walls. The Confederates cut doors through the walls of the two upper floors, which comprised the prisoners' quarters, and they were thus permitted to mingle freely with each other; but there was no communication whatever between the three large rooms on the first floor. Beneath these floors were three cellars of the same dimensions as the rooms above them, and, like them, divided from each other by massive blank walls. For ready comprehension, let these be designated the east, middle and west cellars. Except in the lofts known as "Streight's room" and "Milroy's room," which were occupied by the earliest inmates of Libby in 1863, there was no furniture in the building, and only a few of the early comers possessed such a luxury as an old army blanket or a knife, cup, and tin plate. As a rule, the prisoner, by the time he reached Libby, found himself devoid of earthly goods save the meager and dust-begrimed summer garb in which he had made his unlucky campaign.

At night the six large lofts presented strange war-pictures, over which a single tallow candle wept copious and greasy tears that ran down over the petrified loaf of corn-bread, Borden's condensed-milk can, or bottle in which it was set. The candle flickered on until "taps," when the guards, with unconscious irony shouted, "Lights out!"—at which signal it usually disappeared amid a shower of boots and such other missiles as were at hand. The sleepers covered the six floors, lying in ranks, head to head and foot to foot, like prostrate lines of battle. For the general good, and to preserve something like military precision, these ranks (especially when cold weather compelled them to lie close for better warmth) were subdivided into con-

venient squads under charge of a "captain," who was invested
with authority to see that every man lay "spoon fashion."

No consideration of personal convenience was permitted to
interfere with the general conduct of the "squad." Thus, when
the hard floor could no longer be endured on the right side,—
especially by thin men,—the captain gave the command, "Attention, Squad Number Four! Prepare to spoon! One—two—
spoon!" And the whole squad flopped over on the left side.

The first floor on the west of the building was used by the
Confederates as an office and for sleeping-quarters for the prison
officials, and a stairway guarded by sentinels led from this to
Milroy's room just above it. As before explained, the middle
room was shut off from the office by a heavy blank wall. This
room, known as the "kitchen," had two stoves in it, one of which
stood about ten feet from the heavy door that opened on Carey
Street sidewalk, and behind the door was a fireplace. The room
contained also several long pine tables with permanent seats
attached, such as may be commonly seen at picnic grounds. The
floor was constantly inundated here by several defective and
overworked water-faucets and a leaky trough.

A stairway without banisters led up on the south-west end
of the floor, above which was a room known as the "Chickamauga room," being chiefly occupied by Chickamauga prisoners. The sentinel who had formerly been placed at this
stairway at night, to prevent the prisoners from entering the
kitchen, had been withdrawn when, in the fall of 1863, the
horrible condition of the floor made it untenable for sleeping
purposes.

The uses to which the large ground-floor room east of the
kitchen was put varied during the first two years of the war; but
early in October of 1863, and thereafter it was permanently used
and known as the hospital, and it contained a large number of
cots, which were never unoccupied. An apartment had been
made at the north or front of the room, which served as a doctor's office and laboratory. Like those adjoining it on the west,
this room had a large door opening on Carey Street, which was
heavily bolted and guarded on the outside.

The arrival of the Chickamauga prisoners greatly crowded

the upper floors, and compelled the Confederates to board up a small portion of the east cellar at its southeast corner as an additional cook-room, several large caldrons having been set in a crudely built furnace; so, for a short period, the prisoners were allowed down there in the daytime to cook. A stairway led from this cellar to the room above, which subsequently became the hospital.

Such, in brief, was the condition of things when Col. Rose arrived at the prison. From the hour of his coming, a means of escape became his constant and eager study; and, with this purpose in view, he made a careful and minute survey of the entire premises.

From the windows of the upper east or "Gettysburg room" he could look across the vacant lot on the east and get a glimpse of the yard between two adjacent buildings which faced the canal and Carey Street respectively, and he estimated the intervening space at about seventy feet. From the south windows he looked out across a street upon the canal and James River, running parallel with each other, the two streams at this point being separated by a low and narrow strip of land. This strip periodically disappeared when protracted seasons of heavy rain came, or when spring floods so rapidly swelled the river that the latter invaded the cellars of Libby. At such times it was common to see enormous swarms of rats come out from the lower doors and windows of the prison and make head for dry land in swimming platoons amid the cheers of the prisoners in the upper windows. On one or two occasions Rose observed workmen descending from the middle of the south-side street into a sewer running through its center, and concluded that this sewer must have various openings to the canal both to the east and west of the prison.

The north portion of the cellar contained a large quantity of loose packing-straw, covering the floor to an average depth of two feet; and this straw afforded shelter, especially at night, for a large colony of rats, which gave the place the name of "Rat Hell."

In one afternoon's inspection of this dark end, Rose suddenly encountered a fellow prisoner, Major A. G. Hamilton, of the 12th Kentucky Cavalry. A confiding friendship followed, and the two men entered at once upon the plan of gaining their liberty. They agreed that the most feasible scheme was a tunnel to begin in the rear of the little kitchen-apartment at the southeast corner of Rat Hell. Without more ado they secured a broken shovel and two case-knives and began operations.

Within a few days the Confederates decided upon certain changes in the prison for the greater security of their captives. A week afterward the cook-room was abandoned, the stairway nailed up, the prisoners sent to the upper floors, and all communication with the east cellar was cut off. This was a sore misfortune, for this apartment was the only possible base of successful tunnel operations. Colonel Rose now began to study other practicable means of escape, and spent night after night examining the posts and watching the movements of the sentinels on the four sides of Libby. One very dark night, during a howling storm, Rose again unexpectedly met Hamilton in a place where no prisoner could reasonably be looked for at such an hour. For an instant the impenetrable darkness made it impossible for either to determine whether he had met friend or foe; neither had a weapon, yet each involuntarily felt for one, and each made ready to spring at the other's throat, when a flash of lightning revealed their identity. The two men had availed themselves of the darkness of the night and the roar of the storm to attempt an escape from a window of the upper west room to a platform that ran along the west outer wall of the prison, from which they hoped to reach the ground and elude the sentinels, whom they conjectured would be crouched in the shelter of some doorway or other partial refuge that might be available; but so vivid and frequent were the lightning flashes that the attempt was seen to be extremely hazardous.

Rose now spoke of the entrance from the south-side street to the middle cellar, having frequently noticed the entrance and exit of workmen at that point, and expressed his belief that if an entrance could be effected to this cellar it would afford them the only chance of slipping past the sentinels.

He hunted up a bit of pine-wood which he whittled into a sort of a wedge, and the two men went down into the dark, vacant kitchen directly over this cellar. With the wedge Rose pried a floor board out of its place, and made an opening large enough to let himself through. He had never been in this middle cellar, and was wholly ignorant of its contents or whether it was occupied by Confederates or workmen; but as he had made no noise, and the place was in profound darkness, he decided to go down and reconnoiter.

He wrenched off one of the long boards that formed a table seat in the kitchen, and found that it was long enough to touch the cellar base and protrude a foot or so above the kitchen floor. By this means he easily descended, leaving Hamilton to keep watch above.

The storm still raged fiercely, and the faint beams of a street lamp revealed the muffled form of the sentinel slowly pacing his beat and carrying his musket at "secure" arms. Creeping slowly toward him along the cellar wall, he now saw that what he had supposed was a door was simply a naked opening to the street; and further inspection disclosed the fact that there was but one sentinel on the south side of the prison. Standing in the dark shadow, he could easily have touched this man with his hand as he repeatedly passed him. Groping about, he found various appurtenances indicating that the south end of this cellar was used for a carpenter's shop, and the north end was partitioned off into a series of small cells with padlocked doors, and that through each door a square hole, a foot in diameter, was cut. Subsequently it was learned that these dismal cages were alternately used for the confinement of "troublesome prisoners"— i.e., those who had distinguished themselves by ingenious attempts to escape—and also for runaway slaves, and Union spies under sentence of death.

At the date of Rose's first reconnaissance to this cellar, these cells were vacant and unguarded. The night was spent, and Rose proceeded to return to the kitchen, where Hamilton was patiently waiting for him.

The very next day a rare good fortune befell Rose. By an agreement between the commissioners of exchange, several bales of clothing and blankets had been sent by our government to the famishing Union prisoners on Belle Isle, a number of whom had already frozen to death. A committee of Union officers then confined in Libby, consisting of General Neal Dow, Colonel Alexander von Shrader, Lieut. Col. Joseph F. Boyd, and

Colonel Harry White, having been selected by the Confederates to supervise the distribution of the donation, Col. White had, by a shrewd bit of finesse, "confiscated" a fine rope by which one of the bales was tied, and this he now presented to Colonel Rose. It was nearly a hundred feet long, an inch thick, and almost new.

It was hardly dark the following night before Rose and Hamilton were again in the kitchen, and as soon as all was quiet Rose fastened his rope to one of the supporting posts, took up the floor plank as before, and both men descended to the middle cellar. They were not a little disappointed to discover that where there had been but one sentinel on the south side there were now two. On this and for several nights they contented themselves with sly visits of observation to this cellar, during which Rose found and secreted various tools, among which were a broad-ax, a saw, two chisels, several files, and a carpenter's square. One dark night both men went down and determined to try their luck at passing the guards. Rose made the attempt and succeeded in passing the first man, but unluckily was seen by the second. The latter called lustily for the corporal of the guard, and the first excitedly cocked his gun and peered into the dark door through which Rose swiftly retreated. The guard called, "Who goes there?" but did not enter the dark cellar. Rose and Hamilton mounted the rope and had just succeeded in replacing the plank when the corporal and a file of men entered the cellar with a lantern. They looked into every barrel and under every bench, but no sign of Yankees appeared; and as on this night it happened that several workmen were sleeping in an apartment at the north end, the corporal concluded that the man seen by the sentinel was one of those, notwithstanding their denial when awakened and questioned. After a long parley, the confederates withdrew, and Hamilton and Rose, depressed in spirits, went to bed, Rose, as usual, concealing his rope.

Before the week was out they were at it again. On one of these nights Rose suddenly came upon one of the workmen, and, swift as thought, seized the hidden broad-ax with the intention of braining him if he attempted an alarm; but the poor fellow was too much paralyzed to cry out, and when finally he did recover his voice and his wits, it was to beg Rose, "for God's sake," not to come in there again at night. Evidently the man never mentioned the circumstance, for Rose's subsequent visits, which were soon resumed, disclosed no evidence of a discovery by the Confederates.

Hamilton agreed with Rose that there remained apparently but one means of escape, and that was by force. To overpower the two sentinels on the south side would have been an easy matter, but how to do it and not alarm the rest of the guard, and, in consequence, the whole city, was the problem. To secure these sentinels, without alarming their comrades on the east, west, and north sites of the prison, would require the swift action of several men of nerve acting in concert. Precious time was passing, and possibly further alterations might be decided upon that would shut them off from the middle cellar, as they had already been from their original base of operations. Moreover, a new cause of anxiety now appeared. It soon transpired that their nocturnal prowlings and close conferences together had already aroused the belief among many observant prisoners that a plan of escape was afoot, and both men were soon eagerly plied with quarted inquiries, and besought by their questioners to admit them to their confidence.

Hamilton and Rose now decided to organize an escaping party. A number of men were then sworn to secrecy and obedience by Col. Rose, who was the only recognized leader in all operations that followed. This party soon numbered seventy men. The band was then taken down by Rose in convenient details to the middle cellar or carpenter's shop on many nights, to familiarize each man with the place and with his special part in the plot, and also to take advantage of any favoring circumstances that might arise.

When all had by frequent visits become familiar with the rendezvous, Rose and the whole party descended one night with the determination to escape at whatever hazard. The men were assigned to their several stations as usual, and a selected few were placed by the leader close to the entrance, in front of which the sentinel was regularly passing. Rose commanded strict silence, and placed himself near the exit preparatory to giving the signal. It was an exciting moment, and the bravest heart beat fast. A signal came, but not the one they looked for. At the very moment of action, the man who Rose had left at the floor opening in the kitchen gave the danger signal! The alert leader had, with consummate care, told every man beforehand that he must never be surprised by this signal, it was a thing to be counted upon, and that noise and panic were of all things to be avoided as fatal folly in their operations. As a consequence, when the signal came, Rose quietly directed the men to fall in line and reascend to the kitchen rapidly, but without noise, which they did by the long rope which now formed the easy means of communication from the kitchen to the cellar.

Rose remained below to cover the retreat, and when the last man got up he followed him, replaced the board in the floor and concealed the rope. He had barely done so when a detail of Confederate guards entered the kitchen from the Carey Street door, and headed by an officer, marched straight in his direction. Meantime the party had disappeared up the stairway and swiftly made their way over their prostrate comrades' forms to their proper sleeping places. Rose, being the last up, and having the floor to fix, had now no time to disappear like his companions, at least without suspicious haste. He accordingly took a seat at one of the tables, and, putting an old pipe in his mouth, coolly awaited the approach of the Confederates. The officer of the guard came along, swinging his lantern almost in his face, stared at him for a second, and without a remark or a halt marched past him and ascended with his escort to the Chicka- mauga room. The entrance of a guard and their march around the prison, although afterward common enough after taps, was then an unusual thing, causing much talk among the prisoners, and to the mind of Rose and his fellowplotters was indicative of aroused suspicion on the part of the Confederates.

The whispering groups of men next day, and the number of his eager questioners, gave the leader considerable concern; and Hamilton suggested, as a measure of safety rather than choice, that some of the mischievous talk of escape would be suppressed by increasing the party. This was acted upon; the men, like the rest were put under oath by Rose, and the party was thus increased to four hundred and twenty. This force would have been enough to overpower the prison guard in a few minutes, but the swift alarm certain to ensue in the streets and

spread like wildfire over Richmond, the meager information possessed by the prisoners as to the strength and position of the
nearest Federal troops, the strongly guarded labyrinth of breast-
works that encircled the city, and the easy facilities for instant
pursuit at the command of the Confederates, put the success of
such an undertaking clearly out of the range of probability, unless, indeed, some unusual favoring contingency should arise,
such as the near approach of a cooperation column of Federal
cavalry.

Nor was this an idle dream, as the country now knows, for
even at this period General Kilpatrick was maturing his plans
for that bold expedition for the rescue of the prisoners at Richmond and Belle Isle in which the lamented and heroic young
cripple, Colonel Ulric Dahlgren, lost his life. Rose saw that a
break out of Libby without such outside assistance promised
nothing but a fruitless sacrifice of life and the savage punishment of the survivors. Hence the project, although eagerly and
exhaustively discussed, was prudently abandoned.

All talk of escape by the general crowd now wholly ceased,
and the captives resigned themselves to their fate and waited
with depressed spirits for the remote contingency of an exchange. The quiet thus gained was Rose's opportunity. He
sought Hamilton and told him that they must by some stratagem
regain access to Rat Hell, and that the tunnel project must be at
once revived. The latter assented to the proposition, and the two
began earnestly to study the means of gaining an entrance without discovery into this coveted base of operations.

They could not even get into the room above the cellar they
wanted to reach, for that was the hospital, and the kitchen's
heavy wall shut them off therefrom. Neither could they break
the heavy wall that divided this cellar from the carpenter's shop,
which had been the nightly rendezvous of the party while the
breakout was under consideration, for the breach certainly
would be discovered by the workmen or Confederates, some of
whom were in there constantly during daylight.

There was, in fact, but one play by which Rat Hell could be
reached without detection, and the conception of this device
and its successful execution were due to the stout-hearted Hamilton. This was to cut a hole in the back of the kitchen fireplace;

the incision must be just far enough to preserve the opposite or hospital side intact. It must then be cut downward to a point below the level of the hospital floor, then eastward into Rat Hell, the completed opening thus to describe the letter "S". It must be wide enough to let a man through, yet the wall must not be broken on the hospital side above the floor, nor marred on the carpenter's-shop side below it. Such a break would be fatal, for both of these points were conspicuously exposed to the view of the Confederates every hour in the day. Moreover, it was imperatively necessary that all trace of the beginning of the opening should be concealed, not only from the Confederate officials and guards, who were constantly passing the spot every day, but from the hundreds of uninitiated prisoners who crowded around the stove just in front of it from dawn till dark.

Work could be possible only between the hours of ten at night, when the room was generally abandoned by the prisoners because of its inundated condition, and four o'clock in the morning, when the earliest risers were again astir. It was necessary to do the work with an old jack-knife, and one of the chisels previously secured by Rose. It must be done in darkness and without noise, for a vigilant sentinel paced on the Carey Street sidewalk just outside the door and within ten feet of the fireplace. A rubber blanket was procured, and the soot from the chimney carefully swept into it. Hamilton, with his old knife, cut the mortar between the bricks and pried a dozen of them out, being careful to preserve them whole.

The rest of the incision was made in accordance with the design described, but no conception could have been formed beforehand of the sickening tediousness of cutting an S-shaped hole through a heavy wall with a feeble old jack-knife, in stolen hours of darkness. Rose guarded his comrade against the constant danger of interruption by alert enemies on one side and by blundering friends on the other; and, as frequently happens in human affairs, their friends gave them more trouble than their foes. Night after night passed, and still the two men got up after taps from their hard beds, and descended to the dismal and reeking kitchen to bore for liberty. When the sentinel's call at Castle Thunder and at Libby announced four o'clock, the dislodged bricks were carefully replaced, and the soot previously gathered in the gum blanket was flung in handfuls against the restored wall, filling the seams between the bricks so thoroughly as to defy detection. At last, after many weary nights, Hamilton's heroic patience and skill were rewarded, and the way was open to the coveted base of operations, Rat Hell.

Now occurred a circumstance that almost revealed the plot and nearly ended in tragedy. When the opening was finished, the long rope was made fast to one of the kitchen supporting posts, and Rose proceeded to descend and reconnoiter. He got partly through with ease, but lost his hold in such a manner that his body slipped through so as to pinion his arms and leave him wholly powerless either to drop lower or return—the bend of the hole being such as to cramp his back and neck terribly and prevent him from breathing. He strove desperately, but each effort only wedged him more firmly in the awful vise. Hamilton sprang to his aid and did his utmost to effect his release; but, powerful as he was, he could not budge him. Rose was gasping for breath and rapidly getting fainter, but even in this fearful strait he refrained from an outcry that would certainly alarm the guards just outside the door. Hamilton saw that without speedy relief his comrade must soon smother. He dashed through the long, dark room up the stairway, over the forms of several hundred men, and disregarding consequences and savage curses in the dark and crowded room, he trampled upon arms, legs, faces and stomachs, leaving riot and blasphemy in his track among the rudely awakened and now furious lodgers of the Chickamauga room. He sought the sleeping place of Major George H. Fitzsimmons, but he was missing. He, however, found Lieutenant F. F. Bennett, of the 18th Regulars (since a major in the 9th United States Cavalry), to whom he told the trouble in a few hasty words. Both men fairly flew across the room, dashed down the stairs, and by their united efforts Rose, half dead and quite speechless, was drawn up from the fearful trap.

Hamilton managed slightly to increase the size of the hole and provide against a repetition of the accident just narrated, and all being now ready, the two men entered eagerly upon the work before them. They appropriated one of the wooden spittoons of the prison, and to each side attached a piece of clothesline which they had been permitted to have to dry clothes on.

Several bits of candle and the larger of the two chisels were also taken to the operating-cellar. They kept this secret well, and worked alone for many nights. In fact, they would have so continued, but they found that after digging about four feet their candle would go out in the vitiated air. Rose did the digging, and Hamilton fanned air into him with his hat: even then he had to emerge into the cellar every few minutes to breathe. Rose could dig, but needed the light and air; and Hamilton could not fan, and drag out and deposit the excavated earth, and meantime keep a lookout. In fact, it was demonstrated that there was slim chance of succeeding without more assistance, and it was decided to organize a party large enough for effective work by reliefs. As a preliminary step, and to afford the means of more rapid communication with the cellar from the fireplace opening, the long rope obtained from Colonel White was formed by Hamilton into a rope-ladder with convenient wooden rungs. This alteration considerably increased its bulk, and added to Rose's difficulty in concealing it from curious eyes.

He now made a careful selection of thirteen men beside himself and Hamilton, and bound them in a solemn oath to secrecy and strict obedience. To form this party as he wanted it required some diplomacy, as it was known that the Confederates had on more than one occasion sent cunning spies into Libby disguised as Union prisoners, for the detection of any contemplated plan of escape. Unfortunately, the complete list of the names of the party now formed has not been preserved; but among the party, besides Rose and Hamilton, were Captain John Sterling, 30th Indiana; Captain John Lucas, 5th Kentucky Cavalry; Captain Isaac N. Johnson, 6th Kentucky Cavalry; and Lieutenant F. F. Bennett, 18th Regulars.

The party, being now formed, were taken to Rat Hell and their several duties explained to them by Rose, who was invested with full authority over the work in hand. Work was begun in rear of the little kitchen-room previously abandoned at the southeast corner of the cellar. To systematize the labor, the party was divided into squads of five each, which gave the men one night on duty and two off, Rose assigning each man to the branch of work in which experiments proved him the most proficient. He was himself, by long odds, the best digger of the party; while Hamilton had no equal for ingenious mechanical skill in contriving helpful little devices to overcome or lessen the difficulties that beset almost every step of the party's progress.

The first plan was to dig down alongside the east wall and under it until it was passed, then turn southward and make for the large street sewer next the canal and into which Rose had before noticed workmen descending. This sewer was a large one, believed to be fully six feet high, and if it could be gained, there could be little doubt that an adjacent opening to the canal would be found to the eastward. It was very soon revealed, however, that the lower side of Libby was built upon ponderous timbers, below which they could not hope to penetrate with their meager stock of tools—such, at least, was the opinion of nearly all the party. Rose, nevertheless determined that the effort should be made, and they were soon at work with old penknives and caseknives hacked into saws. After infinite labor they at length cut through the greatlogs, only to be met by an unforeseen and still more formidable barrier. Their tunnel, in fact, had penetrated below the level of the canal. Water began to filter in—feebly at first, but at last it broke in with a rush that came near drowning Rose, who barely had time to make his escape. This opening was therefore plugged up; and to do this rapidly and leave no dangerous traces put the party to their wit's end.

An attempt was next made to dig into a small sewer that ran from the southeast corner of the prison into the main sewer. After a number of nights of hard labor, this opening was extended to a point below a brick furnace in which were incased several caldrons. The weight of this furnace caused a cave-in near the sentinel's path outside the prison wall. Next day, a group of officers were seen eying the break curiously. Rose, listening at a window above, heard the words "rats" repeated by them several times, and took comfort. The next day he entered the cellar alone, feeling that if the suspicions of the Confederates were really awakened a trap would be set for him in Rat Hell, and determined, if such were really the case, that he would be the only victim caught. He therefore entered the little partitioned corner room with some anxiety, but there was no visible evidence of a visit by the guards, and his spirits again rose.

The party now reassembled, and an effort was made to get into the small sewer that ran from the cookroom to the big sewer which Rose was so eager to reach; but soon it was discovered, to the utter dismay of the weary party, that this wood-lined sewer was too small to let a man through it. Still it was hoped by Rose that by removing the plank with which it was lined the passage could be made. The spirits of the party were by this time considerably dashed by their repeated failures and sickening work; but the undaunted Rose, aided by Hamilton, persuaded the men to another effort, and soon the knives and toy saws were at work again with vigor. The work went on so swimmingly that it was confidently believed that an entrance to the main sewer would be gained on the night of Janyuary 26, 1864.

On the night of the 25th two men had been left down in Rat Hell to cover any remaining traces of a tunnel, and when night came again it was expected that all would be ready for the escape between eight and nine o'clock. In the mean time, the two men were to enter and make careful examination of the main sewer and its adjacent outlets. The party, which was now in readiness for its march to the Federal camps, waited tidings from these two men all next day in tormenting anxiety, and the weary hours went by on leaden wings. At last the sickening word came that the planks yet to be removed before they could enter the main sewer were of seasoned oak—hard as bone, and three inches thick. Their feeble tools were now worn out or broken; they could no longer get air to work, or keep a light in the horrible pit, which was reeking with cold mud; in short, any attempt at further progress with the utensils at hand was foolish.

Most of the party were now really ill from the foul stench in which they had lived so long. The visions of liberty that had first lured them to desperate efforts under the inspiration of Rose and Hamilton had at last faded, and one by one they lost heart and hope, and frankly told Colonel Rose that they could do no more. The party was therefore disbanded, and yet the sanguine leader, with Hamilton for his sole helper, continued to work alone. Up to this time thirty-nine nights had been spent in the work of excavation. The two men now made a careful examination of the northeast corner of the cellar, at which point the earth's surface outside the prison wall, being eight or nine feet higher than at the canal or south side, afforded a better place to dig than the latter, being free from water and with clay-top enough to support itself. The unfavorable feature of this point was that the only possible terminus of a tunnel was a yard between the buildings beyond the vacant lot on the east of Libby. Another objection was that, even when the tunnel should be made to that point, the exit of any escaping party must be made through an arched wagon way under the building that faced the street on the canal side, and every man must emerge on the sidewalk in sight of the sentinel on the south side of the prison, the intervening space being in the full glare of the gas lamp. It was carefully noted, however, by Rose, long before this, that the west end of the beat of the nearest sentinel was between fifty and sixty feet from the point of egress, and it was concluded that by walking away at the moment the sentinel commenced his pace westward, one would be far enough into the shadow to make it improbable that the color of his clothing could be made out by the sentinel when he faced about to return toward the eastern end of his beat, which terminated ten to fifteen feet east of the prison wall. It was further considered that as these sentinels had for their special duty the guarding of the prison, they would not be eager to burden themselves with the duty of molesting persons seen in the vicinity outside of their jurisdiction, provided, of course, that the retreating forms—many of which they must certainly see—were not recognized as Yankees. All others they might properly leave for the challenge and usual examination of the provost guard who patrolled the streets of Richmond.

The wall of that east cellar had to be broken in three places before a place was found where the earth was firm enough to support a tunnel. The two men worked on with stubborn patience, but their progress was painfully slow. Rose dug assiduously, and Hamilton alternately fanned air to his comrade and dragged out and hid the excavated dirt, but the old difficulty confronted him. The candle would not burn, the air could not be fanned fast enough with a hat, and the dirt hidden, without better contrivances or additional help.

Rose now reassembled the party, and selected from them a

number who were willing to renew the attempt.* Against the east wall stood a series of stone fenders abutting inward, and these, being at uniform intervals of about twenty feet, cast deep shadows that fell toward the prison front. In one of these dark recesses the wall was pierced, well up toward the Carey Street end.

The earth here was very densely compressed sand, that offered a strong resistance to the broad bladed chisel, which was their only effective implement, and it was clear that a long turn of hard work must be done to penetrate under the fifty foot lot to the objective point. The lower part of the tunnel was about six inches above the level of the cellar floor, and its top about two and a half feet. Absolute accuracy was of course impossible, either in giving the hole a perfectly horizontal direction or in preserving uniform dimensions; but a fair level was preserved, and the average diameter of the tunnel was a little over two feet. Usually one man would dig, and fill the spittoon with earth; upon the signal of a gentle pull, an assistant would drag the load into the cellar by the clothes lines fastened to each side of this box, and then hide it under the straw; a third constantly fanned air into the tunnel with a rubber blanket stretched across a frame, the invention of the ingenious Hamilton; a fourth would give occasional relief to the last two; while a fifth would keep a lookout.

The danger of discovery was continual, for the guards were under instructions from the prison commandant to make occa-

---

*The party now consisted of Colonel Thomas E. Rose, 77th Pennsylvania; Major A. G. Hamilton, 12th Kentucky; Captain Terrance Clark, 79th Illinois; Major George H. Fitzsimmons, 30th Indiana; Captain John F. Gallagher, 2d Ohio; Captain W. S. B. Randall, 2nd Ohio; Captain John Lucas, 5th Kentucky; Captain I. N. Johnson, 6th Kentucky; Major B. B. McDonald, 101st Ohio; Lieutenant N. S. McKean, 21st Illinois; Lieutenant David Garbett, 77th Pennsylvania; Lieutenant J. C. Fislar, 7th Indiana Artillery; Lieutenant John D. Simpson, 10th Indiana; Lieutenant John Mitchell, 79th Illinois; and Lieutenant Eli Foster, 30th Indiana. This party was divided into three reliefs, as before, and the work of breaking the cellar wall was successfully done the first night by McDonald and Clark.

sional visits to every accessible part of the building; so that it
was not unusual for a sergeant and several men to enter the south
door of Rat Hell in the daytime, while the diggers were at labor
in the dark north end. During these visits the digger would
watch the intruders with his head sticking out of the tunnel,
while the others would crouch behind the low stone fenders, or
crawl quickly under the straw. This was, however, so uninviting
a place that the Confederates made this visit as brief as a nom-
inal compliance with their orders permitted, and they did not
often venture into the dark north end. The work was fearfully
monotonous, and the more so because absolute silence was commanded, the men moving about mutely in the dark. The darkness caused them frequently to become bewildered and lost; and
as Rose could not call out for them, he had to often hunt all over
the big dungeon to gather them up and pilot them to their places.

The difficulty of forcing air to the digger, whose body nearly
filled the tunnel, increased as the hole was extended, and compelled the operator to back often into the cellar for air, and for
air that was itself foul enough to sicken a strong man.

But they were no longer harassed with the water and timbers that had impeded their progress at the south end. Moreover,
experience was daily making each man more proficient in the
work. Rose urged them on with cheery enthusiasm, and their
hopes rose high, for already they had penetrated beyond the
sentinel's beat and was nearing the goal.

The party off duty kept a cautious lookout from the upper
east windows for any indications of suspicion on the part of the
Confederates. In this extreme caution was necessary, both to
avert the curiosity of prisoners in those east rooms, and to keep
out of the range of bullets from the guards, who were under a
standing order to fire at a head if seen at a window, or at a hand
if placed on the bars that secured them. A sentinel's bullet one
day cut a hole in the ear of Lieutenant Hammond; another officer
was wounded in the face by a bullet, which fortunately first
splintered against one of the window bars; and a captain of an
Ohio regiment was shot through the head and instantly killed
while reading a newspaper. He was violating no rule whatever,
and when shot was from eight to ten feet inside the window
through which the bullet came. This was a wholly unprovoked

and wanton murder; the cowardly miscreant had fired the shot while he was off duty, and from the north sidewalk of Carey Street. The guards (home guards they were) used, in fact, to gun for prisoner's heads from their posts below pretty much after the fashion of boys after squirrels; and the whizz of a bullet through the windows became too common occurrence to occasion remark unless some one was shot.

Under a standing rule, the twelve hundred prisoners were counted twice each day, the first count being made about nine in the morning, and the last about four in the afternoon. This duty was habitually done by the clerk of the prison, E. W. Ross, a civilian employed by the commandant. He was christened "Little Ross"* by the prisoners, because of his diminutive size. Ross was generally attended by either "Dick" Turner, Adjutant Latouche, or Sergeant George Stansil, of the 18th Georgia, with a small guard to keep the prisoners in four closed ranks during the count. The commandant of the prison, Major Thomas P. Turner (no relative of Dick's) seldom came up stairs.

To conceal the absence of the five men who were daily at work at the tunnel, their comrades of the party off digging duty resorted, under Rose's supervision, to a device of "repeating." This scheme, which was of vital importance to hoodwink the Confederates and avert mischievous curiosity among the uniformed prisoners, was a hazardous business that severely taxed the ingenuity and strained the nerve of the leader and his co-conspirators. The manner of the fraud varied with circumstances, but in general it was worked by five of Rose's men, after being counted at or near the head of the line, stooping down and running toward the foot of the ranks, where a few moments later they were counted a second time, thus making Ross's book balance. The whole five, however, could not always do this undiscovered, and perhaps but three of the number could repeat. These occasional mishaps threatened to dethrone the reason of the puzzled clerk; but in the next count the "repeaters" would succeed in their game, and for the time all went well, until one

---

*"Little Ross" was burned to death, with other guests, at the Spotswood House, Richmond, in 1873.

day some of the prisoners took it into their heads, "just for the fun of the thing," to imitate the repeaters. Unconscious of the curses that the party were mentally hurling at them, the meddlers' sole purpose was to make "Little Ross" mad. In this they certainly met with signal success, for the reason of the mystified clerk seemed to totter as he repeated the count over and over in the hope of finding out how one careful count would show that three prisoners were missing and the next an excess of fifteen. Finally Ross, lashed into uncontrollable fury by the sarcastic remarks of his employers and the heartless merriment of the grinning Yanks before him, poured forth his goaded soul as follows:

"Now, gentlemen, look yere. I can count a hundred as good as any blank man in this yere town, but I'll be blank blanked if I can count a hundred of you blanked Yankees. Now, gentlemen, there's one thing sho: there's eight or ten of you-uns yere that aint yere!"

This extraordinary accusation "brought down the house," and the Confederate officers and guards, and finally Ross himself, were caught by the resistless contagion of laughter that shook the rafters of Libby.

The officials somehow found a balance that day on the books, and the danger was for this once over, to the infinite relief of Rose and his anxious comrades. But the Confederates appeared dissatisfied with something, and came up stairs next morning with more officers and with double the usual number of guards; and some of these were now stationed about the room so as to make it next to impossible to work the repeating device successfully. On this day, for some reason, there were but two men in the cellar, and these were Major B. B. McDonald and Capt. I. N. Johnson.

The count began as usual, and despite the guard in rear, two of the party attempted the repeating device by forcing their way through the center of the ranks toward the left; but the "fun of the thing" had now worn out with the unsuspecting meddlers, who resisted the passage of the two men. This drew the attention of the Confederate officers, and the repeaters were threatened with punishment. The result was inevitable; the count showed two missing. It was carefully repeated with the same result. To the dismay of Rose and his little band, the prison register was now brought up stairs and a long, tedious roll call by name was endured, each man passing through a narrow door as his name was called, and between a line of guards.

No stratagem that Rose could now invent could avert the discovery by the Confederates that McDonald and Johnson had disappeared, and the mystery of their departure would be almost certain to cause an inquiry and investigation that would put their plot in peril and probably reveal it.

At last the "J's" were reached, and the name of I. N. Johnson was lustily shouted and repeated, with no response. The roll call proceeded until the name of B. B. McDonald was reached. To the increasing amazement of everybody but the conspirators, he also had vanished. A careful note was taken of these two names by the Confederates, and a thousand tongues was now busy with the names of the missing men and their singular disappearance.

The conspirators were in a tight place, and must choose between two things. One was for the men in the cellar to return that night and face the Confederates with the most plausible explanation of their absence that they could invent, and the other alternative was the revolting one of remaining in their horrible abode until the completion of the tunnel.

When night came the fireplace was opened, and the unlucky pair were informed of the situation of affairs and asked to choose between the alternatives presented. McDonald decided to return and face the music; but Johnson, doubtful if the Confederates would be hoodwinked by any explanation, voted to remain where he was and wait for the finish of the tunnel.

As was anticipated, McDonald's return awakened almost as much curiosity among the inhabitants of Libby as his disappearance, and he was soon called to account by the Confederates. He told them he had fallen asleep in an out-of-the-way place in the upper west room, where the guards must have overlooked him during the roll-call of the day before. McDonald was not further molested. The garrulous busybodies, who were Rose's chief dread, told the Confederate officials that they had certainly slept near Johnson the night before the day he was missed. Lieutenant J. C. Fislar (of the working party), who also slept next to Johnson, boldly declared this a case of mistaken identity, and confidently expressed his belief to both Confederates and Federals who gathered around him that Johnson had escaped, and was by this time, no doubt, safe in the Union lines. To this he added the positive statement that Johnson had not been in his accustomed sleeping-place for a good many nights. The busybodies who had indeed told the truth, looked at the speaker in speechless amazement, but reiterated their statements. Others of the conspirators, however took Fislar's bold cue and stoutly corroborated him.

Johnson was, of course, nightly fed by his companions and gave them such assistance as he could at the work; but it soon became apparent that a man could not long exist in such a pestilential atmosphere. No tongue can tell how long were the days and nights the poor fellow passed among the squealing rats,— enduring the sickening air, the deathly chill, the horrible, interminable darkness. One day out of three was an ordeal for the workers, who at least had a rest of two days afterward. As a desperate measure of relief, it was arranged, with the utmost caution, that late each night Johnson should come up stairs, when all was dark and the prison in slumber, and sleep among the prisoners until just before the time for closing the fireplace opening, about four o'clock each morning. As he spoke to no one and the room was dark, his presence was never known, even to those who lay next to him; and indeed he listened to many earnest conversations between his neighbors regarding his wonderful disappearance.

As a matter of course, the incidents above narrated made day work on the tunnel too hazardous to be indulged in, on account of the increased difficulty of accounting for absentees; but the party continued the night work with unabated industry.

When the opening had been extended nearly across the lot, some of the party believed they had entered under the yard which was the intended terminus; and one night, when Mc-Donald was the digger, so confident was he that the desired distance had been made, that he turned his direction upward, and soon broke through to the surface. A glance showed him his nearly fatal blunder, against which, indeed, he had been earnestly warned by Rose, who from the first had carefully estimated the intervening distance between the east wall of Libby and the terminus. In fact, McDonald saw that he had broken through in the open lot which was all in full view of a sentinel who was dangerously close. Appalled by what he had done, he retreated to the cellar and reported the disaster to his companions. Believing that discovery was now certain, the party sent one of their number up the rope to report to Rose, who was asleep. The hour was about midnight when the leader learned of the mischief. He quickly got up, went down cellar, entered the tunnel and examined the break. It was not so near the sentinel's path as McDonald's excited report indicated, and fortunately the breach was at a point whence the surface sloped downward toward the east. He took off his blouse and stuffed it into the opening, pulling the dirt over it noiselessly, and in a few minutes there was little surface evidence of the hole. He then backed into the cellar in the usual crab fashion, and gave directions for the required depression of the tunnel and vigorous resumption of the work. The whole made in the roof of the tunnel was not much larger than a rat hole, and could not be seen from the prison. But the next night Rose shoved an old shoe out of the hole, and the day afterward he looked down through the prison bars and saw the shoe lying where he had placed it, and judged from its position that he had better incline the direction of the tunnel slightly to the left.

Meantime Captain Johnson was dragging out a wretched existence in Rat Hell, and for safety was obliged to confine himself by day to the dark north end, for the Confederates often came into the place very suddenly through the south entrance. When they ventured too close, Johnson would get into a pit that he had dug under the straw as a hiding hole both for himself and the tunnelers' tools, and quickly cover himself with a huge heap of short packing straw. A score of times he came near being stepped upon by the Confederates, and more than once the dust of the straw compelled him to sneeze in their very presence.

On Saturday, February 6, a larger party than usual of the Confederates came into the cellar, walked by the very mouth of the tunnel, and seemed to be making a critical survey of the entire place. They remained an unusually long time and conversed in low tones; several of them even kicked the loose straw

about; and in fact everything seemed to indicate to Johnson—
who was the only one of the working party now in the cellar—
that the long averted discovery had been made. That night he
reported matters fully to Rose at the fireplace opening.

The tunnel was now nearly completed, and when Rose conveyed Johnson's message to the party it caused dismay. Even the
stout-hearted Hamilton was for once excited, and the leader
whose unflinching fortitude had thus far inspired his little band
had his brave spirits dashed. But his buoyant courage rose
quickly to its high and natural level. He could not longer doubt
that the suspicions of the Confederates were aroused, but he felt
convinced that these suspicions had not as yet assumed such
definite shape as most of his companions thought; still, he had
abundant reason to believe that the success of the tunnel absolutely demanded its speedy completion, and he now firmly resolved that a desperate effort should be made to that end.
Remembering that the next day was Sunday, and that it was not
customary for the Confederates to visit the operating cellar on
that day, he determined to make the most in his power of the
now precious time. He therefore caused all the party to remain
upstairs, directing them to keep close watch upon the Confederates from all available points of observation, to avoid being
seen in whispering groups,—in short, to avoid all things calculated to excite the curiosity of friends or the suspicion of
enemies,—and to await his return.

Taking McDonald with him, he went down through the fireplace before daylight on Sunday morning and, bidding Johnson
to keep a vigilant watch for intruders and McDonald to fan air
into him, he entered the tunnel and began the forlorn hope. From
this time forward he never once turned over the chisel to a relief.

All day long he worked with the tireless patience of a bea-
ver. When night came, even his single helper, who performed
the double duty of fanning air and hiding the excavated earth,
was ill from his hard, long task and the deadly air of the cellar.
Yet this was as nothing compared with the fatigue of the duty
that Rose had performed; and when at last, far into the night,
he backed into the cellar, he had scarcely strength enough to
stagger across the rope ladder.

He had made more than double the distance that had been

accomplished under the system of reliefs on any previous day, and the non-appearance of the Confederates encouraged the hope that another day, without interruption, would see the work completed. He therefore determined to refresh himself by a night's sleep for the finish. The drooping spirits of his party were revived by the report of his progress and his unalterable confidence.

Monday morning dawned, and the great prison with its twelve hundred captives was again astir. The general crowd did not suspect the suppressed excitement and anxiety of the little party that waited through that interminable day, which they felt must determine the fate of their project.

Rose had repeated the instructions of the day before, and again descended to Rat Hell with McDonald for his only helper. Johnson reported all quiet, and McDonald taking up his former duties at the tunnel's mouth, Rose once more entered with his chisel. It was now the seventeenth day since the present tunnel was begun, and he resolved it should be the last. Hour after hour passed, and still the busy chisel was plied, and still the little wooden box with its freight of earth made its monotonous trips from the digger to his comrade and back again.

From the early morning of Monday, February 8, 1864, until an hour after midnight the next morning, his work went on. As midnight approached, Rose was nearly a physical wreck: the perspiration dripped from every pore of his exhausted body; food he could not have eaten if he had had it. His labors thus far had given him a somewhat exaggerated estimate of his physical powers. The sensation of fainting was strange to him, but his staggering senses warned him that to faint where he was meant at once his death and burial. He could scarcely inflate his lungs with the poisonous air of the pit; his muscles quivered with increasing weakness and the warning spasmodic tremor which their unnatural strain induced; his head swam like that of a drowning person.

By midnight he had struck and passed beyond a post which he felt must be in the yard. During the last few minutes he had directed his course upward, and to relieve his cramped limbs he turned upon his back. His strength was nearly gone; the feeble stream of air which his comrade was trying, with all his might, to send to him from a distance of fifty-three feet could no longer reach him through the deadly stench. His senses reeled; he had not breath or strength enough to move backward through his narrow grave. In the agony of suffocation he dropped the dull chisel and beat his two fists against the roof of his grave with the might of despair—when, blessed boon! the crust gave way and the loosened earth showered upon his dripping face purple with agony; his famished eye caught sight of a radiant star in the blue vault above him; a flood of light and a volume of cool, delicious air poured over him. At that very instant the sentinel's cry rang out like a prophecy—"Half-past one, and all's well!"

Recovering quickly under the inspiring air, he dragged his body out of the hole and made a careful survey of the yard in which he found himself. He was under a shed, with a board fence between him and the east side sentinels, and the gable end of Libby loomed grimly against the blue sky. He found the wag-onway under the south side building closed from the street by a gate fastened by a swinging bar, which, after a good many efforts, he succeeded in opening. This was the only exit to the street. As soon as the nearest sentinel's back was turned he stepped out and walked quickly to the east. At the first corner he turned north, carefully avoiding the sentinels in front of the Pemberton Buildings (another military prison northeast of Libby), and at the corner above this he went westward, then south to the edge of the canal, and thus, by cautious moving, made a minute examination of Libby from all sides.

Having satisfied his desires, he retraced his steps to the yard. He hunted up an old bit of heavy plank, crept back into the tunnel feet first, drew the plank over the opening to conceal it from the notice of any possible visitors to the place, and crawled back to Rat Hell. McDonald was overjoyed, and poor Johnson almost wept with delight, as Rose handed one of them his victorious old chisel, and gave the other some trifle he had picked up in the outer world as a token that the Underground Railroad to God's country was open.

Rose now climbed the rope ladder, drew it up, re-built the fireplace wall as usual, and finding Hamilton, took him over near one of the windows and broke the news to him. The brave fellow was almost speechless with delight, and quickly hunting up the rest of the party, told them that Colonel Rose wanted to see them down in the dining room.

As they had been waiting news from their absent leader with feverish anxiety for what had seemed to them all the longest day in their lives, they instantly responded to the call, and flocked around Rose a few minutes later in the dark kitchen where he waited them. As yet they did not know what news he brought, and they could scarcely wait for him to speak out; and when he announced, "Boys, the tunnel is finished," they could hardly repress a cheer. They wrung his hand again and again, and danced about with childish joy.

It was now nearly three o'clock in the morning. Rose and Hamilton were ready to go out at once, and indeed were anxious to do so, since every day of late had brought some new peril to their plans. None of the rest, however, were ready; and all urged the advantage of having a whole night in which to escape through and beyond the Richmond fortifications, instead of the few hours of darkness which now preceded the day. To this proposition Rose and Hamilton somewhat reluctantly assented. It was agreed that each man of the party should have the privilege of taking one friend into his confidence, and that the second party of fifteen thus formed should be obligated not to follow the working party out of the tunnel until an hour had elapsed. Colonel H. C. Hobart, of the 21st Wisconsin, was deputed to see that the program was observed. He was to draw up the rope ladder, hide it, and rebuild the wall; and the next night was himself to lead out the second party, deputing some trustworthy leader to follow with still another party on the third night; and thus it was to continue until as many as possible should escape.

On Tuesday evening, February 9, at seven o'clock, Colonel Rose assembled his party in the kitchen, and posting himself at the fireplace, which he opened, waited until the last man went down. He bade Colonel Hobart good-bye, went down the hole, and waited until he had heard his comrade pull up the ladder, and finally heard him replace the bricks in the fireplace and depart. He now crossed Rat Hell to the entrance into the tunnel, and placed the party in the order in which they were to go out. He gave each a parting caution, thanked his brave comrades for their faithful labors, and, feelingly shaking their hands, bade them Godspeed and farewell.

He entered the tunnel first, with Hamilton next, and was promptly followed by the whole party through the tunnel and into the yard. He opened the gate leading toward the canal, and signaled the party that all was clear. Stepping out on the sidewalk as soon as the nearest sentinel's back was turned, he walked briskly down the street to the east, and a square below was joined by Hamilton. The others followed at intervals of a few minutes, and disappeared in various directions in groups usually of three.

The plan agreed upon between Rose and Hobart was frustrated by information of the party's departure leaking out; and before nine o'clock the knowledge of the existence of the tunnel and of the departure of the first party was flashed over the crowded prison, which was soon a convention of excited and whispering men. Colonel Hobart made a brave effort to restore order, but the frenzied crowd that now fiercely struggled for precedence at the fireplace was beyond human control.

Some of them had opened the fireplace and were jumping down like sheep into the cellar one after another. The colonel implored the maddened men at least to be quiet, and put the rope ladder in position and escaped himself.

My companion, Sprague, was already asleep when I lay down that night; but my other companion, Duenkel, who had been hunting for me, was very much awake, and, seizing me by the collar, he whispered excitedly the fact that Colonel Rose had gone out at the head of a party through a tunnel. For a brief moment the appalling suspicion that my friend's reason had been dethroned by illness and captivity swept over my mind; but a glance toward the window at the east and showed a quiet but apparently excited group of men from other rooms, and I now observed that several of them were bundled up for a march. The hope of regaining liberty thrilled me like a current of electricity. Looking through the window, I could see the escaping men appear one by one on the sidewalk below, opposite the exit yard, and silently disappear, without hindrance or challenge by the prison sentinels. While I was eagerly surveying this scene, I lost track of Duenkel, who had gone in search of further information, but ran against Lt. Harry Wilcox, of the 1st New York, whom I knew, and who appeared to have the "tip" regarding the tunnel. Wilcox and I agreed to unite our fortunes in the escape. My shoes were nearly worn out, and my clothes were thin and ragged. I was ill prepared for a journey in midwinter through the enemy's country; happily I had my old overcoat, and this I put on. I had not a crumb of food saved up, as did those who were posted; but as I was ill at the time, my appetite was feeble.

Wilcox and I hurried to the kitchen, where we found several hundred men struggling to be first at the opening in the fireplace. We took our places behind them, and soon two hundred more closed us tightly in the mass. The room was pitch dark, and the sentinel could be seen through the door cracks, within a dozen feet of us. The fight for precedence was savage, though no one spoke; but now and then fainting men begged to be released. They begged in vain: certainly some of them must have been permanently injured. For my own part, when I neared the stove I was nearly suffocated; but I took heart when I saw but three more men between me and the hole. At this moment a sound as of tramping feet was heard, and some idiot on the outer edge of the mob startled us with the cry, "The guards, the guards!" A fearful panic ensued and the entire crowd bounded toward the stairway leading up to their sleeping quarters. The stairway was unbanistered, and some of the men were forced off the edge and fell on those beneath. I was among the lightest in that crowd; and when it broke and expanded I was taken off my feet, dashed to the floor senseless, my head and one of my hands bruised and cut, and my shoulder painfully injured by the boots of the men who rushed over me. When I gathered my swimming wits I was lying in a pool of water. The room seemed darker than before; and, to my grateful surprise, I was alone. I was now convinced that it was a false alarm, and quickly resolved to avail myself of the advantage of having the whole place to myself. I entered the cavity feet first, but found it necessary to remove my overcoat and push it through the opening, and it fell in the darkness below.

I had now no comrade, having lost Wilcox in the stampede. Rose and his party, being the first out, were several hours on their journey; and I burned to be away, knowing well that my salvation depended on my passage beyond the city defenses before the pursuing guards were on our trail, when the inevitable discovery should come at roll-call. The fact that I was alone I regretted; but I served with McClellan in the Peninsula campaign of 1862, I knew the country well from my frequent inspection of war maps, and the friendly north star gave me my bearings. The rope ladder had either become broken or disarranged, but it afforded me a short hold at the top; so I balanced myself, trusted to fortune, and fell into Rat Hell, which was a rayless pit of darkness, swarming with squealing rats, several of which I must have killed in my fall. I felt a troop of them run over my face and hands before I could regain my feet. Several times I put my hand on them, and once I flung one from my shoulder. Groping around, I found a stout stick or stave, put my back to the wall, and beat about me blindly but with vigor.

In spite of the hurried instructions given me by Wilcox, I had a long and horrible hunt over the cold surface of the cellar walls in my efforts to find the entrance to the tunnel; and in two minutes after I began feeling my way with my hands I had no idea in what part of the place was the point where I had fallen: my bearings were completely lost, and I must have made the circuit of Rat Hell several times. At my entrance the rats seemed to receive me with cheers sufficiently hearty, I thought; but my vain efforts to find egress seemed to kindle anew their enthusiasm. They had received large reinforcements, and my march around was now received with deafening squeaks. Finally, my exploring hands fell upon a pair of heels which vanished at my touch. Here at last was the narrow road to freedom! The heels proved to be the property of Lt. Charles H. Morgan, 21st Wisconsin, a Chickamauga prisoner. Just ahead of him in the tunnel was Lt. William L. Watson of the same company and regiment. With my cut hand and bruised shoulder, the passage through the cold, narrow grave was indescribably horrible, and when I reached the terminus in the yard I was sick and faint. The passage seemed to me to be a mile long; but the crisp, pure air and the first glimpse of freedom, the sweet sense of being out of doors, and the realization that I had taken the first step toward liberty and home, had a magical effect in my restoration.

I have related before, in a published reminiscence,* my experience and that of my two companions above named in the
journey toward the Union lines, and our recapture; but the more
important matter relating to the plot itself has never been published. This is the leading motive of this article, and therefore I
will not intrude the details of my personal experience into the
narrative. It is enough to say that it was a chapter of hairbreadth
escapes, hunger, cold, suffering, and, alas! failure. We were run
down and captured in a swamp several miles north of Char-
lottesville, and when we were taken our captors pointed out to
us the smoke over a Federal outpost. We were brought back to
Libby, and put in one of the dark, narrow dungeons. I was afterward confined in Macon, Georgia; Charleston, and Columbia,
South Carolina; and in Charlotte, North Carolina. After a captivity of just a year and eight months, during which I had made
five escapes and was each time retaken, I was at last released
on March 1, 1865, at Wilmington, North Carolina.

Great was the panic in Libby when the next morning's roll
revealed to the astounded Confederates that 109 of their captives
were missing; and as the fireplace had been rebuilt by some one
and the opening of the hole in the yard had been covered by the
last man who went out, no human trace guided the keepers
toward the solution of the mystery. The Richmond papers having
announced the "miraculous" escape of 109 Yankee officers from
Libby, curious crowds flocked thither for several days, until
someone, happening to removed the plank in the yard, revealed
the tunnel. A terrified negro was driven into the hole at the point
of the bayonet, and thus made a trip to Rat Hell that nearly
turned him white.

Of the original 15 who began the tunnel, four were killed. Forty-

---

*Philadelphia Times, October 28, 1882.

eight of the 109 men who escaped were captured, including Col. Rose, and returned to Libby Prison. In July 1864 Col. Rose was exchanged for a Confederate Colonel and returned to his regiment to serve for the rest of the war.

MEN AT WAR

THE NAVY

Admiral Porter Takes Fort Fisher

The Confederacy enjoyed a victory in December 1864 when an amphibious expedition under General Benjamin Butler had tried to capture Fort Fisher in Wilmington, North Carolina. It was the one remaining seaport which the South could use to continue trade with the outside world. Under the command of Admiral David Porter, the Federal fleet bombarded the fort which protected the entrance of Cape Fear River, and General Butler put his troops ashore. The answering fire from the fort was so heavy that General Butler panicked and withdrew his troops. He came to the conclusion that the fort was too strong to be taken.

Grant wanted Fort Fisher and so he tried again. He removed General Butler from command, added fifteen hundred troops and gave the task to General A. H. Terry. The directive was similar to that given General Butler. Grant did not order a direct assault, but he left tactical details entirely to the discretion of the commanding officer.

Admiral Porter was again in charge of the naval unit, and because of weather difficulties, waited five days before reaching his destination. In the morning, the troops disembarked, and by three o'clock they were beached without the loss of a single man. The next day, a reconnaissance was made to within five hundred yards of the fort, and a small advance work was taken and turned into a defensive line against any attempt that might be made from the fort.

On Sunday, they prepared for the assault, but in the meantime, the fleet kept up a terrible fire upon the fort, and attacked in three columns. The first was led by the *Brooklyn*, with 116 guns; the second by the *Minnesota*, 176 guns; while the third, composed of gunboats, carried 123—in all, over four hundred guns played with fearful precision on the hostile fort. When the firing was most rapid, shells fell at the rate of four every second! Under the tremendous fire, guns were dismounted, embrazures blown open, and traverses disappeared with amazing rapidity.

A force of marines and sailors, numbering about two thousand, was to assault from the sea-side at the same time Terry's columns advanced from the land-side. For three hours previous to the assault, the four hundred guns of the fleet worked to their utmost capacity. The parapet was twenty-five feet thick and twenty feet high, surrounded by a strong palisade. About two hundred yards in advance of this was strung a line of torpedoes, eighty-five feet apart, each one containing a hundred pounds of powder and all connected by wires. Shells from the fleet had cut the wires leading to those that lay in the path of the assaulting columns. The shells also broke down a part of the palisade so the attackers had almost a clear sweep to the ramparts.

At length, everything being ready, at three o'clock the signal was given, and the three brigades dashed forward, following one another about three hundred yards apart, making, in their final rush, for the west end on the landing side. As they started, Porter ran up his signal which set all the steam-whistles shrieking. This was the signal to change the fire of the fleet from the fort, and concentrate it on the batteries to the left and above, to avoid hitting friendly troops. Smoke hung over the mighty armada out of which arose the shriek of countless steam whistles and incessant explosions, and the brigades drove on. Marines and sailors on the sea-side dashed forward but were stopped before the ramparts. Terry's troops, however, mounted those in front, and engaged in severe hand to hand combat.

They fought until the sun went down, and then continued fitfully in the light of the flashes from muskets, and flaming shells. The garrison was forced back, step by step, and at half-past nine the fort was cleared. Terry's signal torches flamed from the summit, announcing to Porter that the place had been won. About midnight, General Whitney and Colonel Lamb, the commanders with the garrison, eighteen hundred in number, surrendered. Seventy-three guns were taken along with equipage and stores. The Union loss was 646 killed and wounded, the

Confederacy suffered 400 in losses. In the morning, the magazine blew up, killing and wounding several hundred more men. In the fleet the loss was about two hundred. The other forts in the vicinity now fell into Union hands one after another, surrendering eighty-three cannons.

Admiral Porter, who was involved in both attacks on Fort Fisher, reveals more of himself than he intended to as he relates his experience in this batle. His memoirs are entitled *Incidents and Anecdotes of the Civil War* (D. Appleton & Co., 1886).

In October, 1864, I (Admiral David Porter) took command of the North Atlantic squadron, with directions to bombard Fort Fisher and the other defenses at the mouth of Cape Fear River.

From my study of the subject I was satisfied that the reduction of these works could only be accomplished by a combined military and naval force, and General Grant had promised that a body of troops should be ready at the proper time—when all the naval vessels had assembled in Hampton Roads.

General Grant was anxious to do everything he could to forward the expedition; but as the troops would have to be taken from General Butler's command, which occupied an important position on the left bank of the James River, they could not be removed until arrangements were made for other troops to take their place.

I was walking with General Grant at City Point, on the James River, when I espied General Butler approaching, and said to Grant, "Please don't introduce me to Butler. We had a little difficulty at New Orleans, and although I attach no importance to the matter, perhaps he does."

"Oh!" said Grant, "you will find Butler quite willing to forget old feuds, and, as the troops who are to accompany you will be taken from his command, it will be necessary for you to communicate with him from time to time." So when General Butler came up the introduction took place. The general was very pleasant, and I invited him to lunch with me on board the vessel in which I had come up the river; so a good understanding was apparently established between us.

From my knowledge of General Butler's peculiarities, I thought it best we should not co-operate in so important an affair as the attack on Fort Fisher, for when men have once had an encounter of sharp words they are not likely ever again to be in complete accord with each other; and the general and myself had had a little difficulty at New Orleans at a time when he had not been long enough in military employment to understand the courtesy due from the officers of either branch of the service to the other. I presume I had my peculiarities as well as the general, one of them being a determination not to submit to rudeness from anyone.

As far as I was concerned, I did not intend to let past differences stand in the way, but I feared the general had not forgotten the trouble, and that it might interfere with the important operations that were intended.

I therefore suggested to General Grant the propriety of sending some one in command of the land forces with whom I would be in entire accord, and Grant thereupon said he would send General Weitzel in command, a selection with which I was quite satisfied.

General Butler made himself very agreeable in his intercourse with me, and was apparently very busy in making preparations for embarking the troops that were to go to Fort Fisher. We visited each other and hobnobbed together. I was pleased with his zeal for the success of the expedition, and as General Weitzel was always with him when he visited my flag-ship, I took it for granted that Weitzel's going in command of the troops was a fixed fact.

Butler made many visits, but the troops were not forthcoming, though winter was approaching, and it was necessary we should commence operations before it became too stormy on the coast. The fleet was all ready, and, as time passed, my patience was becoming exhausted.

In a leisure interval I went up the James River to Dutch Gap in the flag-ship *Malvern* to give orders to the vessels that would be left there in my absence. The cutting of the canal at Dutch

Gap was a very good idea, contrary to the general impression, and should have been undertaken earlier in the war.

While I was at Dutch Gap, General Butler came up to see me in the *Greyhound*, which was his headquarters when afloat. This vessel deserved her name, for she was a long, lean looking craft, and the fastest steamer on the river.

The general informed me that Mr. Fox, Assistant Secretary of the Navy, wished to see me without delay at Hampton Roads on important business, and, as my flag ship was rather a slow vessel, he would take me down in the *Greyhound*. To this I agreed.

The *Greyhound* had been lying about an hour at the bank when we started down river.

The vicinity of Dutch Gap was a kind of neutral ground between the two armies, where prisoners were exchanged, and all sorts of people seemed to be hanging around the neighborhood. I never saw so many hang-dog-looking-rascals congregated together in one place. The Confederates doubtless had spies there all the time among the adventurers who always follow in the wake of a great army.

I found General Schench on board the *Greyhound* as Butler's guest; he suffered from his wounds, and was taking a little excursion for the benefit of his health.

There were no arms on board the *Greyhound* to my knowledge except General Butler's sword, which, though a formidable looking weapon, was of no use to any one except the owner, who seldom laid it aside.

The general's boat's crew wore *his* uniform, but had not so much as a pop-gun among them

There was a captain and a pilot, an engineer, several firemen and coal-heavers, a couple of deck-hands, and a cook and steward.

I never carried a sword or pistol at any time; neither did General Schenck; so here was a vessel, totally unarmed, carrying two major-generals up and down the James River with nothing to protect them, to say nothing of an admiral who seldom traveled in such a careless fashion.

The two generals immediately sat down to a political discussion, while I thought I would take a turn through the upper saloon of the *Greyhound*, which was fitted like most passenger steamers of her class, although her saloon may have been a little more gorgeous than usual. She cost the Government only about $500. a day, and carried the general with great speed from point to point where his services were required. Every general of importance had a vessel for this purpose, but the *Greyhound* was the gem of them all.

It was about half an hour after we started down the river that I went up to the saloon, and there I found half a dozen of those cut throat looking fellows, such as haunted Dutch Gap, scattered through the apartment.

I was so much struck with the appearance of these men and the confusion they exhibited that I said to one of them, "What are you doing here? Does the *Greyhound* carry first class passengers?" The fellow glared impudently at me and said, "We are just lookin' around to see how you fellers live; we ain't doin' no harm."

Not wishing to let these men see that I suspected them, I walked about quietly, as if amusing myself, while they, one after another disappeared below.

I went immediately to General Butler and said, "General, I don't particularly care to be captured just now, as I have important business on hand, and I don't suppose you do either; but you have a cargo of the worst looking wretches on board this vessel that ever I laid eyes on; hadn't you better look after them before they do any harm?"

The general acted promptly and ordered the captain to roundto at Bermuda Hundreds, and turned our passengers over to a guard to give an account of themselves, much to their disgust. After a thorough search to see that there were no stowaways on board, we proceeded on our way, no one attaching much importance to the fellows whom we had put ashore, as it was supposed they were merely loafers trying to get to Hampton Roads free of expense.

We had left Bermuda Hundreds five or six miles behind us when suddenly an explosion forward startled us, and in a moment large volumes of smoke poured out of the engine-room.

The engineer at once closed the throttle valve, stopping the vessel, and opened the safety valve; the steam rushed out, and the *Greyhound* howled louder than her living namesake would have done.

The generals stopped their conversation, and the crew seized the planks lying about the decks and jumped overboard.

"What's that?" exclaimed General Butler.

"Torpedo!" I answered. "I know the sound."

The vessel was now in flames amidships and the upper saloon filled with smoke like that from coal tar. We were cut off completely from the crew, whom we did not know had jumped overboard.

I was in full vigor at that time, and possessed considerable bodily strength. The general's gig hung at the port quarter, its bow resting on a house abaft the wheel. I put my shoulder under the boat and raised it from its rest, while the steward hauled in the slack of the tackle. When the boat was clear of the wheel house I lowered the after-tackle and left the boat hanging within two feet of the water. I then lowered a smaller boat on the starboard side, put the steward and stewardess in her, and bade them look out for themselves. In the meantime some of the gig's crew had swam around the gangway, and we all got into the boat and shoved off, with the exception of the captain of the steamer, who worked his way aft, hauled down the colors and seated himself on the rudder, whence we took him off.

From the moment of the explosion until the time of our leaving the *Greyhound* was certainly less than five minutes, yet the flames made such progress that the general's aide, who had gathered up some of his papers and was the last one to get into the boat, had his hand burned.

We picked up the rest of the men who were floating in the water, and then lay on our oars watching the conflagration. The *Greyhound* was now wrapped in flames from one end to the other, and, in newspaper parlance, was a "grand spectacle."

There was one melancholy event connected with the destruction of the *Greyhound*. General Butler had two or three fine horses on board, and their cries when the flames reached them were dreadful to hear, but their sufferings lasted only a short time, and their last groans were unheard amid the roaring of the flames, the crashing of timbers, and the noise of the steam, which continued blowing off to the last.

I think I saved General Butler a ducking on that occasion, if not his life; but I am afraid he forgot the service, although I would have worked as hard to get him out of that vessel, even had I known beforehand he would try to injure me.

Shortly afterward an army transport, loaded with troops for Hampton Roads, came along, and General Butler proposed we should take passage in her; but I had had enough of army steamers for one day, and, knowing that we should soon meet a navy tug, I proposed to pull on down the river. In half an hour we met the tug, went on board, and turned her back to Fortress Monroe.

The firemen were just going to dinner as we embarked, but kindly volunteered to relinquish their meal to us; so we sat down to pork and beans served in tin plates with iron spoons, and enjoyed it as much as if it had been a dinner at Delmonico's.

I do not know that there was ever any investigation into the loss of the Greyhound. My theory was that the fellows put ashore at Bermuda Hundreds had planned to capture General Butler and destroy the Greyhound, and I believe they were provided with torpedoes to throw among the coal, which they could easily do when the firemen's backs were turned. They could also have saturated the wood work in the vicinity of the engine and fire-rooms with tar-oil with very little chance of detection.

When the torpedo was thrown into the furnace with the coal, it soon burst, blowing the furnace doors open and throwing the burning mass into the fire-room, where it communicated with the woodwork. Perhaps the shell may have contained some volatile matter which caught the saturated wood. We were furnished with such shells ourselves during the war, but never used them. Only a few months ago the inventor inquired of me how many had been expended by the navy during the war, probably with the idea of claiming a royalty.

In whatever manner the Greyhound was set on fire, I am sure it was not one of the ordinary accidents to which all ships are liable. In devices for blowing up vessels the Confederates were far ahead of us, putting Yankee ingenuity to shame.

When we reached Hampton Roads a large assembly of the general's friends was there to congratulate him on his escape from death, but the rest of us were unnoticed. I slipped on board one of the vessels of the squadron and invited myself to take tea with the captain, but resolved to keep clear of army steamers in the future.

We waited patiently for the soldiers promised by General Grant. It was no use to attack Fort Fisher without them, for, although we might disable the guns, we could not take possession of the place. The defenders would stow themselves away in bombproofs, and would be safe against our fire. All I wanted of the army was to occupy the works after I had finished with them. I supposed they would have some fighting to do, but did not think they would meet with any great loss.

One day General Butler came on board the *Malvern*, accompanied by General Weitzel, some of his staff, and a reporter, and said that he had an important communication to make to me.

I had a faint hope that there was now a prospect of getting the fleet off to Fort Fisher. I saw plainly that I could not get away until General Butler chose to send his troops, for at that time General Butler was in the zenith of his power and seemed to do pretty much as he pleased.

When we were all in the cabin, including Captain K. R. Breese, my fleet-captain, General Butler said, "The communication I have to make is so important that I deem it necessary to observe the greatest secrecy." Then he and Weitzel and the stenographic reporter whispered together. This was a common practice with these gentlemen when they visited my ship, as if they hesitated about taking me into their confidence; but I was willing to stand almost any nonsense if I could only get off, although by nature not of the most patient disposition.

"Mr. Reporter," said the general, "don't you miss one syllable that I say, and put it down exactly as I say it. Weitzel, you pay attention. Remember, this proposition is altogether mine. I have never mentioned it to anybody except you." Then he whispered for a while to Weitzel, and took his seat, evidently much excited—something like a hen that has laid an egg.

My patience was rapidly evaporating when the stenographer got down to his work, the general watching every word he wrote.

General Butler seemed so intent on his project, and so earnest, that I began to be curious to hear all about it. I had not the faintest idea what he was driving at. It certainly could not be a balloon attack, for we had no balloons, and couldn't get them without an act of Congress. Perhaps, thought I, he intends to introduce rattlesnakes into Fort Fisher on the sly; but this idea I at once dismissed; there was nothing in the Constitution which would authorize such a proceeding.

I whispered to Captain Breese, "The general is going to propose his 'petroleum bath,' such as he has already proposed to use on James River. He is going to attack Fort Fisher from seaward by setting afloat tons of petroleum when the wind is on shore, and, by igniting it, knock the rebs out of their boots!" I thought the absurdity of such an idea would be a great recommendation, especially as it would cost a great deal of money, for at that time there was great competition in Washington as to which department could make the largest expenditure.

At length the reporter stood up, and read what he had taken down. The amount of it was that the general proposed to blow up Fort Fisher with a "powder-boat" laden with one hundred and fifty tons of powder. He argued the subject with so much eloquence, and showed such a knowledge of pyrotechnics, that no one could controvert his opinions.

When the matter of the proposed powder-boat had been submitted, I saw at once that here was something to simplify matters very much, requiring no act of Congress or interference of the Committee on the Conduct of the War!

The army and navy had plenty of bad powder and worthless vessels—in fact, material for a half a dozen powder-boats if necessary.

I don't know whether the general claimed the powder-boat as an original idea, but there is nothing new under the sun, and such a means of attack has been employed before.

I arose from my seat, and in a short speech accepted the general's plan, at the same time eulogizing the head that could conceive such a brilliant idea. The navy and the powder-boat would be all sufficient, and I rather like the notion, as the expedition would be entirely a naval affair, and I was not anxious to repeat my Red River experience on the Atlantic coast.

I think I stood higher in General Butler's estimation at that moment than I have ever done before or since, for, on the whole, he didn't seem to fancy me, as I had an unpleasant way of speaking my mind freely and not permitting anyone to interfere with my business.

I don't hesitate to say that I encouraged this scheme of a powder-boat, for in it I saw the road to success, and I was pleased to see that, notwithstanding General Butler's enthusiasm at the idea of blowing up Fort Fisher, he was not at all disinclined to have the navy go along, and *also the contingent of troops that had been originally proposed!*

Many persons have ridiculed General Butler's plan, but in war it is worth while to try everything, and some of our most scientific officers in Washington were so much impressed with the idea of the powder-boat that they carefully investigated the subject. The result of their calculations went to show that if a hundred and fifty tons of powder, confined in an inclosed space, could be *at once* exploded at a short distance from Fort Fisher, the concussion would displace so much air and so rapidly that it would kill every living thing in the vicinity, and wipe the sand fort out of existence.

At this lapse of time I have forgotten how much faith I really had in the project, but I must have been somewhat excited for I telegraphed to Captain Wise, Chief of the Bureau of Ordnance, Navy Department, that I wanted fifteen thousand tons of powder to blow up Fort Fisher, instead of one hundred and fifty tons, the amount asked for by General Butler. I was vexed at Wise's answer: "Why don't you make a requisition for Niagra Falls and Mount Vesuvius? They will do the job for you."

This little mistake of two ciphers would indicate that I was not so phlegmatic as usual, so I really think I must have believed in the scheme.

After General Butler and his staff had departed, Captain Breese said to me: "Admiral, you certainly don't believe in that idea of a powder-boat. It has about as much chance of blowing up the fort as I have of flying!"

"And who knows," I said, "whether a machine may not soon be perfected to enable us all to fly, as it only requires a forty-horse power in a cubic foot of space, and a propeller that will make such a vacuum that the air will rush in and drive something along."

Breese sighed as he walked out of the cabin, and I thought I heard him say, "All bosh!"—but one has to be a little deaf occasionally.

In answer to a telegram, I was told by the Navy Department to take any steamer I wanted for blowing up, for both the War and Navy Department highly approved the powder-boat scheme; in fact, General Butler had a right to be proud of the support he received from some of the most "scientific" men in both branches of the service.

I sent a tug to Newbern, North Carolina, for the steamer *Louisiana*, a valuable vessel, worth at least a thousand dollars! I calculated that by passing hawsers around her and "setting them taut," she would hold together long enough to get to Fort Fisher.

Next day the powder-boat arrived at Hampton Roads, and Captain Jeffers, of the Ordnance Bureau, came from Washington to take charge of loading her and laying the "Gomer fuse," which would ignite any quantity of powder quicker than lightning— that is, if the fuse went off, which it sometimes failed to do.

Several young army officers fresh from West Point also appeared on the scene, bringing with them a cart-load of books relating to explosives, and in the course of their researches one of them discovered that the illustrious Chi-Fung, a Chinese general, had blown up an enemy's fort with gunpowder several centuries before the discovery of America, but whether he used a powder-boat history did not say.

The day the steamer arrived I sent an officer to General Weitzel's camp to find out quietly if anything different from usual was going on. He returned shortly after and informed me that they were telling off the contingent that was to go to Fort Fisher, that transports were assembling near Dutch Gap, and everybody was talking hopefully of what the powder-boat would do. The soldiers seemed to fancy they would have an easy job, as the fort and all its contents would be blown away.

"Breese," I said to the fleet-captain, "I hope now you believe in the powder-boat. Issue an order for all the vessels to be ready to sail at noon tomorrow, and have two steamers on hand to tow the powder-boat down."

I then visited the powder-boat, and never saw greater enthusiasm. Officers were hard at work in their shirt-sleeves, and the "Gomer fuse," like a huge tape-worm, was working its way through piles of powder-bags. Every bag had a piece of fuse around it, so that there would be no mistake about its going off.

In the cabin of the powder-boat was a peculiar clock to fire the fuse at any time desired. There were candles that would burn a given number of minutes and then explode, and there were hand grenades that would fall at a given time and set the vessel on fire.

These were fine contrivances; but I ordered half a cord of pine-knots piled up in the cabin, to be ignited by the last man who left the ship, and this was what finally did the work.

The powder-boat left that night, and next day at noon the fleet, consisting of seventy-five or eighty well-armed vessels, got under way from Hampton Roads, the flag-ship *Malvern* bringing up the rear.

As the flag-ship quitted the anchorage the transports were sighted with the troops aboard.

We all arrived at the rendezvous near Fort Fisher, and every one was enjoined to be cautious.

The fleet lay some ten miles off shore, but the commanding officers of vessels were advised not to have too much steam up for fear of bursting their boilers when the explosion took place. One captain asked if it would not be prudent to send down top-gallant masts and yards, and brace the lower yards sharp up. I told him, "No," for there might be a gun or two left in the works after the explosion, and he would need his sail to get out in case a shot should perforate his boilers.

General Butler's transports lay at New Inlet, some distance to the northward, but I supposed he would soon be on the ground to stand by and charge the ruined works after the explosion.

At ten o'clock on the night succeeding our arrival the powder-boat was towed in abreast of the fort and anchored near the shore, the clock was started, candles lighted, hand grenades fixed, and the wood-pile ignited—not a soul in the fort aware of the terrible fate that awaited them. In ten minutes the powder-boat blew up, and the ships stood in to the attack.

The night the powder-boat was exploded a boat from shore came off with four deserters from the enemy. I asked what effect the explosion had on the people in the fort.

"It was dreadful," said one of the men; "it woke up every-body in Fort Fisher!"

But I do believe, notwithstanding, that the explosion had its effect on the enemy, for next morning, when the ships attacked, the Confederates fought as if they meant business, and the pow-der-boat waked them up to some purpose.

It was not General Butler's fault that the scheme was not a success. Something was wrong in the powder, or it could not all have exploded; for while standing on the deck of the Malvern the morning after the surrender of Fort Fisher, the earth works seemed to be in motion, the light was obscured by smoke and sand, amid which I could see bodies of many people carried up in the air, and I heard a great explosion which shook the earth. Then I learned that Fort Fisher had blown up and killed a number of our men—yet only four tons of powder exploded.

This would indicate that the conception of the powder-boat was a good one, and, if it could only have been got near enough to the fort or inside, and *all* the powder exploded, it would have demolished the works and their occupants.

I shall always feel under the greatest obligations to the pow-der-boat, for, although it failed to blow up Fort Fisher, it did what nothing else could have done—it started the expedition off. Considering all things, it was a cheap experiment in pyro-technics, for the powder cost not more than sixty thousand dol-lars, the vessel was absolutely worthless.

Had she not gone up in a blaze of glory she might today have figured on the navy-list as an effective vessel of war, while slowly decaying at her berth in Rotten Row.

After the failure to capture Fort Fisher I wrote to General Grant, "Send me the same soldiers with another general, and we will have the fort." So the soldiers were sent under command of General Terry, and after a fight that did credit to all concerned, we succeeded on January 15, 1865.

Then we worked our way up the Cape Fear River, all of which has been duly recorded in the official reports of the day.

After Cape Fear River was in our possession it struck me that it would be a good plan to set a trap for blockade-runners, who could not have heard of the change of affairs, and I put the indefatigable Lieutenant Cushing at work to establish decoy signals and range lights, and this, with the assistance of the "intelligent contraband," who was always on hand, Cushing soon accomplished.

On the night of the 19th of January two long, light colored objects were seen moving up the Cape Fear River, and in a few moments came to anchor near the flag-ship. These were the Stag and Charlotte, two blockade-running steamers, and they had hardly got their anchors down before our boats boarded them and summoned them to surrender.

The officers and passengers of the Charlotte were just sitting down to an elegant supper, in honor of their safe arrival, when the boarding officer walked into the cabin and announced to the astonished company that they were prisoners.

"The Yankees have got us, by thunder!" exclaimed one of the revelers, while consternation for the moment reigned round the board.

Among the passengers were several distinguished Englishmen, one or two of the officers of the British army, in search of adventures, and they were not particularly delighted at the turn affairs had taken.

The captain of the steamer had been captured before, and took his present mishap as a matter of course; but one of his passengers could not be made to comprehend how one of her Majesty's merchant vessels could be taken possession of in a friendly port while peaceable passengers were eating supper.

"Look here, sir," said he to the boarding officer, "aren't you joking? You certainly wouldn't dare to interfere with one of her Majesty's vessels; the Admiralty would quick send a fleet over here and dampen you fellows. This is all a joke, I know it is, and I want to go on shore at once."

"You have very singular ideas of what constitutes a joke,"

said the boarding officer. "I don't think you could understand one unless it was fired at you out of a thirty-two pounder."

"But," said the Englishman, "how can you fire a joke out of a thirty-two pounder?"

This remark "brought down the house," and the captain of the blockade-runner suggested that they had better eat supper first and discuss the joke afterward.

This affair turned out to be a very lucrative night's work, as the *Stag* and *Charlotte* were filled with all kinds of valuable goods, including many commissions for the "ladies of the court."

In the cabin of one vessel was a pile of bandboxes in which were charming little bonnets marked with the owner's names. It would have given me much pleasure to have forwarded them to their destination, but the laws forbade our giving aid and comfort to the enemy, so all the French bonnets, cloaks, shoes and other feminine *bric-a-brac* had to go to New York for condemnation by the Admiralty Court, and were sold at public auction.

These bonnets, laces, and other vanities rather clashed with the idea I had formed of the Southern ladies, as I had heard that all they owned went to the hospitals, and they never spent a cent on their personal adornment; but human nature is the same the world over, and the ladies will indulge in their little vanities in spite of war and desolation.

It looked queer to me to see boxes labeled, "His Excellency, Jefferson Davis, President of the 'Confederate States of America.'" The packages so labeled contained Bass ale or Cognac brandy, which cost "His Excellency" less than we Yankees had to pay for it. Think of the President drinking imported liquors while his soldiers were living on pop-corn and water!

I had supposed that blockade-runners were mainly filled with arms, ammunition, and clothing for troops; but the *Charlotte, Stag*, and *Blenheim*, captured by us at the mouth of the Cape Fear River, were not entirely laden with army supplies. The main cargo of one vessel was composed of articles for ladies' use, and all three were plentifully stocked with liquors and table luxuries.

There were many dreadful sights at Fort Fisher, and much

hard work to engross our time and thoughts, yet there were ridiculous incidents as well.

After the surrender of the fort all the smaller vessels of the fleet had to cross the bar of Cape Fear River, where at most there was but eleven feet of water. In the attempt they got fast in the mud, some twenty of them mixed up in apparently inextricable confusion, but in a few hours they were all across "the rip" and at anchor inside Cape Fear River.

Early next morning (February 18, 1865) an attack was made on Fort Anderson, a well-built star fort armed with nineteen heavy guns and situated on the right bank of the river. Like their other works, Fort Anderson was not well protected in the rear. The Confederates, it would seem, did not calculate their forts would be taken, thinking them proof against an enemy's fire and not anticipating that troops would ever be landed in their rear. If such were their calculations, the enemy were grievously disappointed.

In the attack on Fort Fisher we had burst nearly all the Parrott guns in the fleet; so I had telegraphed to Captain Wise, chief of the Ordnance Bureau, to send me twenty eleven-inch smoothbores, shot and shell, triangles for hoisting, etc., and in four days the articles arrived in a fast steamer from New York, which shows how promptly the Ordnance Bureau did business during the war. It was four days then before we could commence operations on Fort Anderson.

The night before we attacked that place I had a mock monitor constructed very much like the one which did such good service on the Mississippi. I knew that the enemy had the channel planted with torpedoes, and piles were driven in such a manner that vessels would have to pass right over where the torpedoes were sunk. At about 11 P.M. I had the monitor towed up, and let go within two hundred yards of the enemy's works.

The monitor floated with the flood-tide to within a short distance of the batteries, when the enemy opened fire with heavy guns and musketry, and exploded some of the torpedoes, all of which did the monster no harm, and she finally floated off toward Wilmington, not troubling herself to keep in the channel, but crossing flats where there were only a few inches of water!

All the next afternoon the monitor *Montauk* lay close in to the fort, keeping up a constant fire, while we mounted our eleven inch guns; and this was the monitor that the enemy thought had passed by in the previous night.

Just before dark that evening a veracious "contraband" paddled alongside the *Malvern* in a canoe and informed me that the enemy had a powerful ram and torpedo-vessel ready to come down upon us after dark that night.

I was surprised at not having heard of this ram before, but I prepared to receive her. Every vessel was to keep two boats ready, the boats' crews armed for boarding, and each boat was provided with a heavy net on a pole, with which to foul the torpedo-vessel's propeller.

The idea was for the boats to get alongside, cripple the enemy's propeller, and then carry the vessel by boarding. Two picket-boats were kept about six hundred yards ahead of the leading vessel, and a strict watch was kept on board the gunboats; but the picket-boats got so far ahead that they missed what they were watching for.

The *Malvern* lay in the middle of the line. I had no idea that any torpedo-boat would trouble us, and was just going to bed when shouts attracted my attention, and I heard orders for the boats to shove off from several vessels. Then came pistol-shots and hurrahs enough to account for half a dozen torpedo-boats.

"Thank fortune!" I said to Captain Breese, "I have been looking out for rams and torpedo-boats for the last three years, and have never yet seen one; but I think we'll get this fellow sure if they only carry out my orders."

By this time the river was alive with boats dashing by in desperate efforts to reach the scene of conflict, and, as they came up with the enemy, they joined in with louds cheers. "There he goes!" I heard them shout. "Head him off!" "Here he comes!" "Give him a volley!" This shouting and firing continued for several minutes, and I wondered why they did not board the enemy, saying to the captain, "That thing will get a crack at some of the vessels above us, and if they sink one it will block the game on us, for there is only room for one vessel to go along at a time. The channel has but eleven feet of water, and is only sixty feet wide. Why don't they board, as I ordered them to do?"

Then the vessels above commenced firing howitzers and

musketry. "That is sheer folly," I said. "They will never capture the thing in that way. That vessel is probably a turtleback, with an inch thickness of iron. He'll sink one of those vessels as sure as a gun. Jump into the boat, pull up there, and tell them to board the thing, whatever it is, at all hazards."

The captain shoved off, and in five minutes the strange vessel seemed to be coming down on us. "Look out!" I heard them shout, "Give it to him!" "Now's your chance!" Then a volley of musketry and three cheers.

"Here he comes!" shouted the lookout in the forecastle, "and all the boats after him," and, sure enough, the boats were all pulling after the thing and making a great clatter as they laid to their oars.

All the vessels had lanterns over the side, and one vessel incautiously burned a "Coston signal" which for a moment made everything as light as day.

To my great relief a shout arouse, "We've got him! Tie on to him! Double-bank him with boats!" and such shouting and cheering as only sailors can accomplish.

The struggle ended, the enemy was ours. I heard an officer give the order to "take the enemy in tow and stop their noise."

I thought to myself, "I must issue an order tomorrow rebuking the officers and men for making so much noise," and when Captain Breese returned alongside I tried to appear indifferent.

"Well, sir, we got him," said the captain.

"And a time they had of it. Why didn't those fellows do as I told them—jam his screw with the nets?" I inquired.

"He hadn't any screw, sir," replied the captain.

"Then what had he?" I inquired.

The captain laughed. "It was something worse than a ram; it was the biggest bull I ever saw. He was swimming across the channel when he was first espied. I don't wonder they took him for a torpedo-boat, he got through the water at such a rate."

"A bull!" I exclaimed. "And so I am not to see a ram after all. Tell them to keep a good lookout, notwithstanding the capture of the bull," and I laughed heartily at this absurd episode—so much more ridiculous in reality than even in the narration.

That evening General Schofield, who had assumed command of the army after the capture of Fort Fisher, had landed some troops to take Fort Anderson in the rear, and at eight next morning (February 18th) I attacked Fort Anderson with all the gun-boats, which, with their newly mounted eleven-inch guns, soon silenced the enemy's guns, and the Confederates abandoned the work and fled, to avoid capture by our troops coming up in their rear.

Off we went again on our way up river till at a point where the water was shoal. Fort Strong, on the left bank, opened on us and succeeded in boring some good holes in our vessels; but, with the aid of our eleven-inch guns, in twenty minutes we had all the firing to ourselves, the enemy evacuating the fort, on which we hoisted our flag. An hour later the army marched into Wilmington, and we were masters of the situation.

I reached Wilmington on the afternoon of February 22, 1865, soon after the army had entered the city. The river-bank was covered with negroes, and, as soon as the vessels arrived, a salute was fired in honor of the day, causing the darkies to suddenly scatter in all directions, under the impression that we were bombarding the town.

While we were at Fort Strong a contraband informed us that the enemy were going to let a hundred torpedoes drift down upon us at night and blow us all to pieces! I therefore ordered a double line of fishing nets spread across the river, so as to intercept any visitors of this sort. It was a bright moonlight night, and, although we had little faith in the negro's story, we kept a good lookout all the same.

At about eight o'clock I saw a barrel drifting down the river, and, hailing the Shawmut, directed them to send a boat and see what it was. Acting Ensign Trufant was in command of the boat, and, pulling close to the barrel, fired his pistol into it, whereupon it exploded, dangerously wounding the officer and killing two and wounding several of the crew.

The barrel was a floating torpedo which in some unaccountable manner had got past the nets, and the contraband's information was correct.

A short time afterward a torpedo caught in the *Osceola's* wheel and knocked the wheel-house to pieces, knocked down some of her bulkheads and disturbed things generally.

The torpedo-nets intercepted many of the same kind of devices, which were sunk next morning by firing musketry at them from a safe distance. But for the information given by the contraband which led to the precaution of setting the nets, I might have lost several of my vessels that night.

The night after we arrived at Wilmington we had another alarm. The vessel highest up the river opened fire on something, the next one took it up, and so did all the others until it came to my vessel, when I discovered through my night-glass a large steam launch floating down stream. She was towed alongside, and it proved to be the same launch in which I had sent Cushing to blow up the *Albemarle* a few weeks previous.

After the destruction of the *Albemarle* the torpedo-vessel fell into the hands of the enemy, and was sent to Cape Fear River to operate against our vessels; but the Confederates were not lucky with torpedo-boats, so she again fell into our hands.

The events occurring on the Cape Fear River and about Fort Fisher and Wilmington could make an interesting book, but I can spare but little space for them here. I will, however, mention one incident which occurred the day after the capture of Fort Fisher.

I was in a steam launch on the river, directing in person how to get over the bar, when I saw a large steamer anchor near the flag ship, while the latter fired a salute of fifteen guns, which meant that some high functionary had come into port. I soon learned that Mr. Stanton, the Secretary of War, had arrived. He had been to Savannah to see General Sherman, and stopped in at Fort Fisher, not knowing it had fallen.

I immediately went on board to see Mr. Stanton, whom I found seated at the head of the dinner-table with a napkin under his chin. He arose and put his arms around my neck and kissed me—imagine such a thing of Mr. Stanton! "I love you," he said, "the President loves you, the people love you, for you have—" but I refrain from stating the reason assigned by Mr. Stanton for the deep affection with which I was universally regarded; but it was not for my part in the capture of Fort Fisher.

"What can I do for you?" said Mr. Stanton. "Ask anything, and you shall have it if it's in my power to give it."

"Thank you," I said, "I want nothing for myself, but you can do me a great favor by promoting General Terry on the spot.

He has done his duty like a good soldier, and his reward should not be postponed."

Mr. Stanton ordered General Terry to be sent for immediately, and, while we were awaiting his arrival, Mr. Stanton opened his heart to me on a subject which, as it was strictly confidential, I forbear to repeat.

When General Terry came on board, the Secretary of War received him with great warmth, and after some conversation, retired with his private secretary into the after-cabin, where he remained for about twenty minutes.

General Terry had been up all the preceding night, and was worn out with fatigue; and his brother, who accompanied him on board went to sleep with his head leaning against the cabin-door, where he slept and snored to the amusement of the company.

When the secretary reappeared he presented the general with an official document containing an appointment of Major-General of Volunteers, and then shook the general's brother by the shoulder. "Wake up, young man," he said; "here's something for you."

Young Terry opened his eyes and stammered an apology for falling asleep in the presence of such high functionaries, but, when he looked at the paper given him by Mr. Stanton, he rubbed his eyes as if he thought himself dreaming. "By jove," he said, "I went to sleep a captain and woke up a major." I think General Terry and his brother were two as contented men as I had seen for some time.

Mr. Stanton was a much abused man, yet when he did anything to reward an officer he did it gracefully and liberally— unlike the head of the Navy Department, who, so far from thanking me for my efforts at Fort Fisher, wrote me a rude letter because I had given the five oldest officers of the squadron commendatory letters when we parted after the capture of the fort.

General Terry took no horses with him to Fort Fisher. He was lame at the time, and could not sit on a horse. I accordingly sent an officer to Smithville to procure me a horse and buggy— the best he could find. The officer departed at once in a double banked boat, and, on arriving at the little town, found a doctor's horse and gig standing in front of that gentleman's house. The officer jumped into the buggy and drove off—not a very polite thing to do, but it was a case of military necessity—and, getting horse and buggy into the boat, brought them both down to me. There chanced to be nobody around at the time, as the town was nearly deserted, so no one witnessed the abstraction of the doctor's equipage; but when the unfortunate physician came out of the house he couldn't understand what had become of his horse and buggy. He could not suppose that the reliable animal had run away, and no one around there would have stolen him, so for some time the doctor was in a high state of excitement.

General Terry was much pleased with the horse, and could have been seen early and late traveling around in the doctor's gig, attending to military matters, for Terry had no liking for fuss and feathers and cared little for outward appearance as long as he was comfortable.

When we were done with the horse and buggy they were sent back one morning before daylight, and when the owner arose from his slumbers he found the faithful steed standing patiently at the door with a good supply of oats in the vehicle.

The Monitor and the Merrimac

The Secretary of the Navy under Jefferson Davis, Stephen R. Mallory of Florida, knew he was in trouble. He was responsible for a Navy that didn't exist. There was no money to buy ships, and even if money were available, there were no shipyards or naval architects to build them. Even if he could contract with foreign ship builders, it would be months before a single ship was delivered. He hastily supervised the making over of merchant ships to men-of-war, but all the attempts ended in disaster. The vessels lacked speed, maneuverability, and the capabilities of carrying adequate large guns and cannon ball.

It was less than a month after the firing on Fort Sumter that Mallory began to look for a solution. In France, a new battleship, La Gloire, had just been constructed, and Great Britain had just launched The Warrior; both were ordinary men-of-war covered wholly or in part with iron plates from four to five inches thick. Wooden ships in war, he knew, could always be sunk. They might win one battle, but at the next meeting, a lucky shot from a large gun would sink the ship. The answer lay in iron vessels, but where would Mallory get the necessary foundries and shipyards? Carelessness, treachery, and fate came to the aid of the Confederate Secretary of the Navy.

In 1855, the United States built at different Navy yards three powerful steam frigates, the Merrimac, the Roanoke, and the Minnesota. They were all nearly alike: 3,500 tons, carrying from forty to fifty heavy guns. In April 1861, the Merrimac was at the Norfolk Navy Yard undergoing repairs when that place was abandoned. She was set on fire, scuttled, and sunk only soon to be raised by the Confederates. Upon examination it was learned that the upper works was so far damaged as to be worthless, but the bottom part, the hull and the boilers, were almost without injury. These could be adapted for a shot-proof steam ship more quickly and for about one third of the cost it would take to construct such a vessel from the beginning. The central part of the hull was cut down to within three feet of the water line to form the gun deck, and the hull was plated with iron to a depth of six feet below the water line. Upon the gun deck a casemate was built using pine beams a foot square and fifteen feet long. They were placed side by side, like rafters, at an inclination of forty-five degrees. These projected over the sides of the vessel like the eaves of a house. Upon these beams were placed two layers of oak planks four inches thick, one layer horizontal, the other vertical. This was first overlaid with ordinary flat bars of iron four and a half inches thick. A layer of railroad iron was added. The flat space on top was rendered bomb-proof by plates of wrought iron. From this roof projected a small smokestack. The armament consisted of eight eleven-inch guns, four on each side, and a one hundred pound rifled Armstrong gun at each end. The ends of the vessel were cut down still lower as to be two feet below water. At her bow, well under water, she had a massive cast-iron ram.

The *Merrimac* had a speed of fiften knots, but now, with all the armor, the speed was cut to less than half that. She was sluggish to handle, and took a half hour to make a full turn. Of her crew of almost three hundred men, fifty to sixty were always laid up in shore hospitals from sea sickness, and lack of oxygen because of the poor ventilation; in addition, several men were always laid up in the ship's sick bay. People who watched the building of the *Merrimac* commented that she would either capsize as soon as she got into the water, suffocate the crew, or at the first firing of a shell, everyone aboard would go deaf.

On that fateful morning of March 8, 1862, the *Merrimac*, rechristened the *Virginia*, set sail to prove herself to the Confederacy and show the world that a new era had come to naval warfare.

News of the construction of an iron boat was not long in filtering through to the Federal government. The slow process of creating something to meet the challenge began in the halls of

Congress. Bids were asked for and received from boat building companies, and the prices staggered the legislators. Just before the closing date of the congressional session, the house voted and appropriated 1.5 million dollars for the building of one or more iron clad ships.

The commission approved three different vessels. The *Ironsides* was a regular man-of-war covered with four and a half inch solid plates. She was to be 240 feet long, about 3,500 tons, and carry twenty heavy guns broadside. She would be completed in a year at the cost of $780,000.

The *Galena* was to be a steamer of seven hundred tons, brigantine rigged, pierced for eighteen guns. Her frame to be of solid timber eighteen inches thick, covered with two to four inches of plate-thin rolled iron. Her cost: $235,000. (Later it was found that the armor was totally inadequate to resist heavy guns.)

Of a completely different class was the *Monitor* proposed by John Ericsson. Her design was so new and different that the approval was cautious and guarded. The Commission said, "This is novel, but seems based upon a plan which will render the battery shot and shell proof. We are somewhat apprehensive that her best properties for sea are not such as a sea-going vessel should possess; but she may be moved from place to place on our coast in smooth water. We recommend that an experiment be made with one battery of this description on the terms proposed, with a guaranty and forfeiture in case of a failure in any of the points and properties of the vessel as proposed."

So confident was Ericsson of the perfect success of his ship that he proposed to name her the *Monitor* in order to "admonish the South of the fate of the Rebellion, Great Britain of her fading naval supremacy, and the English government of the folly of spending millions of dollars in fixed fortifications for defense." The price of the *Monitor* was to be $275,000.

John Ericsson was sixty years old when construction began on the *Monitor*; however, he skipped about like a school boy of sixteen. No workman could put in a bolt or lay down a plate without his inspection and approval. So diligently did he press the work on the ship that it was launched, with her engines aboard, on the 30th of January, one hundred days after the keel was laid.

The *Monitor* was 140 feet long, 30 feet wide at its broadest part, and 12 feet deep. The hull was constructed of a double thickness of iron, three-eighths of an inch thick, strengthened by iron ribs and knees. An Indian canoe is almost a perfect miniature of this hull, and just as frail for a cannon ball could pierce the thin iron as easily as a pistol shot could pierce the bark of a canoe. But this frail hull was protected so that when afloat no shot could reach it. Five feet below the top, an iron shelf, strongly braced, projected nearly four feet from the sides. This shelf was filled up with oaken blocks three and a half feet thick over which were bolted five series of iron plates, each an inch thick. This armor-shelf or platform projected sixteen feet at the stern in order to cover the rudder and the propeller, and ten feet at the bow to protect the anchor. The entire length of the deck was 166 feet, breadth forty-two. When afloat the entire hull and three feet of the armor platform were submerged. To the eye the vessel was merely a low raft, rising only two feet above water. No shot from a hostile vessel could reach the vulnerable hull without passing through the invulnerable armor.

The *Monitor* had two eleven-inch guns, the heaviest ordnance ever placed aboard a vessel. Ericsson had them set in a revolving turret invented years earlier by a farm boy, Theodore R. Timby, when he was sixteen. But the invention, at that time was deemed useless and abandoned. Ericsson, in his genius, saw an answer in the revolving turret, for he could bring his guns to bear on target in an action without turning the entire vessel.

The turret of the *Monitor* was constructed of plates of iron an inch thick, about three feet wide and nine feet long. Eight of these plates constituted its thickness. It was therefore nine feet high, and eight inches thick with a diameter of about twenty feet. The two port holes, side by side, were oval, just large enough horizontally to allow the gun to be run out, with sufficient vertical height to give room for the elevation of the guns to secure the range for different distances. It was made to revolve upon a central shaft by means of a separate engine. When not in action, by driving back a wedge, it rested firmly upon a metallic ring upon the deck. The guns were loaded within the turret and only run out to be discharged. The deck was perfectly flat, without even a permanent railing. The smokepipe and draftpipe for admitting air to the hull could be lowered below deck. When the vessel was prepared for action the deck presented a smooth surface broken only by the huge round turret and a low square pilot house near the bow. The vessel drew ten feet of water and was rated at 776 tons.

Two full months were spent in fitting the armaments and testing. On the fifth of March, sudden orders were presented, and the *Monitor* set off for Fortress Monroe. She reached her destination the evening of the eighth of March. The following day she engaged in battle for the first time, and forever changed the future history of war on the high seas.

The following three accounts, from a reporter's viewpoint on land, and from officers stationed aboard both vessels, give a new dimension to the naval engagement.

"The *Merrimac*'s Day of Triumph and Defeat," a newsman's report from Newport News Point, is taken from *The Civil War in Song & Story* by Frank Moore (P. F. Collier, 1865). "How the *Merrimac* Fought the *Monitor*" is taken from an article of the same name by Lt. Arthur Sinclair, C.S.N., in *Hearst's Magazine* 24:6 (1913). "How the *Monitor* Fought the *Merrimac*" is taken from *Aboard the U.S.S. Monitor 1862* by Acting Paymaster William F. Keeler, U.S.N. Edited by Robert W. Daly. ©1964, U.S. Naval Institute, Annapolis, Maryland. Reprinted by permission.

THE *MERRIMAC*'S DAY OF TRIUMPH AND DEFEAT

On Saturday, the 8th of March 1862, about noon, the United States frigate, *Cumberland,* lay off in the roads at Newport News, about three hundred yards from shore, the *Congress* being two hundred yards south of her. The morning was mild and pleasant, and the day opened without any noteworthy incident.

Soon after eleven o'clock a dark looking object was seen coming round Craney Island through Norfolk Channel, and making straight for the two Union war vessels. It was instantly recognized as the *Merrimac*. The officers of the *Cumberland* and of the *Congress* had been on the lookout for her for some time, and were as well prepared for the impending fight as wooden vessels could be.

As the strange looking craft came ploughing through the water right onward towards the port bow of the *Cumberland*, she resembled a huge, half submerged crocodile. Her sides seemed of solid iron, except where the guns pointed from the narrow ports, and rose slantingly from the water like the roof on a house, or the arched back of a tortoise. Probably the entire height of the apex from the water's edge was ten perpendicular feet. At her prow could be seen the iron ram projecting straight forward somewhat above the water's edge, and apparently a mass of iron. Small boats were slung or fastened to her sides, and the rebel flags from one staff, and a pennant to another at the stern. There was a smoke-stack near her middle; but no side-wheels or machinery was visible, and all exposed parts of the formidable craft were heavily coated with iron.

Immediately on the appearing of the Merrimac, both Union vessels made ready for action. All hands were ordered to places, and the Cumberland was swung across the channel, so her broadside would bear on the hostile craft. The armament she could use against the Merrimac was about eleven nine and ten-inch Dahlgren guns, and two pivot guns of the same make. The enemy came on at the rate of four or five knots an hour. When within a mile, the Cumberland opened on her with her pivot guns, and soon after with broadsides. Still she came on, the balls bounding from her sides like India rubber, making apparently no impression except to cut away the flag staff.

The Merrimac passed the Congress, discharging a broadside at her, one shell from which killed and disabled every man at gun No. 10 but one, and made directly for the Cumberland, which she struck on the port bow just starboard of the main chains, knocking a hole in the side near the water line as large as the head of a hogshead, and driving the vessel back upon her anchors with great force. The water at once commenced pouring into the hold, and rose so rapidly as to reach in five minutes the sickbay on the berth-deck. Almost at the moment of the collision the Merrimac discharged from her forward gun an eleven-inch shell. The shell raked the whole gun-deck, killing ten men at Gun No. 1, among whom was Master Mate John Harrington, and cutting off both arms and legs of Quarter Gunner Wood. The water rushed in from the hole made below, and in five minutes the ship began to sink by the head. Shell and solid shot from the Cumberland were rained on the Merrimac as she passed ahead, but the most glanced harmlessly from the incline of her iron-plated bomb-roof.

As the Merrimac rounded to and came up, she again raked the Cumberland with heavy fire. At this fire sixteen men at Gun No. 10 were killed or wounded, and were all subsequently carried down in the sinking ship.

Advancing with increased momentum, the Merrimac struck the Cumberland on the starboard side, smashing her upper works and cutting another hole below the water line.

The ship now began rapidly to settle, and the scene became most horrible. The cockpit was filled with the wounded, whom it was impossible to bring up. The forward magazine was under water, but powder was still supplied from the after magazine, and the firing kept steadily up by men who knew that the ship was sinking under them. They worked desperately and unremittingly, and amid the din and horror of the conflict gave cheers for their flag and the Union, which were joined in by the wounded. The decks were slippery with blood, and arms and legs and chunks of flesh were strewed about. The Merrimac lay off at easy point-blank range, discharging her broadsides alternately at the Cumberland and the Congress. The water by this time had reached the after magazine of the Cumberland. The men, however, kept at work, and several cases of powder were passed up, and the guns kept in play. Several men in the after shell-room lingered there too long in their eagerness to pass up shell, and were drowned.

The water had at this time reached the berth or main gun-deck, and it was felt hopeless and useless to continue the fight longer. The word was given for each man to save himself; but after this order Gun No. 7 was fired, when the adjoining Gun,

No. 6, was actually under water. This last shot was fired by an active little fellow named Matthew Tenney, whose courage had been conspicuous throughout the action. As his port was left open by the recoil of the gun, he jumped to scramble out; but the water rushed in with so much force that he was washed back and drowned. When the order was given to cease firing, and to look out for their safety in the best way possible, numbers scampered through the port holes, whilst others reached the spar deck by the companionways. Some were unable to get out by either of these means, and were carried down by the rapidly sinking ship. Of those who reached the upper deck, some swam off to the tugs that came out from Newport News.

The Cumberland sank in water nearly to her cross-trees. She went down with her flag still flying—a memento of the bravest, most daring, and yet most hopeless defence that has ever been made by any vessel belonging to any navy in the world. The men fought with a courage that could not be excelled. There was no flinching, no thought of surrender.

The whole number lost of the Cumberland's crew was one hundred and twenty.

The Cumberland being thoroughly demolished, the Merrimac left her—not, to the credit of the rebels it ought to be stated, firing either at the men clinging to the rigging, or at the small boats on the propeller *Whildin*, which were busily employed rescuing the survivors of her crew—and proceeded to attack the Congress. The officers of the Congress, seeing the fate of the Cumberland, and aware that she also would be sunk if she remained within reach of the iron beak, of the Merrimac, had got all sail on the ship, with the intention of running her ashore. The tugboat Zouave also came out and made fast to the Cumberland, and assisted in towing her ashore.

The Merrimac then surged up, gave the Congress a broadside, receiving one in return, and getting astern, raked the ship fore and aft. This fire was terribly destructive, a shell killing every man at one of the guns except one. Coming again broadside to the Congress, the Merrimac ranged slowly backward and forward, at less than one hundred yards distant, and fired broadside after broadside into the Congress. The latter vessel replied manfully and obstinately, every gun that could be brought to bear being discharged rapidly, but with little effect upon the iron monster. Some of the balls caused splinters of iron to fly from her mailed roof, and one shot, entering a port-hole, dismounted a gun. The guns of the Merrimac appeared to be specially trained on the after magazine of the Congress, and shot after shot entered that part of the ship.

Thus slowly drifting down with the current and again steaming up, the Merrimac continued for an hour to fire into her opponent. Several times the Congress was on fire, but the flames were kept down. Finally the ship was on fire in so many places, and the flames gathering such force, that it was hopeless and suicidal to keep the defence any longer. The national flag was sorrowfully hauled down, and a white flag hoisted at the peak.

After it was hoisted the Merrimac continued to fire, perhaps not discovering the white flag, but soon after ceased firing.

A small rebel tug that followed the Merrimac out of Norfolk then came alongside the Congress, and a young officer gained the gun-deck through a port-hole, announced that he came on board to take command, and ordered the officers on board the tug.

The officers of the Congress refused to go on board, hoping from the nearness to the shore that they would be able to reach it, and unwilling to become prisoners whilst the least chance of escape remained. Some of the men, supposed to number about forty, thinking the tug was one of our vessels, rushed on board. At this moment the members of an Indiana regiment at Newport News, brought a parrott gun down to the beach and opened fire upon the rebel tug. The tug hastily put off, and the Merrimac again opened fire upon the Congress. The fire not being returned from the ship, the Merrimac commenced shelling the woods and camps at Newport News, fortunately, however, without doing much damage, only one or two casualties occurring.

By the time all were ashore, it was seven o'clock in the evening, and the Congress was in a bright sheet of flame, fore and aft. She continued to burn until twelve o'clock at night, her guns, which were loaded and trained, going off as they became heated. A shell from one struck a sloop at Newport News, and blew her up. At twelve o'clock the fire reached her magazines, and with a tremendous concussion her charred remains blew up. There were some five tons of gunpowder in her magazine.

After sinking the Cumberland and firing the Congress, the Merrimac, with the Yorktown and Jamestown, stood off in the direction of the steam frigate Minnesota, which had been for some hours aground, about three miles below Newport News. This was about five o'clock on Saturday evening. The rebel commander of the Merrimac, either fearing the greater strength of the Minnesota, or wishing, as it afterwards appeared, to capture this splendid ship without doing serious damage to her, did not attempt to run the Minnesota down, as he had run down the Cumberland. He stood off about a mile distant, and with the Yorktown, and Jamestown threw shell and shot at the frigate. The Minnesota, though, from being aground, unable to manoeuvre, or bring all her guns to bear, was fought splendidly. She threw a shell at the Yorktown, which set her on fire, and she was towed off by her consort, the Jamestown. From the reappearance of the Yorktown next day, the fire must have been suppressed without serious damage. The after cabins of the Minnesota were torn away in order to bring two of her large guns to bear from her stern ports, the position in which she was lying enabling the rebels to attack her there with impunity. She received two serious shots; one, an eleven-inch shell, entered near the waist, passed through the chief engineer's room, knocking both rooms into ruins, and wounding several men. Another shot went clear through the chain plate, and another passed through the mainmast. Six of the crew were killed outright on board the Minnesota, and nineteen wounded. The men, though fighting at great disadvantage, stuck manfully to their guns, and exhibited a spirit that would have enabled them to compete successfully with any ordinary vessel.

About nightfall, the Merrimac, satisfied with her afternoon's work of death and destruction, steamed in under Sewall's Point. The day thus closed most dismally for the Union side, and with the most gloomy apprehensions of what would occur the next day. The Minnesota was at the mercy of the Merrimac; and there appeared no reason why the iron monster might not clear the Roads of the fleet, destroy all the stores and warehouses on the beach, drive the troops into the Fortress, and

command Hampton Roads against any number of wooden vessels the Government might send there. Saturday was a terribly
dismal night at Fortress Monroe.

About nine o'clock Ericsson's battery, the Monitor, arrived
at the Roads; and upon her performance was felt that the safety
of their position in a great measure depended. Never was a
greater hope placed upon apparently more insignificant means;
but never was a great hope more triumphantly fulfilled. The
Monitor was the reverse of formidable, lying low on the water,
with a plain structure amidships, a small pilot-house forward,
a diminutive smoke-pipe aft: at a mile's distance she might be
taken for a raft, with an army ambulance amidships.

When Lieutenant Worden was informed of what had occurred, though his crew were suffering from exposure and loss
of rest from a stormy voyage around from New York, he at once
made preparations for taking part in whatever might occur next
day.

Before daylight on Sunday morning, the Monitor moved up
and took a position alongside the Minnesota, lying between the
latter ship and the Fortress, where she could not be seen by the
rebels, but was ready, with steam up, to slip out.

Up to this time, on Sunday, the rebels gave no indication of
what were their further designs. The Merrimac lay up towards
Craney Island, in view, but motionless. At one o'clock she was
observed in motion, and came out, followed by the Yorktown
and Jamestown, both crowded with troops. The object of the
leniency towards the Minnesota on the previous evening thus
became evident. It was the hope of the rebels to bring the ships
aboard the Minnesota, overpower her crew by the force of numbers, and capture both vessel and men.

As the rebel flotilla came out from Sewall's Point, the Monitor stood out boldly towards them. It is doubtful if the rebels
knew what to make of the strange looking battery, or if they
despised it. Even the Yorktown kept on approaching, until a
thirteen-inch shell from the Monitor sent her to the right about.
The Merrimac and the Monitor kept on approaching each other,
the latter waiting until she would choose her distance, and the
former apparently not knowing what to make of her funny looking antagonist. The first shot from the Monitor was fired when

about one hundred yards distant from the Merrimac, and this distance was subsequently reduced to fifty yards, and at no time during the furious cannonading that ensued were the vessels more than two hundred yards apart.

It is impossible to reproduce the animated descriptions given of this grand contest between two vessels of such formidable offensive and defensive powers. The scene was in plain view from Fortress Monroe, and in the main facts all the spectators agree. At first the fight was furious and the guns of the Monitor were fired rapidly. As she carried but two guns, whilst the Merrimac had eight, of course she received two or three shots for every one she gave. Finding that her antagonist was much more formidable than she looked, the Merrimac attempted to run her down. The superior speed and quicker turning qualities of the Monitor enabled her to avoid these shocks, and to give the Merrimac, as she passed, a shot. Once the Merrimac struck her near amidships, but only to prove that the battery could not be run down nor shot down. She spun around like a top; and as she got her bearing again, sent one of her formidable missiles into her huge opponent.

The officers of the Monitor, at this time, had gained such confidence in the impregnability of their battery, that they no longer fired at random, nor hastily. The fight then assumed its most interesting aspects. The Monitor ran round the Merrimac repeatedly, probing her sides, seeking for weak points, and reserving her fire with coolness, until she had the right spot and the exact range, and made her experiments accordingly. In this way the Merrimac received three shots, which seriously damaged her. Neither of these shots rebounded at all, but cut their way clean through iron and wood into the ship. Soon after receiving the third shot, the Merrimac turned towards Sewall's Point, and made off at full speed.

The Monitor followed the Merrimac until she got well inside Sewall's Point, and then returned to the Minnesota.

The Merrimac then took the Patrick Henry and Jamestown in tow and proceeded to Norfolk. In making the plunge at the Monitor, she had lost her enormous iron beak and damaged her machinery, and was leaking considerably.

Thus ended the most terrific naval engagement of the war.

The havoc made by the Merrimac among the wooden vessels of the Federal navy was appalling; but the providential arrival of the Monitor robbed the rebel craft of its terrors, and the destruction of that one Saturday afternoon in March was the last serious mischief she ever did.

HOW THE MERRIMAC FOUGHT THE MONITOR*

As long as men go down to the sea in ships, as long as they will fling at each other the thunders of war and thrill at a flag unlowered even unto death, so long shall one naval battle stand forth in the eyes of men, celebrated and tremendous—the duel between the Monitor and the Merrimac. On the night of March 9th, 1862, panic raced north to Washington, to New York. Fright! and the wires were hot with it. A new sea monster had smashed and mangled a whole fleet, single-handed. An entire seaboard was at its mercy. All that night the wires burned with terror, and in the gray dawn the North sat ashen-faced and nerveless, staring at Hampton Roads. Then a marvelous thing happened: out upon the Merrimac darted the Monitor and for—but that's in the story below. On board the Merrimac was a young man—in the very heart of the inferno, mind you, for that was in the temper of him. Later he was to fight in the Alabama when she swept the high seas; before him his grandfather had fought on Lake Erie. His father and Buchanan were planning the Merrimac; "Take me," said the youth. Buchanan turned to his mother, and she replied—but that's in the story, too. Arthur Sinclair was in the midst of it, and now he tells you the facts. No wonder it's thumping good—here is the man to tell, and here is the battle that changed the warfare of the seas for all time.

Before the sun was fairly up on March 9, 1862, the first naval battle between Ironclads the world had ever seen, was on.

---

*With introductory remarks from Hearst's Magazine.

With the first gun fired by the *Monitor* upon the *Merrimac* that quiet Sunday morning the combined navies of the world passed into the scrapheap of useless and forgotten things.

It was eleven o'clock on the night of March 8th, 1862, that I had my first view of the *Monitor* in Hampton Roads. With one of the pilots of the *Merrimac* I stood on the gun-deck of the ship looking out through an open port toward that part of the harbor where the Federal frigate, *Congress*, which we had set on fire with red-hot shot earlier in the day, was illuminating the waters. As we looked, there passed between us and the doomed and blazing frigate a strange craft thrown into strong relief by the flames. It was wholly unlike anything I had dreamed of in connection with ships, and in my surprise I opened my mouth to express my astonishment when the pilot slapped the breech of one of our Dahlgren smooth bores and exclaimed, "That's the Ericsson battery for a bale of our money!"

He did not call her the *Monitor*, and if he had I doubt if I should have known what he meant, for while it was vaguely rumored that the North was building some type of armored vessel, and that John Ericsson had designed her, we did not even know she had been completed.

The craft passed into the shadow, and we lost sight of her. To us she was merely the Ericsson battery. Next day by unanimous consent she had been dubbed the "cheesebox on a raft," a description that suited her quite as well as our humorous appellation, "Noah's Ark," suited us.

"What can she do with us? How is she armed?" were the questions that rang through my head that night, and when the dawn appeared I was up and looking for her, as in fact was practically every man aboard. The morning was hazy, and it was not until the mist had lifted that we saw our rival lying close in behind the *Minnesota*, which had grounded late the day before in endeavoring to escape from our fire. There she lay. Within a few hours we were at handgrips with her.

Before the sun was fairly up the first naval battle between ironclads the world had ever seen was on. With the first gun, fired by the *Monitor*, that quiet Sunday morning the combined navies of the world passed over into the scrap heap of useless and forgotten things. The ships of England, France, Austria, Spain; all were as hopelessly out of class as the Spanish Armada. A new type of fighting ship had been born and before noon had proved its worth. Two great war machines, each radically different from the other, had come into being unknown to each other, and from them both arose the modern battleship.

I had returned to my home in Norfolk from service with Admiral Lynch's fleet, having been ordered to report to Richmond after Admiral Stringham's capture of Fort Hatteras, and was on waiting orders. The *Merrimac* had been raised and was being armored after plans conceived by Lieutenant John M. Brooke, Chief Engineer J. Ashton Ramsay, Chief Engineer Williamson, and others, and she was a source of mighty interest to me. On the night of Friday, March 7th, a group of officers gathered at the house of my father, Captain Arthur Sinclair, on Washington Street, to discuss the grave question as to the capacity of the *Merrimac*. Could four inches of iron stand a heavy fire?

Captain Franklin Buchanan had been ordered to commission her, and she lay ready in the navy yard basin. It had been decided that the trial of the new ship must be on the morrow, and the conversation turned on the possibilities of her beak or prow, a cast iron affair of 1,500 pounds weight that had been affixed to her bow below the water line. This prow was an after thought, hence not built into the ship, but bolted on to the stem.

I will remember my father nodding his head emphatically and remarking to Captain Buchanan, "The prow's the thing, Buck, Ram 'em! Give 'em the ram!"

I was twenty-four, held a sailing master's certificate, and the talk of a single vessel, of a type new and untried that should attempt to lift the blockade established by the Federal forces inflamed my imagination. I came forward into the circle of light about the table.

"Take me with you tomorrow, Captain Buchanan," I begged, and the group looked at me. Captain Buchanan smiled slowly and turned to my mother. I recall that he did not consult my father.

"How about that, Lelia?" he asked quietly.

She looked up at him with steady eyes and there was not a tremor in her voice.

"My boy's service is sworn to his country, Captain," she answered. "Take him."

My father nodded his head with satisfaction, and early next morning I stepped aboard the ship as she lay at the yard and reported myself to Lieutenant Catesby Jones, her executive officer. I was forthwith mustered into her company as volunteer aide to her commander, and at eleven that morning we slipped down the Elizabeth River, past Craney Island, on our way to raise the blockade. We were accompanied by the two gunboats, *Beaufort* commanded by Lieutenant Commander W. H. Parker, and *Raleigh* commanded by Lieutenant Commander J. W. Alexander.

The ship's engines were not all they might have been. Submergence had not improved them, and I doubt if we could have gotten over seven knots an hour from the vessel at the best. We made probably five down the river. All along the banks the soldiers of the batteries lined the shore to cheer us, and every point of vantage was occupied to watch the battle that they knew was sure to come.

Out of the river we turned and headed directly up the Roads to where the Federal frigates *Cumberland* and *Congress* lay blocking the entrance to the James River. As we swung out into the broad waters we could plainly see the excitement we created. Signals went flying to mastheads everywhere. On one of the frigates, I forget which, clothing was drying, and this disappeared as if by magic as she beat to quarters and cleared for action. The great harbor fairly bustled. Captain Buchanan came along the deck and lifted his hand.

"I intend to do my duty, men," he said, "and I expect you to do yours. Quarters!"

I have always believed that he intended an indirect reference to the known fact that his brother, McKean Buchanan was an officer on the *Congress*, which we were soon to engage, but of that I have of course no confirmation. He went aft, and I fell to pacing up and down the deck, conflicting thoughts racing through my head. I wondered whether this ship on which we of the South had built such high hopes of opening the blockade,

and thus securing European recognition, would prove successful. I felt an arm laid across my shoulders and a quiet voice
addressed me. I looked up and found Lieutenant Robert D. Minor beside me.

"Arthur, we"ll be in action shortly. Don't forget that you are
the son of one Captain Arthur Sinclair, and the grandson of
another, both gallant sailors, my boy." He left me with a friendly
tap on the arm, and I felt a lump rise in my throat. It was his
brave way of encouraging a youngster, and I've loved his memory
for it ever since.

It was not light test we were bound for. Hundreds of guns
would be directed at us and upon our capacity to withstand that
terrific hammering seemed to rest the fate of the vessel and the
Cause. We were headed directly for the two ships, and could
see others making sail in our direction. The Congress opened
first and was followed by the Cumberland. The former lay a little
off our course, while the latter lay directly ahead, and we made
straight for her.

"Hold your fire!" Captain Buchanan ordered quietly, and
the instructions were passed along. The solid shot from the two
frigates created a terrific clangor as it struck our armor and ric-
ochetted or glanced off upward to fall the other side of the vessel, or dropped beside her to hurl up showers of spray. The racket
was deafening. As we drew in we opened with the bow rifle and
tore a terrific hole in the Cumberland. A moment later we had
driven our prow deep into her side, and were being borne downward as she sank. The Captain gave the order to reverse the
engines to E. V. White, who was stationed on deck at bell and
tube, and we began to back out. As we ripped our way from the
doomed vessel we left the beak in her side. She instantly began
to founder, but her brave crew never ceased from fighting. They
served their guns and poured shot and shell with calm delib-
eration upon us. They fought their ship until the decks sank
with them, still fighting, and the greater number went down
with the ship, her ensign flying from her gaff.

"By God, they're men!" said someone, I never knew who,
and we turned our attention to the Congress, which had
grounded. By this time a hundred or more guns were directed
at us and the uproar of all that shot striking our armor was

describable. The *Congress* fought desperately, but a few shots put
her out of commission. We sent a boat aboard her to help with
her wounded, and while thus engaged, presumably through a
mistake on shore, some of their batteries opened, and, a heavy
rifle fire accompanying it, made an evil situation. We were
forced to abandon the mission. It was just here that Captain
Buchanan, wishing to get a clear view of what was going on,
called out to me and sprang up the after ladder leading to the
grating which bridged our armored sides at the top.

"Come on, lad," he called to me.

At the moment his head reached the top rung I cried to him,
"Don't go up, sir! They are firing all about us!"

The rifle balls were rattling like giant hail upon the armor.

"Damn it, come on! Follow me!" he cried and had just set
his foot upon the grating when a rifle bullet passed through his
thigh, and he collapsed into my arms. He was a big man and
too heavy for me to support, so I managed to ease him to the
deck and sent for Dr. D. B. Philips, our surgeon, who took him
in hand.

Lieutenant Jones hastened up and Captain Buchanan lifted
his hand.

"Take her on," he said with clenched teeth. "Give her the
hot shot. They'll have to look after their wounded themselves."

They carried him below. The order was instantly given for
the hot shot, which were prepared by being rolled into a furnace
on a grating, and then hoisted on deck in an iron bucket, and
with these the *Congress* was set on fire, her crew and that of
another vessel escaping in boats. It was here that Lieutenant
Minor was drilled through the body with a rifle ball and carried
below. Half an hour later I was astonished to see a stout, tall
figure, stripped to the waist, and deathly pale stagger up from
below, leap on a gun carriage, and seize a rammer. Blood was
streaming from a wound in his back.

"Give 'em hell, boys!" he cried, and to my amazement I saw
that it was Lieutenant Minor who had escaped from the sick
bay, torn off his bandages, and come on deck again. He fell unconscious and was carried again below, eventually to recover.

Dusk now began to fall, and the *Minnesota*, which we had
by then engaged, had run ashore where we could not follow her

because of our great draught, 24 feet, so we had to leave without a serious attack on her. We steamed over to Sewall's Point and there dropped anchor, close beneath our batteries. It was necessary to send our half dozen wounded ashore to the hospital near Portsmouth, and our last remaining boat was called away. As Captain Buchanan was carried on deck he beckoned me.

"You stay here with Captain Jones, Mr. Sinclair," he said. "When the scrimmage is over come up to the hospital and bring me the report. I'll want you to carry it to Norfolk and Richmond.

I am sure that, knowing my mother would be anxious, he wished to give me the chance of seeing her and relieving her mind. A thoughtful, true gentleman was Captain Franklin Buchanan. When the boat had gone we turned to and cleaned ship. There was not much damage. A shot from the Cumberland had smashed the muzzles from two of our guns, there were many dents in our armor, and we had lost an anchor, but of serious damage there was none. The Merrimac had proved her worth, and the rest would be merely a question of a few hours. I recall leaning over a gun breach and thinking this ship would end the war and then came the Monitor.

As I have stated, I was up betimes that Sunday morning to see the Monitor, or Ericsson battery, as the pilot had called her. When I found her lying slightly behind the Minnesota, to me she seemed a freak. What could that tin can tied to a shingle do to our impregnable vessel? A wisp of thin smoke was curling from her stack, set aft. Behind her were the frowning batteries and escarpments of Fortress Monroe, and at a little distance rose the topmasts of the ill-fated but gallant Cumberland with her silent crew sleeping the long sleep beside their guns. An odd thing the Monitor looked with her massive turret amidships and her rough pilot house well forward on decks that were all but submerged. Submerged decks were no novelty to us, for we had them fore and aft and under a foot or so of water. Suddenly she began to move. She was going to give us battle. One bearded veteran with a grimy rag about his forehead peered through a port about which we were clustered and spat into the water.

"Huh, she's a blasted toy!" he exlaimed and turned away. We were under way almost as soon as she was. I remember looking at my watch. It was just eight. Captain Jones was quietly about his duties. It had been decided to complete the destruction of the *Minnesota*, and toward her we headed. We gathered way slowly, the men at their stations, the marines, for whom there were no duties, grouped idly about. The *Patrick Henry* and the *Teaser* had come down the river the afternoon before and had joined us, and now they too got under way. Together we steamed toward the *Minnesota*. The pilots were to have put us within half a mile of her. Captain Jones had intended to stand off, reduce her to a wreck, and engaged the fort. We opened fire on her at something under a mile. The *Monitor* came toward us, and instinctively the two vessels seemed to recognize each other as foes.

Neither now fired until they were close aboard, then the *Monitor* opened, and as she did so we went ashore on the Middle Ground. The first of the *Monitor*'s shots struck fairly and glanced off, but it shook us up. She continued to fire, and we then replied, the while trying to back off the shoal. I watched her curiously and she puzzled me. We could see nothing of her guns until they suddenly appeared through the turret apertures, were fired and disappeared as the turret revolved rapidly. Our guns were directed at that turret, our only target, or at least the one we believed hid the heart of the ship.

On our gun deck there were grime, smoke, flashes of flame, an inferno of noise, terrific clanging crashes as the heavy solid shot struck us, the ripping sound of splintering wood as the heavy oak backing gave beneath the terrific hammering, and the wild cheers of the men. The air was choking. There was a vital danger spot in us had the *Monitor* but known it. Originally our protective armor had been carried two feet below the water line. Now, with the consumption of coal and water, we had risen quite two feet, and had the *Monitor*'s fire been directed at our water line she must inevitably have sunk us.

Captain Jones was everywhere, seeing, ordering, encouraging and fighting his ship like a man who knew his business to the last decimal point. We were still aground. The engineers had fastened down the safety valves, and the boilers were humming madly with the pressure. The screw was churning wildly astern, and the ship shook and jarred as if in agony. Around us and again around us the *Monitor* circled, pounding us at every possible angle, searching always for the weak spot where she could plant a shot that would cripple us. The *Minnesota* joined in the play. Our gunboats had withdrawn.

Suddenly we came off the shoal and the tune of battle changed slightly. Even now the vessels were hardly a hundred yards apart at any time, and generally they were close aboard. The range was point blank, and shot after shot reached its target. The *Monitor* continued to circle us, driving her bulk repeatedly into our stern and trying to reach either screw or rudder. The grinding shock of the two iron monsters as they came together, breathing fire and smoke, was almost nauseating at times. I carried orders here, there, everywhere. We manoeuvered in the narrow channel and finally turned. The *Monitor* was close ahead.

"Stand by!" cried Captain Jones. "We'll ram her!"

The bells clanged down in the engine room, and we gathered way slowly. The distance was too short, however, to secure any speed that would give our hull the weight, and we struck her a glancing blow amidships with our unprotected bow, and glanced off. Had we struck her fairly I am not sure what the result would have been. We might have forced her under water, or capsized her, but we should certainly have been badly damaged in the process. As we slid by her we fired our rifled Brooke bow gun, and this shot, as we learned later, smashed the conning tower and disabled Lieutenant Worden, the *Monitor*'s commander.

As we drew apart Boatswain Hasker went below with the carpenter and succeeded in stopping the leak from the crushed bow. Chief Engineer Ashton Ramsay has said that the impact was imperceptible below decks and he did not notice much water coming in, even after he had been directed to make an examination by Captain Jones.

At about the moment we rammed the *Monitor* our flag staff at the stern was shot away, and the ensign went overboard. I dimly recall a burst of cheering from the Federal encampment, wild shouts that echoed over the water, and this I later learned was caused by the belief that we had surrendered. The instant it was known that the staff was gone a man was sent above with new colors, and these he made fast to the funnel, which by the way had been riddled with shot.

As I have stated, there were no duties for our marines. One of them sat on the deck with his back against the oak sheathing that supported the armored side. A round shot hit outside immediately at this point, and the resulting impact transmitted through the iron and wood was sufficient to drive him clear across the deck to the other side of the ship, but without injury, where he lay for a few minutes stunned.

"My land, but that mule suah can kick!" he exclaimed when he recovered, and was careful to keep away from such an unpleasant experience in the future.

There was no cessation of firing. The *Monitor* plugged away, her turret revolving and her guns firing with great regularity. Our men tried hard for her portholes in that turret, but they were difficult to hit as she seemed to fire "on the fly" as it were, and there were shields that dropped over the ports. The bombardment was terrific, and it did not seem possible that guns carrying heavy projectiles could be fired at a distance of a few yards and not do terrific execution. I caught a glimpse of the *Monitor*'s turret once as she manoeuvred past us, trying again for our steering gear. Our fire had battered her severely, but her armor was intact, though she bore our marks in the shape of deep indentations. When a shot would strike her she seemed to shiver. When one of her 180-pound balls struck us it jarred the whole structure. I am sure if her fire could have been concentrated at one spot for a time she could have broken through us. The uproar was simply beyond description, for the roar of the guns was almost in the ears. Our men were compelled to load and swab their guns from the *outside*, and had there been rifle fire or machine guns, as today, they would have dropped like flies. As it was we lost not a single man.

Once more we scraped by the *Monitor*, and now we came between her and the *Minnesota*, immediately opening upon the latter with our port broadside. The *Monitor* gallantly rushed to her assistance, and being capable of quick handling, spun about and scurried close under our stern, giving us a good jar in the process. As she passed some man, whom I have never been able to identify, remarked, "If we could just jump aboard that dish with a sledge and some wedges we'd plug her turret."

The idea must have been well disseminated, for a little later it was heard on every hand, and some days later four boats were actually equipped with the tools to do this very thing.

I cannot attempt to describe the whole of that titanic battle which reminded me more of two knights in armor smashing at each other with heavy maces than anything else. No man can see but that small portion which lies beneath his eyes, and all see from a different angle. My station was with Captain Jones, and I was here and there so the whole picture is disjointed and fragmentary. As we fired into the *Monitor* we sent one shot into the *Dragon*, a steamer lying close to the *Minnesota*, and this blew up her boiler, but our distance was too great for effective firing at the larger ship. Our pilots could place us no nearer. The *Monitor* fired once more when she passed us, and continued on toward the *Minnesota*, still aground upon the shoal where we could not reach her, and where the *Monitor* with her light draught could go easily. We continued to fire at the *Minnesota*, and then it became plain, greatly to our astonishment that the *Monitor* had withdrawn from the fight. We could not understand this, for we knew we had not damaged her. The fight had lasted nearly four hours; we had fired hundreds of shots at each other, and neither vessel had been injured, nor had either lost a man. Gradually we ceased firing at the *Monitor*, and then remained upon the ground, cruising back and forth for an hour or more, but the *Monitor* did not appear again. Captain Jones finally turned to me.

"She has gone, and I am sure she will not come back."

We sent an occasional shot in the direction of the *Minnesota*, and then steamed in the direction of Sewall's Point again. We waited for the *Monitor* till noon when we steamed to the navy yard to be refitted. Commander Josiah Tatnall then took command of her, and on April 11th he returned with her to the Roads expecting to have a return encounter with the *Monitor*. The latter did not come out. On May 8th, the *Monitor* with other vessels attacked the batteries at Sewall's Point, and retired. Two days later Norfolk was evacuated, and the *Merrimac* was destroyed by Commander Tatnall.

While I have no desire to reopen any controversy that has been waged about this battle, yet a letter that has a most important bearing on it has come into my hands, which to my knowledge has never seen public print. As you know, Captain G. V. Fox, to who it is addressed, was during the war Assistant Secretary of the U. S. Navy, and made his headquarters at old Point for a portion of the time. He and Captain Jones had been shipmates in the old navy. Twelve years after the battle Captain Fox asked Captain Jones for a report of the battle. When this was supplied him he sent it with other reports to Captain John Ericsson who returned the documents to Captain Fox with the following letter:

New York, Nov. 24th, 1874

My dear Sir:

I am at a loss to understand why you have opened a fresh discussion about the *Monitor* and *Merrimac* fight, so happily disposed of by several patriotic writers to the satisfaction of the country—I may say to the satisfaction of the whole world.

No one knows better than yourself the shortcomings of that fight, ended at the moment the crew had become well trained and the machinery got in good working order. Why? Because you had a miserable executive officer who, in place of jumping into the pilot house when Worden was blinded, ran away with his impregnable vessel. The displacements of the plate of the pilot house, which I had designed principally to keep out spray in bad weather, was really an advantage, by allowing fresh air to enter the cramped, iron-walled cabin—certainly that displacement offered no excuse for discontinuing the fight—the revolving turret and the good steering qualities of the *Monitor* making it unnecessary to fire over the pilot house.

Regarding the Rebel statement before me I can only say that if published it will forever tarnish the lustre of your naval administration, and amaze our people, who have been told that the *Merrimac* was a terrible ship, which, but for the *Monitor*, would have destroyed the Union fleet and burnt the Atlantic cities—in fact, that the *Monitor* saved the country.

Need I say that Jones's statement will be published in the professional journals of all civilized countries, and call forth sneers and condemnation from a legion of *Monitor* opponents?

How the changes will be rung on the statement of the *Merrimac's* commanding officer that the *Cumberland* could have sunk his vessel (admitted to be unseaworthy, the hull being covered by only one inch plating) yet the *Monitor* was unable to inflict any damage, not a man on board the *Merrimac* wounded or killed. But the *unarmed Cumberland* destroyed two guns, wounding and killing several of the *Merrimac's* crew.

Again the *Monitor*, when challenged to come out, "hugged the shore under the guns of the fort." Counter statements, even if believed, would never be published. But I have said enough. Should the Rebel statement be published, its effects will be more damaging than probably any incident of my life. Please find your several documents enclosed.

Yours truly, J. Ericsson.

Captain G. V. Fox, Boston

In 1885 Dana Green, who replaced Lieutenant Worden when he was blinded, published the following letter from Assistant Secretary Fox:

U.S.S. Roanoke, Old Point, March 10, 1862.

Dear Mr. Green:

Under the extraordinary circumstances of the contest of yesterday, and the responsibilities devolving upon me, and your extreme youth,* I have suggested to Captain Marston to send on board the *Monitor* as temporary commanding officer, Lieutenant Selfridge, until the arrival of Commodore Goldsborough, which will be in a few days.

I appreciate your position, and you must appreciate mine, and serve with the same zeal and fidelity. With kindest wishes for your all,

Most truly, G. V. Fox

---

*Mr. Green was 22 years old and had seen less than three years of service.

I believe this letter from Captain Fox to Mr. Green to be self-explanatory in view of the facts, I have related, as can be.

In 1884 or thereabouts the officers and men of the *Monitor* put in a claim to Congress for the distribution of the value of the *Merrimac* ($200,000) among them on the ground that they had destroyed her. The Committee on Naval Affairs investigated the claim, and wholly denied it.

I have no further comment to make. I think there can be none. Of my own statements I am sure, for they are deeply engraved upon my mind, even after 51 years. The other matter is documentary evidence and admits of no contradiction. The *Monitor* did not defeat the *Merrimac*, false reports to the contrary notwithstanding, nor by the same token did the *Merrimac* do hurt to her opponent. The battle, the first between ironclads, was a draw, and in justice nothing more or less can be said.

HOW THE *MONITOR* FOUGHT THE *MERRIMAC*

Wednesday Morning,
March 5th, 1862

Capt. Worden has just come on board & says the Commodore has just had a dispatch saying that a heavy storm was raging on the coast & it was not safe to go to sea. So here we shall remain until tomorrow & probably longer as we have every indication of a gathering storm.

I made my last visit on shore this morning as I suppose, to bring off the mail matter for the ship. I found among others your good long one of the 1st & I need not assure you how eagerly it was opened & read, though it was more than two hours before I had time to read it through, it seemed as if the Paymaster never was in such demand.

I had shut myself in my state room for the sake of being alone & quiet—first came my boy to make my bed & clean up

the room. I dismissed him without ceremony. Then came the
Surgeon, just as I had fairly commenced & seated himself to
read the morning paper & have a chat. One of the masters followed to hear the news.

"Ah," says the M. D., "a letter from your girl hey?"

"Yes," says I, "& I wish you would let me read it." I had no
sooner disposed of him than my steward (Ellis Roberts) presented himself to know something about the day's rations. Then
came the lieutenant to get some information of some men who
deserted day before yesterday.

I got through with him & had taken up your letter once
more when I heard Capt. Worden enquiring for the Paymaster &
found he wanted some papers made out for the Department,
through with this & some of the men wanted some money which
involved an examination of their accounts. Then I had to go on
board of the Frigate *Sabine* to see her Paymaster, from there to
the *North Carolina* & when I got back to my stateroom once more
I found my darkey had been putting my room to rights &, as is
always the case at such times, turned everything upside down
& loosing your letter. I blowed him up, found your letter, read
that & felt better natured. . . .

Perhaps you would like to know just how my room looks—
I wish you could look into it & see for yourself. As you can't &
as I have none of "Porte Crayon's" skill, I must perforce use pen
& ink. Here is a plan that will give you a little idea—A is my
desk, B is the door let down to write on, the iron chest is placed
underneath, C is the door, D is the shelf in which is my wash-
bowl, underneath is another shelf in which are holes cut (remember that at sea nothing is placed *on* a shelf, but *in it*) for
my slop jar, tumbler, water pitcher, soap dish &c &c, all of nice
white ware with "Monitor" on each in gilt letters. Over the wash
bowl is a small shelf for hair brush, comb &c. Over this shelf, &
the bottom resting on it & reaching nearly to the top of my room,
is a large looking glass in a gilt frame. The floor of my room is
covered with oil cloth on which is a tapestry rug & on this again
is a fine, soft goat's hair mat. E. is my berth, wide enough to be
comfortable, & just so long that when my head touches one end,
my feet touch the other. In front of it is a handsome rail, 8 or 9
inches high, turning down on hinges when I wish, the top of

the rail being about on a level with my chin, so I have something of a climb to get into bed. F. F. are two closets, 3 shelves each, back of the berth, but they are so high up & so far back that it is unhandy to get at them. Under the berth are four drawers. The berth, drawers, & closets are all of black walnut, the curtains are lace & damask, or an imitation I suppose. For a seat I have a camp stool covered with a piece of tapestry carpet.

Capt. Ericcson fitted our rooms up at his own expense & has been very liberal. I have been on board of nearly all the vessels that have left the Yard since I have been here & have seen no room as handsomely fitted up as ours. The only objection is they are too dark. I have all my writing to do by candlelight & lamps are always burning in the ward room. If the sun ever shines again it may light up a little better.

The room is about a foot higher than I can reach. A register is in the floor for the purpose of admitting fresh air when we desire it, so you see we are providing against suffocation—the air is forced under the floor by the blowers in the engine room.

I should think from your account there would soon be war in La Salle. I hope you nor none of my friends will get mixed up in it—nothing would pain me more than to see our pleasant little circle broken up from some such foolish thing. . . .

Our rooms are all open at the top, for ventilation, & the doors are blinds, so that as far as sounds are concerned we might as well be in one room. While writing now, every word spoken by the circle around the ward room table is audible as if they were seated by my elbow. This does not assist one to concentrate his thoughts & very likely is the occasion of not a very few mistakes . . .

Yours, William

U. S. Steamer *Monitor*
Off Sandy Hook
March 6th, 1862

4 o'clock P.M. We have just parted with our pilot & may consider ourselves at sea. We have a fine westerly wind, a

smooth sea & as fair a sky as we could expect in the month of March.

We are in tow of the tug *Seth Low* & convoyed by the U. S. Steam Gun Boats, *Currituck* & *Sachem*, who are ordered to accompany us the whole distance. Our boat proves to be much more buoyant than we expected & no water of consequence has yet found its way on deck. Our hatchways are covered with glass hatches battened down & the only means of access to the deck is up through the top of the tower & then down to the deck.

9 P.M. I have just returned from the top of the turret. The moon is shining bright, the water smooth & everything seems favourable. The green lights of the gun boats are on our lee beam but a short distance off & the tug is pulling lustily at our big hawser about 400 feet ahead. A number of sail are visible in different directions, their white sails glistening in the moon light. Not a sea has yet passed over our deck, it is as dry as when we left port. We had a merry company at the supper table, the Captain telling some of his experiences as a Midshipman.

Friday, March 7th. When I awoke this morning I found much more motion to the vessel & could see the green water through my deck light as the waves rolled across the deck. A number were complaining of seasickness, among them Capt. Worden & the Surgeon.

The water had worked under the tower during the night & drowned out the Sailors whose hammocks were hung on the berth deck immediately below. The water was coming down this morning from under the tower & from the hatches & deck lights & various other openings making it wet & very disagreeable below—in the engine room it was still worse.

From the top of the tower, where our seasick ones were laid out, a number of sail were in sight, our companions the gun boats maintaining about the same relative position to us they had last night—they were rolling badly.

Towards noon the wind, which blew quite fresh in the morning, increased, blowing a gale from the no'west & of course getting up quite a heavy sea. The gun boats would occasionally roll the muzzles of their guns under & as far as motion was concerned they were much more uncomfortable than ourselves. To form a correct idea of our position you must bear in mind that our deck is a flat, level surface barely a foot above the water in still calm weather, with nothing whatever to keep the seas off our deck.

Now the top of every sea that breaks against our side rolls unobstructed over our deck dashing & foaming at a terrible rate. The wind continued to increase after dinner with a heavier sea pouring across our deck with an almost resistless force, every now & then breaking against our smoke pipes, which are only about six feet high, sending a torrent of water down on our fires.

Our decks are constantly covered with a sea of foam pouring from one side to the other as the deck is inclined, while at short intervals a dense green sea rolls across with terrible force, breaking into foam at every obstruction offered to its passage.

Now we scoop up a huge volume of water on one side & as it rolls to the other with the motion of the vessel, is met by a sea coming from the opposite direction, the accumulative weight seeming sufficient to bury us forever.

The steady & monotonous clank, clank of the engines assure us that they are still at work & the tug ahead is still pulling at the hawser, but as the day advances some anxious faces are seen. Things continued in this way till about 4 o'clock when on turning to go down from the turret I met one of our engineers coming up the steps, pale, black, wet & staggering along gasping for breath. He asked me for brandy & I turned to go down & get him some & met the Sailors dragging up the fireman & other engineers apparently lifeless.

I got down as soon as possible & found the whole between decks filled with steam & gas & smoke, the Sailors were rushing up stifled with the gas. I found when I reached the berth deck that it came from the engine room, the door of which was open.

As I went to shut it one of our Sailors said he believed that one of the engineers was still in there—no time was to be lost, though by this time almost suffocated myself I rushed in over heaps of coal & ashes & fortunately found the man lying insensible. One of the Sailors who had followed me helped pull him out & close the door. We got him up to the top of the tower but he was nearly gone.

To understand correctly the nature of our troubles you should get a correct idea of the boat. I enclose a draft of the deck & space below the deck which may assist you some.

Immediately under the blower pipes E.E., which are about 2 ft. by 2½ ft. sq. on the upper deck, are the blowers which take air down through the pipes & force it into the room aft of the bulkhead C.C. This room is tight, the openings to the deck being kept closed. Communication is had with the other part of the ship through small oval openings closed by iron doors about where the letters C.C. are.

The air being forced into this room by powerful blowers & having no other outlet goes into the ash pit of the boilers & up through the fires & so out of the smoke stacks D.D. supplying a strong draft & keeping up combustion.

So much water found its way down the blower pipes E.E. that it wet the belts with which the fans were driven & so stretched them as to make them so loose they would not work. This deprived the furnaces of their draft & of course the engine room was soon filled with carbonic acid gas, mingled with the steam of the water which ran down the smoke pipes into the fires.

As long as the doors through the iron partition were closed there was no escape for the gas, but as soon as they were opened by the men who were trying to escape from the engine room, the gas & steam rushed through & completely filled the whole lower part of the vessel.

We got all the men who were in the engine room stretched out on the top of the turret & put up an old piece of sail as an awning or a protection from the wind & spray which occasionally reached us. It was a sorry looking company which crowded the only *habitable* spot on our vessel.

Our colors were set union down to bring the gun boats to our assistance, but they rolled so on the heavy sea, they could help us none—things for a time looked pretty blue, as though we might have to "give up the ship."

We succeeded finally in getting the ventilation started once more & the blowers going, the M. D. in the meantime attending to the sick ones on top of the turret. Evening had now come on & we managed to get the gas out so that we got below once more with the sick. Our supper was crackers & cheese & water.

My mechanical genius came in play, as I took charge of the engines till morning when the engineers were sufficiently recovered to attend to their duties. Of course there was no sleep on board that night.

Towards morning the wind moderated & the water became more smooth. Breakfast tasted good I assure you. Weather was a little more pleasant & the water smoother through the day, still it continued to roll over the deck—it seemed singular to sit in my room & hear the huge waves roll over my head & look up through the little deck light as the mass of water darkened the few straggling rays.

A little after noon Cape Charles was seen & about 4 P.M. Cape Henry. About the same time we imagined we heard heavy firing in the distance, of course all began to speculate as to the cause.

As we neared the land, clouds of smoke could be seen hanging over it in the direction of the Fortress, & as we approached still nearer little black spots could occasionally be seen suddenly springing into the air, remaining stationary for a moment or two & then gradually expanding into a large white cloud— these were shells & tended to increase the excitement. As the darkness increased, the flashes of guns lit up the distant horizon & bursting shells flashed in the air.

We soon took a pilot & then learned that the *Merrimac* was out & making terrible havock among the shipping—how slow we seemed to move—the moments were hours. Oh, how we longed to be there—but our iron hull crept slowly on & the monotonous clank, clank, of the engine betokened no increase of its speed. No supper was eaten that night as you may suppose.

As we neared the harbour the firing slackened & only an occasional gun lit up the darkness—vessels were leaving like a covey of frightened quails & their lights danced over the water in all directions.

We stopped by the *Roanoke* frigate (Captain John Marston)

& rec'd orders to proceed at once to Newport News to protect the *Minnesota* (Captain Henry Van Brunt) which was aground there, so we went up & anchor near her. Capt. Worden went on board & on his return we heard for the first time of the havoc made by the *Merrimac* & the terrible excitement prevailing among the shipping in the harbour & among the troops ashore.

Everything on board of us had been prepared for action as far as possible as we came up the harbour & the report every little while through the night that the *Merrimac* was coming kept all hands to quarters through the night. No one slept.

The first rays of morning light saw the *Minnesota* surrounded by tugs into which were being tumbled the bags & hammocks of the men & barrels & bags of provisions, some of which went into the boats & some into the water, which was covered with barrels of rice, whiskey, flour, beans, sugar, which were thrown overboard to lighten the ship.

One of the little tugs (USS *Dragon*) alongside had the engine & the whole inside blown out by the explosion of a shell in the previous day's fight.

After getting up our anchor we steamed slowly along under the towering side of the *Minnesota*. The men were clambering down into the smaller boats—the guns were being thrown overboard & everything seemed in confusion. Her wooden sides shewed terrible traces of the conflict.

As a light fog lifted from the water it revealed the *Merrimac* with her consorts lying under Sewall's Point. The announcement of breakfast brought also the news that the *Merrimac* was coming & our coffee was forgotten.

Capt. Worden inquired of the *Minnesota* what he intended to do. "If I cannot lighten my ship off I shall destroy her," Capt. Van Brunt replied. "I will stand by you to the last if I can help you," said our Capt. "No Sir, you cannot help me," was the reply.

The idea of assistance or protection being offered to the huge thing by the little pigmy at her side seemed absolutely ridiculous & I have no doubt was so regarded by those on board of her, for the replies came down curt & crispy. As the *Merrimac* approached, we slowly steamed out of the shadow of our towering friend no ways daunted by her rather ungracious replies.

Every one on board of us was at his post except the doctor & myself who having no place assigned us in the immediate working of the ship were making the most of our time in taking a good look at our still distant but approaching foe. A puff of smoke arose from her side & a shell howled over our heads & crashed into the side of the *Minnesota.* Capt. Worden, who was on deck, came up & said more sternly than I ever heard him speak before, "Gentlemen, that is the *Merrimac,* you had better go below."

We did not wait a second *invitation* but ascended the tower & down the hatchway, Capt. W. following. The iron hatch was closed over the opening & all access to us cut off. As we passed down through the turret the gunners were lifting a 175 lb. shot into the mouth of one of our immense guns. "Send them that with our compliments, my lads," says Capt. W.

A few straggling rays of light found their way from the top of the tower to the depths below which was dimly lighted by lanterns. Every one was at his post, fixed like a Statue, the most profound silence reigned—if there had been a coward heart there its throb would have been audible, so *intense* was the stillness.

I experienced a peculiar sensation, I do not think it was fear, but it was different from anything I ever knew before. We were enclosed in what we supposed to be an impenetrable armour—we knew that a powerful foe was about to meet us—ours was an untried experiment & our enemy's first fire might make it a coffin for us all.

Then we knew not how soon the attack would commence, or from what direction it would come, for with the exception of those in the pilot house & one or two in the turret, no one of us could see her. The suspense was awful as we waited in the dim light expecting every moment to hear the crash of our enemy's shot.

Soon came the report of a gun, then another & another at short intervals, then rapid discharge. Then a thundering broadside & the infernal howl (I can't give it a more appropriate name) of the shells as they flew over our vessel was all that broke the silence & made it seem still more terrible.

Mr. Green says, "Paymaster ask the Capt. if I shall fire." The reply was, "Tell Mr. Green not to fire till I give the word, to be cool & deliberate, to take sure aim & not waste a shot."

O, what a relief it was, when at the word, the gun over my head thundered out its challenge with a report which jarred our vessel, but it was music to us all.

The fight had been opened by the *Merrimac* firing on the *Minnesota* who replied by the broadside we first heard. As we lay immediately between the two, we had the full benefit of their shot—the sound of them at least, which if once heard will never be forgotten I assure you. It would not quiet the nerves of an excitable person I think.

Until we fired, the *Merrimac* had taken no notice of us, confining her attentions to the *Minnesota*. Our second shot struck her & made the iron scales rattle on her side. She seemed for the first time to be aware of our presence & replied to our solid shot with grape & canister which rattled on our iron decks like hail stones.

One of the gunners in the turret could not resist the temptation when the port was open for an instant to run out his head, he drew it in with a broad grin. "Well," says he, The d——d fools are firing canister at us."

The same silence was enforced below that no order might be lost or misunderstood.

The vessels were now sufficiently near to make our fire effective & our two heavy pieces were worked as rapidly as possible, every shot telling—the intervals being filled by the howling of the shells around & over us, which was now incessant.

The men at the guns had stripped themselves to their waists & were covered with powder & smoke, the perspiration falling from them like rain.

Below, we had no idea of the position of our unseen antagonist, her mode of attack, or her distance from us, except what was made known through the orders of the Capt.

"Tell Mr. Green that I am going to bring him on our Starboard beam close along side."

"That was a good shot, went through her water line."

"Don't let the men expose themselves, they are firing at us with rifles."

"That last shot brought the iron from her sides."

"She's too far off now, reserve your fire till you're sure."

"If you can elevate enough, try the wooden gun boat."

"You struck her." (We learned afterward the the shot killed four men & wounded the Captain.)

"They're going to board us, put in a round of canister."

"Can't do it," replies Mr. Green, "both guns have solid shot."

"Give them to her then."

Bang goes one of the guns.

"You've made a hole through her, quick give her the other."

Snap goes the primer.

"Why don't you fire?"

"Can't do it, the cartridge is not rammed home."

"Depress the gun & let the shot roll overboard."

"It won't do it."

In the meantime two or three more primers snap.

"How long will it take to get the shot out of that gun?"

"Can't tell, perhaps 15 minutes."

And we hauled off, as the papers say, "to let our guns cool."

We were soon ready for her again as the order from Capt. W. indicated—"Port bow close aboard, load & fire as fast as possible."

"A splendid shot, you raked them then."

"Look out now they're going to run us down, give them both guns."

This was the critical moment, one that I had feared from the beginning of the fight—if she could so easily pierce the heavy oak beams of the *Cumberland*, she surely could go through the ½ inch iron plates of our lower hull.

A moment of terrible suspense, a heavy jar nearly throwing us from our feet—a rapid glance to detect the expected gush of water—she had failed to reach us below the water & we were safe.

The sounds of the conflict at this time were terrible. The

rapid firing of our own guns amid the clouds of smoke,* the howling of the *Minnesota's* shells, which was firing whole broadsides at a time just over our heads (two of her shot struck us), mingled with the crash of solid shot against our sides & the bursting of shells all around us. Two men had been sent down from the turret, who were knocked senseless by balls striking the outside of the turret while they happened to be in contact with the inside.

At this time a heavy shell struck the pilot house—I was standing near, waiting an order, heard the report which was unusually heavy, a flash of light & a cloud of smoke filled the house. I noticed the Capt. stagger & put his hand to his eyes— I ran up to him & asked him if he was hurt.

"My eyes," says he. "I am blind."

With the assistance of the Surgeon I got him down & called Lieut. Green from the Turret. A number of us collected around him, the blood was running from his face, which was blackened with the powder smoke.

He said, "Gentlemen I leave it with you, do what you think best. I cannot see, but do not mind me. Save the *Minnesota* if you can."

The quartermaster at the wheel (Williams), as soon as Capt. W. was hurt, had turned from our antagonist & we were now some distance from her. We held a hurried consultation & "*fight*" was the unanimous voice of all.

Lieut. Green took Capt. W.'s position & our bow was again pointed for the *Merrimac*. As we neared her she seemed inclined to haul off & after a few more guns on each side, Mr. Green gave the order to stop firing as she was out of range & hauling off. We did not pursue as we were anxious to relieve Capt. W. & have more done for him than could be done aboard.

---

*The *Monitor's* gunners could load and fire the 168 pound solid shot in their XI-inch Dahlgrens every seven to eight minutes. In all, the *Monitor* fired forty-one rounds in action approximately from 8 A.M. to 1 P.M., and twenty hit the battered Confederate ironclad. The *Monitor* was struck 23 times—twice by the *Minnesota*.

Our iron hatches were slid back & we sprang out on deck which was strewn with fragments of the fight. Our foe gave us a shell as a parting fire which shrieked just over our heads & exploded about 100 feet beyond us.

In a few minutes we were surrounded by small steamers & boats from Newport News, the Fortress, the various men of war, all eager to learn the extent of our injuries & congratulate us on our victory. They told us of the intense anxiety with which the conflict was witnessed by thousands of spectators from the shipping & from the shore & their astonishment was no less on learning that though we were somewhat marked we were uninjured & ready to pen the fight again.

The *Merrimac* had a black flag flying during the fight. This was the Commodore's flag. She was crowded with men, accounts varied in number, some placing it as high as 400 & from that down to 200 (14 officers & 260 men).

The battle commenced at 1/2 past 8 A.M. & we fired the last gun at 10 minutes past 12 M.

Capt. W. was taken off in a tug boat, in charge of an acquaintance to go to Washington. Our Stewards went immediately to work & at our usual dinner hour the meal was on the table, much to the astonishment of visitors who came expecting to see a list of killed & wounded & a disabled vessel, instead of which was a merry party around the table enjoying some good beef steak, green peas, etc.

"Well, gentlemen," says Sec'y Fox, "you don't look as though you were just through one of the greatest naval conflicts on record."

"No Sir," says Lieut. Greene, "We haven't done much fighting, merely drilling the men at the guns a little."

Never was a set of men more completely sold than those on board the *Merrimac*. She came out in the morning evidently expecting to find an easy prey in the *Minnesota* without any idea of finding a new antagonist. At first she would scarcely condescend to notice us till we gave her a taste of our quality from our 11 inch Dahlgrens, when she replied with grape & canister probably thinking that would demolish her puny looking foe. I believe I have already told you the compliments paid us by Gen.

Wool & Sec'y Fox—all regarded us as their deliverers nor doubt could the rebels have succeeded in their designs it would have been a disastrous thing for the country.

They could have destroyed & driven off the shipping in the harbour, shelled out the Rip Rags, & Fortress Munroe itself would have been at their mercy as Gen. Wool afterwards told us. They would have attacked Gen. Mansfield's army at Newport News in front while Magruder took them in the rear. This & still more extensive plans of operations had been laid by them when our appearance blocked the game.

The night after the fight I stood watch for one of the officers who I thought needed rest more than I did till 12 o'clock when I turned in & had the first sleep for three nights.

The night we arrived I was on deck & witnessed the explosion of the burning *Congress*, a scene of the most terrible magnificence. She was wrapped in one sheet of flame, when suddenly a volcano seemed to open instantaneously, almost beneath our feet & a vast column of flame & fire shot forth till it seemed to pierce the skies. Pieces of burning timbers, exploding shells, huge fragments of the wreck, grenades & rockets filled the air & fell sparkling & hissing in all directions. It did not flash up & vanish in an instant, but seemed to remain for a moment or two an immense column of fire, one end on the earth the other in the heavens. It soon vanished & a dense thick cloud of smoke hid every thing from view. We were about two miles from the wreck & the dull heavy explosion seemed almost to lift us out of the water.

I think we get more credit for the mere fight than we deserve, any one could fight behind an impenetrable armour— many have fought as well behind wooden walls or behind none at all. The credit, if any is due, is in daring to undertake the trip & go into the fight, in an untried experiment & in our unprepared condition.

We were all exhausted before the fight commenced, for want of food & rest—the men had never been drilled at the guns & were not prepared to act in concert—we were unacquainted with our own powers, offensive & defensive & knew nothing of our antagonist except the terrible exhibition of her destructive powers given the previous day. Before we left Brooklyn we heard every kind of derisive epithet applied to our vessel—she was called a "silly experiment," an "iron coffin for her crew" & we were styled fool hardy for daring to make the trip in her, & this too by naval men. But we did dare & we have won & what is more none of us were ordered to the vessel till we had expressed our willingness to go, or in other words we volunteered.

We have had a letter from Capt. Worden's wife, she says that he is very weak & nervous, but the doctors say he will recover his sight though he may be confined for some time. . . .

(*Marginalia*) I fear this will scarcely be intelligible—it has been written while listening to discussions & conversations—sense and nonsense more distracting to me than the *Merrimac's* guns. If read to any out of the family you must apologize.

I send lots of love & kisses to you all. Direct to Hampton Roads instead of Fortress Munroe.

(No signature)

U. S. Steamer *Monitor*
Hampton Roads
March 9th, 1862
2 o'clock P.M.

My Dear Wife & Children,

I have but a few minutes to spare just to say that I am safe. We have had an engagement with the *Merrimac* continuing for three hours & have driven her off, we think in a sinking condition. We have three men disabled, among them & the worst is our noble Captain who has lost his sight, I hope only temporarily. The first opportunity I get you shall have full details & my own experience. With my best & kindest to you all.

William

We fought her at *20 feet* distance a part of the time, the two vessels were touching. My hands are all dirt & powder smoke as you will discover by the paper—

U. S. Steamer *Monitor*
off Fortress Munroe
March 11th, 1862

Dear Anna,

I am full of business & have no time to write in detail. I want to say that I am well & to request you to direct my letters to Fortress Munroe as I shall get them much sooner.

For the first time I have been ashore & have just ret'd. You cannot conceive of the feeling there—the *Monitor* is on every one's tongue & the expressions of gratitude & joy embarrassed us they were so numerous.

Says one gentleman to me—after taking me by the hand & inquiring if I "was from the *Monitor*"—"My insurance is worth $2000. You can draw on me at any time for that Amount & it shall be honoured."

It was told from one to another as I passed along—"he's an officer from the *Monitor*"—& they looked at me as if I was some strange being.

At the store where I went to get fresh provisions for the crew the gentleman told me, "Tell your Ward Room officers to come and see me whenever they come ashore. I have first rate quarters & they are allways welcome without expense. The safety of all I have is due to them."

At the close of the action our deck was covered with fragments of shell. I enclose a few small pieces to Henry in a paper. How anxious you must all have been when the telegraph first brought you news of the terrible conflict.

We shall remain here as *guardians of Fortress Munroe* & the small amount of shipping which will remain in harbour, all have been ordered off in apprehension of the reappearance of the *Merrimac*. We shall remain here to meet her. We are *ready, willing & anxious* for another interview.

We are now commanded by Lieut. (Thomas O.) Selfridge from the sunken frigate *Cumberland*. His description of the fight as we were at the supper table last night was intensely interesting, 130 men were lost.

Yesterday I had the pleasure of shaking hands with Gen. Wool (commanding at Fortress Munroe), who came aboard with his staff. As he was about leaving he turned to us (the officers) who stood in a group & taking off his hat said, "Gentlemen you have made heroes of yourselves."

Asst. Sec'y Fox also paid us a visit. The officers were called together to be introduced & he said while shaking hands, "Gentlemen I want you to remember that millions of property is entrusted to your care."

During the action I acted as aid to Capt. Worden conveying his orders to different parts of the vessel & although I played a humble part I had all I could do, but I did it well I know, for I had both Capt. Worden's & Lieut. Greene's emphatic declarations to that effect. I am writing a detailed account of the whole thing which I will send home as soon as complete.

With the kindest love to yourself, the children & all friends—

William

WOMEN AT WAR

Diary of a Pro-Union
Woman of the Confederacy

These excerpts are from a diary kept by a woman during the Civil War. Because she favored the Union while living in the Confederacy, she discreetly left out names of people and many places, lest disclosure cause embarrassment or worse. The diary was published twenty years after the war, but feeling was still strong enough to make anonymity necessary. Today the names are not as important as the picture the diary presents of the spirit, the hardship, and the boredom of those who fought the war behind the lines the only way they knew—the only way they could. The excerpts are taken from *Famous Adventures & Escapes of the Civil War* (The Century Co., 1893).

New Orleans, Dec. 1, 1860. I understand it now. Keeping journals is for those who cannot, or dare not, speak out. So I shall set up a journal, being only a rather lonely young girl in a very small and hated minority. On my return here in November, after a foreign voyage and absence of many months, I found myself behind in knowledge of the political conflict, but heard the dread sounds of disunion and war muttered in threatening tones. Surely no native-born woman loves her country better than I love America. The blood of one of its Revolutionary patriots flows in my veins, and it is the Union for which he pledged his "life, fortune, and sacred honor" that I love, not any divided, or special section of it. So I have been reading attentively and seeking light from the foreigners and natives on all questions at issue. Living from birth in slave countries, both foreign and American, and passing through one slave insurrection in early childhood, the saddest and also the pleasantest features of slavery have been familiar. If the South goes to war for slavery, slavery is doomed in this country. To say so is like opposing one drop to a roaring torrent.

Sunday, Dec., 1860. In this season for peace I had hoped for a lull in the excitement, yet this day has been full of bitterness. "Come, G.," said Mrs. ——— at breakfast, "leave your church for today and come with us to hear Dr. ——— on the situation. He will convince you."

"It is good to be convinced," I said, "I will go."

The church was crowded to suffocation with the elite of New Orleans. The preacher's text was, "Shall we have fellowship with the stool of iniquity which frameth mischief as a law?" The sermon was over at last, and then followed a prayer. Forever blessed by the fathers of the Episcopal Church for giving us a fixed liturgy! When we met at dinner Mrs. F. exclaimed, "Now, G., you heard him prove from the Bible that slavery is right and that therefore secession is. Were you not convinced?" I said, "I was so busy thinking how completely it proved too that Brigham Young is right about polygamy that it quite weakened the force of the argument for me." This raised a laugh, and covered my retreat.

Jan. 26, 1861. The solemn boom of cannon today announced that the convention have passed the ordinance of secession. We must take a reef in our patriotism and narrow it down to State limits. Mine still sticks out all around the borders of the State. It will be bad if New Orleans should secede from Louisiana and set up for herself. Then indeed I would be "cabined, cribbed, confined." The faces in the house are jubilant today. Why is it so easy for them and not for me to "ring out the old, ring in the new?" I am out of place.

Jan. 28, Monday. Sunday has not got to be a day of special excitement. The gentlemen save all the sensational papers to regale us with at the late Sunday breakfast. Rob opened the battle yesterday morning by saying to me in his most aggressive manner, "G., I believe these are your sentiments"; and then he read aloud from the "Journal des Debats" expressing in rather contemptuous terms the fact that France will follow the policy of nonintervention. When I answered, "Well, what do you expect? This is not their quarrel," he raved at me, ending by a declaration that he would willingly pay my passage to foreign parts if I would like to go. "Rob," said his father, "keep cool; don't let that threat excite you. Cotton is king. Just wait till they feel the pinch a little; their tone will change."

I went to Trinity Church. Some Union people who are not Episcopalians go there now because the pastor has not so much chance to rail at the Lord when things are not going to suit. But yesterday was a marked Sunday. The usual prayer for the President and congress was changed to the "governor and people of this commonwealth and their representatives in convention assembled."

The city was very lively and noisy this evening with rockets and lights in honor of secession. Mrs. F., in common with the neighbors, illuminated. We walked out to see the houses of others gleaming amid the dark shrubbery like a fairy scene. The perfect stillness added to the effect, while the moon rose slowly with calm splendor. We hastened home to dress for a soiree, but on the stairs, Edith said, "G., first come and help me dress Phoebe and Chloe (the negro servants). There is a ball tonight in aristocratic colored society. This is Chloe's first introduction to New Orleans circles, and Henry Judson, Phoebe's husband, gave five dollars for a ticket for her." Chloe is a recent purchase from Georgia. We superintended their very stylish toilets, and Edith said, "G., run into your room, please, and write a pass for Henry. Put Mr. D.'s name to it." "Why, Henry is free," I said. "That makes no difference; all colored people must have a pass if out late. They choose a master for protection, and always carry his pass. Henry chose Mr. D., but he's lost the pass he had."

Feb. 24, 1861. The toil of the week is ended. Nearly a month has passed since I wrote here. Events have crowded upon one another. On the 4th the cannon boomed in honor of Jefferson Davis's election, and day before yesterday Washington's birthday was made the occasion of another grand display and illumination, in honor of the birth of a new nation and the breaking of that Union which he labored to cement. We drove to the racecourse to see the review of troops. A flag was presented to the Washington Artillery by ladies. Senator Judah Benjamin made an impassioned speech. The banner was orange satin on one side, crimson silk on the other, the pelican and brood embroidered in pale green and gold. Silver crossed cannon surmounted it, orange-colored fringe surrounded it, and crimson tassels drooped from it. It was a brilliant, unreal scene; with military bands clashing triumphant music, elegant vehicles, high-stepping horses, and lovely women richly appareled.

Wedding cards have been pouring in till the contagion has reached us; Edith will be married next Thursday. The wedding dress is being fashioned, and the bridesmaids and groomsmen have arrived. Edith has requested me to be special mistress of ceremonies on Thursday evening, and I have told this terrible little rebel, who talks nothing but blood and thunder, yet faints at the sight of a worm, that if I fill that office no one shall mention war or politics during the whole evening on pain of expulsion.

March 10, 1861. The excitement in this house has risen to fever-heat during the past week. The four gentlemen have each a different plan for saving the country, and now that the bridal bouquets have faded, the three ladies have again turned to public affairs; Lincoln's inauguration and the story of the disguise in which he traveled to Washington is a never-ending source of gossip. The family board being the common forum, each gentleman as he appears first unloads his pockets of papers from all the Southern States, and then his overflowing heart to his eager female listeners, who in turn relate, inquire, sympathize, or cheer. If I dare express a doubt that the path to victory will be a flowery one, eyes flash, cheeks burn, and tongues clatter, till all are checked up suddenly by a warning rap for "Order, order!"

from the amiable lady presiding. Thus we swallow politics with every meal. We take a mouthful and read a telegram, one eye on table, the other on the paper. One must be made of cool stuff to keep calm and collected, but I say but little. The war has banished small talk. Through all this black servants move about quietly, never seeming to notice that this is all about them.

"How can you speak so plainly before them?" I say.

"Why, what matter? They know that we shall keep the whip-handle."

April 13, 1861. More than a month has passed since the last date here. This afternoon I was seated on the floor covered with loveliest flowers, arranging a floral offering for the fair, when the gentleman arrived and with papers bearing news of the fall of Fort Sumter, which, at her request, I read to Mrs. F.

April 20. The last few days have glided away in a halo of beauty. But nobody has time or will to enjoy it. War, war! is the one idea. The children play only with toy cannons and soldiers; the oldest inhabitant goes by every day with his rifle to practice; the public squares are full of companies drilling, and are now the fashionable resorts. We have been told that it is best for women to learn how to shoot too, so as to protect themselves when the men have all gone to battle. Every evening after dinner we adjourn to the back lot and fire at a target with pistols. Yesterday I dined at Uncle Ralph's. Some members of the bar were present, and were jubilant about their brand new Confederacy. It would soon be the grandest government ever known. Uncle Ralph said solemnly, "No, gentlemen; the day we seceded the star of our glory set." The words sunk into my mind like a knell, and made me wonder at the mind that could recognize that and yet adhere to the doctrine of secession.

In the evening I attended a farewell gathering at a friend's whose brothers are to leave this week for Richmond. There was music. No minor chord was permitted.

April 25. Yesterday I went with Cousin E. to have her picture taken. The picture galleries are doing a thriving business. Many companies are ordered off to take possession of Fort Pickens (Florida), and all seem to be leaving sweethearts behind them. The crowd was in high spirits; they don't dream that any destinies will be spoiled. When I got home Edith was reading from the daily paper of the dismissal of Miss G. from her place as teacher for expressing abolition sentiments, and that she would be ordered to leave the city. Soon a lady came with a paper setting forth that she has established a "company"—we are nothing if not military—for making lint and getting stores of linen to supply the hospitals.

My name went down. If it hadn't, my spirit would have been wounded as with sharp spears before night. Next came a little girl with a subscription paper to get a flag for a certain company. The little girls, especially the pretty ones, are kept busy trotting around with subscription lists. Latest of all came little Guy, Mr. F.'s youngest clerk, the pet of the firm as well as of his home, a mere boy of sixteen. Such senseless sacrifices seem a sin. He chattered brightly, but lingered about, saying good-by. He got through it bravely until Edith's husband incautiously said, "You didn't kiss your little sweetheart," as he always called Ellie, who had been allowed to sit up. He turned and suddenly broke into agonizing sobs, and then ran down the steps.

May 10. I am tired and ashamed of myself. Last week I attended a meeting of the lint society to hand in the small contribution of linen I had been able to gather. We scraped lint till it was dark. A paper was shown, entitled the "Volunteer's Friend," started by the girls of the high school, and I was asked to help the girls with it. I positively declined. Today I was pressed into service to make red flannel cartridge-bags for ten-inch columbiads. I basted while Mrs. S. sewed, and I felt ashamed to think that I had not the moral courage to say, "I don't approve of your war and won't help you, particularly in the murderous part of it."

May 27. This has been a scenic Sabbath. Various companies

about to depart for Virginia occupied the prominent churches to have their flags consecrated. The streets were resonant with the clangor of drums and trumpets. E. and myself went to Christ Church because the Washington Artillery were to be there.

June 13. Today has been appointed a Fast Day. I spent the morning writing a letter on which I put my first Confederate postage-stamp. It is of a brown color and has a large 5 in the center. To-morrow must be devoted to all my foreign correspondents before the expected blockade cuts us off.

June 29. I attended a fine luncheon yesterday at one of the public schools. A lady remarked to a school official that the cost of provisions in the Confederacy was getting very high, butter especially, being scarce and costly. "Never fear, my dear madam," he replied. "Texas alone can furnish butter enough to supply the whole Confederacy; we'll soon be getting it from there." It's just as well to have this sublime confidence.

July 15. The quiet of midsummer reigns, but ripples of excitement break around us as the papers tell of skirmishes and attacks here and there in Virginia. "Rich Mountain" and "Carrick's Ford" were the last. "You see," said Mrs. D. at breakfast to-day, "my prophecy is coming true that Virginia will be the seat of war." "Indeed," I burst out, forgetting my resolution not to argue, "you think yourselves lucky if this war turns out to have any seat in particular."

So far, no one especially connected with me has gone to fight. How glad I am for his mother's sake that Rob's lameness will keep him at home. Mr. F., Mr. S., and Uncle Ralph are beyond the age for active service, and Edith says Mr. D. can't go now. She is very enthusiastic about other people's husbands being enrolled, and regrets that her Alex is not strong enough to defend his country and his rights.

July 22. What a day! I feel like one who has been out in a high wind, and cannot get my breath. The newsboys are still shouting with their extras, "Battle of Bull's Run! List of the killed! Battle of Manassas! List of the wounded!" Tender-hearted Mrs. F. was sobbing so she could not serve the tea; but nobody cared for tea. "O, G.!" she said, "three thousand of our own, dear Southern boys are lying out there."

"My dear Fannie," spoke Mr. F., "they are heroes now. They died in a glorious cause, and it is not in vain. This will end it. The sacrifice had to be made, but those killed have gained immortal names."

Then Rob rushed in with a new extra, reading of the spoils captured, and grief was forgotten. Words cannot paint the excitement. Rob capered about and cheered; Edith danced around ringing the dinner-bell and shouting, "Victory!" Mrs. F. waved a small Confederate flag, while she wiped her eyes, and Mr. D. hastened to the piano and in his most brilliant style struck up "Dixie," followed by "My Maryland" and the "Bonnie Blue Flag."

"Do not look so gloomy, G.," whispered Mr. S. "You should be happy to-night; for, as Mr. F. says, now we shall have peace."

"And is that the way you think of the men of your own blood and race?" I replied. But an utter scorn came over me and choked me, and I walked out of the room. What proof is there in this dark hour that they are not right? Only the emphatic answer of my own soul. To-morrow I will pack my trunk and accept the invitation to visit at Uncle Ralph's country house.

Sept. 25. When I opened the door of Mrs. F's room on my return, the rattle of two sewing machines and a blaze of color met me.

"Ah, G., you are just in time to help us: these are coats for Jeff Thompson's men. All the cloth in the city is exhausted; these flannel-lined oil-cloth table-covers are all we could obtain to make overcoats for Thompson's poor boys. They will be very warm and serviceable."

"Serviceable—yes! The Federal army will fly when they see those coats! I only wish I could be with the regiment when these are shared around." Yet I helped make them.

Seriously, I wonder if any soldiers will ever wear these remarkable coats—the most bewildering combination of brilliant, intense reds, greens, yellows, and blues in big flowers meandering over as vivid grounds; and as not table-cover was large enough to make a coat, the sleeves of each were of a different color and pattern. However, the coats were duly finished. Then we set to work on gray pantaloons, and I have just carried a bundle to an ardent young lady who wishes to assist. A slight gloom is settling down, and the inmates here are not quite so cheerfully confident as in July.

Oct. 22. When I came to breakfast this morning Rob was capering over another victory—Ball's Bluff. He would read me, "We pitched the yankees over the bluff," and ask me in the next breath to go to the theatre this evening. I turned on the poor fellow.

"Don't tell me about your victories. You vowed by all your idols that the blockade would be raised by October 1, and I notice the ships are still serenely anchored below the city."

"G., you are just as pertinacious yourself in championing your opinions. What sustains you when nobody agrees with you?"

Oct. 28. When I dropped in at Uncle Ralph's last evening to welcome them back, the whole family were busy at a great center table copying sequestration acts for the Confederate Government. The property of all Northerners and Unionists is to be sequestrated, and Uncle Ralph can hardly get the work done fast enough. My aunt apologized for the rooms looking chilly; she feared to put the carpets down, as the city might be taken and burned by the Federals. "We are living as much packed up as possible. A signal has been agreed upon, and the instant the army approaches we shall be off to the country again."

Great preparations are being made for defense. At several other places where I called the women were almost hysterical. They seemed to look forward to being blown up with shot and shell, finished with cold steel, or whisked off to some Northern prison. When I got home Edith and Mr. D. had just returned also.

"Alex," said Edith, "I was up at your orange-lots today, and the sour oranges are dropping to the ground, while they cannot get lemons for our sick soldiers."

"That's my kind, considerate wife," replied Mr. D.

"Why didn't I think of that before? Jim shall fill some barrels to-morrow and take them to the hospital as a present from you."

Nov. 10. Surely this year will ever be memorable to me for its perfection of natural beauty. Never was sunshine such pure gold, or moonlight such transparent silver. The beautiful custom prevalent here of decking the graves with flowers on All Saint's day was well fulfilled, so profuse and rich were the blossoms. On All-hallow eve Mrs. S. and myself visited a large cemetery. The chrysanthemums lay like great masses of snow and flame and gold in every garden we passed, and were piled on every costly tomb and lowly grave. The battle of Manassas robed many of our women in mourning, and some of those who had no graves to deck were weeping silently as they walked through the scented avenues.

A few days ago Mrs. E. arrived here. She is a widow of Natchez, a friend of Mrs. F.'s, and is traveling home with the dead body of her eldest son, killed at Manassas. She stopped two days waiting for a boat, and begged me to share her room and read her to sleep, saying she couldn't be alone since he was killed; she feared her mind would give way. So I read all the comforting chapters to be found till she dropped into forgetfulness, but the recollection of those weeping mothers in the cemetery banished sleep for me.

Nov. 26. The lingering summer is passing into those misty autumn days I love so well, when there is gold and fire above and around us. But the glory of the natural and the gloom of the moral world agree now well together. This morning Mrs. F. came to my room in dire distress. "You see," she said, "cold weather is coming on fast, and our poor fellows are lying out at night with nothing to cover them. There is a wail for blankets, but there is not a blanket in town. I have gathered up all the spare bed-clothing, and now want every available rug or table-cover in the house. Can't I have yours, G.? We must make these small sacrifices of comfort and elegance, you know, to secure independence and freedom."

"Very well," I said, denuding the table. "This may do for a drummer boy."

Dec. 26, 1861. The foul weather cleared off bright and cool in time for Christmas. There is a midwinter lull in the movement of troops. In the evening we went to the grand bazaar in the St. Louis Hotel, got up to clothe the soldiers. The bazaar has furnished the gayest, most fashionable war-work yet, and has kept social circles in a flutter of pleasant, heroic excitement all through December. Everything beautiful or rare garnered in the homes of the rich was given for exhibition, and in some cases for raffle and sale. There were many fine paintings, statues, bronzes, engravings, gems, laces—in fact, heirlooms and bric-a-brac of all sorts. There were many lovely creole girls present, in exquisite toilets, passing to and fro through the decorated rooms, listening to the band blast out the Anvil Chorus.

Jan. 2, 1862. I am glad enough to bid '61 good-by. Most miserable year of my life! What ages of thought and experience have I not lived in it!

The city authorities have been searching houses for firearms. It is a good way to get more guns, and the homes of those men suspected of being Unionists were searched first. Of course they went to Dr. B's. He met them with his own delightful courtesy. "Wish to search for arms? Certainly, gentlemen." He conducted them all through the house with smiling readiness, and after what seemed a very thorough search bowed them politely out. His gun was all the time safely reposing between the canvas folds of a cot-bed which leaned folded up together against the wall, in the very room where they had ransacked the closets.

Queerly, the rebel families have been the ones most anxious to conceal all weapons. They have dug graves quietly at night in the back yards, and carefully wrapping the weapons, buried them out of sight. Every man seems to think he will have some private fighting to do to protect his family.

Friday, Jan. 24, 1862. (On Steamboat W., Mississippi River.)—With a changed name I open you once more, my journal. It was a sad time to wed, when one knew not how long the expected conscription would spare the bridegroom. The women-folk knew how to sympathize with a girl expected to prepare for her wedding in three days, in a blockaded city, and about to go far from any base of supplies. They all rallied round me with tokens of love and consideration and sewed, mended, and packed as if sewing soldier clothes. And they decked the whole house and the church with flowers. Music breathed, wine sparkled, friends came and went. It seemed like a dream, and comes up now again out of the afternoon sunshine where I sit on deck. The steamboat slowly plows its way through lumps of floating ice,—a novel sight to me,—and I look forward wondering whether the new people I shall meet will be as fierce about the war as those in New Orleans. That past is to be all forgotten and forgiven; I understand thus the kindly acts that sought to brighten the threshold of a new life.

Feb. 15. We reached Arkansas Landing at nightfall. Mr. Y., the planter who owns the landing, took us right up to his residence. He ushered me into a large room where a couple of candles gave a dim light, and close to them, and sewing as if on a race with Time, sat Mrs. Y. and a little negro girl, who was so black and sat so stiff and straight she looked like an ebony image. This was a large plantation; the Y.'s knew H. very well, and were very kind and cordial in their welcome and congratulations. Mrs. Y. apologized for continuing her work; the war had pushed them this year in getting the negroes clothed, and she had to sew by dim candles, as they could obtain no more oil. She asked if there were any new fashions in New Orleans.

Next morning we drove over to our home in this village. It is the county-seat, and was, till now, a good place for the practice of H.'s profession. It lies on the edge of a lovely lake. The adjacent planters count their slaves by the hundreds. Some of them live with a good deal of magnificence, using service of plate, having smoking-rooms for the gentlemen built off the house, and entertaining with great hospitality. The Baptists, Episcopalians, and Methodists hold services on alternate Sundays in the courthouse. All the planters and many others near the lake shore keep a boat at their landing, and a raft for crossing vehicles and horses. It seemed very piquant at first, this taking our boat to go visiting, and on moonlight nights it was charming. The woods around are lovelier than those in Louisiana, though one misses the moaning of the pines. There is fine fishing and hunting, but these cotton estates are not so pleasant to visit as sugar plantations.

But nothing else has been so delightful as, one morning, my first sight of snow and a wonderul new, white world.

Feb. 27. The people here have hardly felt the war yet. There are but two classes. The planters and the professional men form one; the very poor villagers the other. There is no middle class. Ducks and partridges, squirrels and fish, are to be had. H. has bought me a nice pony, and cantering along the shore of the lake in the sunset is a panacea for mental worry.

March 11, 1862. The serpent has entered our Eden. The rancor and excitement of New Orleans have invaded this place. If an incautious word betrays any want of sympathy with popular plans, one is "traitorous," "ungrateful," "crazy." If one remains silent and controlled, then one is "phlegmatic," "cool-blooded," "unpatriotic." Cool-blooded! Heavens! if they only knew. It is very painful to see lovable and intelligent women rave till the blood mounts to face and brain. The immediate cause of this access of war fever has been the battle of Pea Ridge. They scout the idea that Price and Van Dorn have been completely worsted. Those who brought the news were speedily told what they ought to say. "No, it is only a serious check; they must have more men sent forward at once. This country must do its duty." So the women say another company must be raised.

We were guests at a dinner-party yesterday. Mrs. A. was very talkative. "Now, ladies, you must all join in with a vim and help equip another company."

"Mrs. L.," she said, turning to me, "are you not going to send your husband? Now use a young bride's influence and persuade him; he would be elected one of the officers."

"Mrs. A.," I replied, longing to spring up and throttle her, "the Bible says, 'When a man hath married a new wife, he shall not go to war for one year, but remain at home and cheer up his wife.'"

"Well, H.," I questioned, as we walked home after crossing the lake, "can you stand the pressure, or shall you be forced into volunteering?"

"Indeed," he replied, "I will not be bullied into enlisting by women, or by men. I will sooner take my chance of conscription and feel honest about it. You know my attachments, my interests are here; these are my people. I could never fight against them; but my judgment disapproves their course, and the result will inevitably be against us."

This morning the only Irishman left in the village presented himself to H. He has been our wood-sawyer, gardener, and factotum, but having joined the new company, his time recently has been taken up with drilling. H. and R. R. feel that an extensive vegetable garden must be prepared while he is here to assist, or we shall be short of food, and they sent for him yesterday.

"So, Mike, you are really going to be a soldier?"

"Yes, sor; but faith, Mr. L., I don't see the use of me going to shtop a bullet when sure an' I'm willin' for it to go where it plazes."

April 30. The last two weeks have glided quietly away without incident, except the arrival of new neighbors—Dr. Y., his wife, two children, and servants. That a professional man prospering in Vicksburg should come now to settle in this retired place looks queer. Max said:

"H., that man has come here to hide from the conscript officers. He has brought no end of provisions, and is here for the war. He has chosen well, for this county is so cleaned of men it won't pay to send the conscript officers here."

Our stores are diminishing and cannot be replenished from without; ingenuity and labor must evoke them. We have a fine garden in growth, plenty of chickens, and hives of bees to furnish honey in lieu of sugar. A good deal of salt meat has been stored in the smokehouse, and, with fish from the lake, we expect to keep the wolf from the door. The season for game is about over, but an occasional squirrel or duck comes to the larder, though the question of ammunition has to be considered. What we have may be all we can have, if the war lasts five years longer; and they say they are prepared to hold out till the crack of doom. Food, however, is not the only want. I never realized before the varied needs of civilization. Every day something is out. Last week but two bars of soap remained, so we began to save bones and ashes. Annie said: "Now, if we only had some china-berry trees here, we shouldn't need any other grease. They are making splendid soap at Vicksburg with china-balls. They just put the berries into the lye and it eats them right up and makes a fine soap." I did long for some china-berries to make this experiment. H. had laid in what seemed a good supply of kerosene, but it is nearly gone, and we are down to two candles kept for an emergency. Annie brought a receipt* from Natchez for making candles of rosin and wax, and with great forethought brought also the wick and rosin. So yesterday we tried making candles. We had no molds, but Annie said the latest style in Natchez was to make a waxen rope by dipping, then wrap it around a corn cob. But H. cut smooth blocks of wood around four inches square, into which he set a polished cylinder about four inches high. The waxen ropes were coiled round the cylinder like a serpent, with the head raised about two inches; as the light burned down to the cylinder, more of the rope was unwound. To-day the vinegar was found to be all gone, and we have started to make some. For tyros we succeed pretty well.

---

*recipe

(In the month of May the Mississippi River rose to flood levels
inundating their home, and destroying their food stores. A
swamp fever spread destroying cattle, and chickens. The young
married couple headed south to Vicksburg for New Orleans had
fallen to the Union forces by this time, and even now there was
fighting outside of Vicksburg.)

Oak Ridge, July 26, Saturday. It was not till Wednesday that H.
could get into Vicksburg, ten miles distant, for a passport, without which we could not go on the cars. We started Thursday
morning. I had to ride seven miles on a hard-trotting horse to
the nearest station. The day was burning at white heat. When
the station was reached my hair was down, my hat on my neck,
and my feelings were indescribable.

On the train one seemed to be right in the stream of war,
among officers, soldiers, sick men and cripples, adieus, tears,
laughter, constant chatter, and, strangest of all, sentinels posted
at the locked car doors demanding passports. There was no train
south from Jackson that day, so we put up at the Bowman House.
The excitement was indescribable. All the world appeared to be
traveling through Jackson. People were besieging the two hotels,
offering enormous prices for the privilege of sleeping anywhere
under a roof. There were many refugees from New Orleans,
among them some acquaintances of mine. The peculiar styles
of (women's) dress necessitated by the exigencies of war gave
the crowd a very striking appearance. In single suits I saw
sleeves of one color, the waist of another, the skirt of another;
scarlet jackets and gray skirts; black waists and blue skirts; black
skirts and gray waists; the trimming chiefly gold braid and buttons, to give a military air. The gray and gold uniforms of the
officers, glittering between, made up a carnival of color. Every
moment we saw strange meetings and partings of people from
all over the South. Conditions of time, space locality, and estate
were all loosened; everybody seemed floating he knew not
whither, but determined to be jolly, and keep up an excitement.
At supper we had tough steak, heavy, dirty-looking bread, Confederate coffee. The coffee was made of either parched rye or
corn-meal, or of sweet potatoes cut in small cubes and roasted.

This was the favorite. When flavored with "coffee essence," sweetened with sorghum, and tinctured with chalky milk, it made a curious beverage which, after tasting, I preferred not to drink. Everyone else was drinking it and an acquaintance said, "Oh, you'll get bravely over that. I used to be a Jewess about pork, but now we just kill a hog and eat it, and kill another and do the same. It's all we have."

Friday morning we took the down train for the station near my friend's house. At every station we had to go through the examination passes, as if in a foreign country.

The conscript camp was at Brookhaven, and every man had been ordered to report there or to be treated as a deserter. At every station I shivered mentally, expecting H. to be dragged off. Brookhaven was also the station for dinner. I choked mine down, feeling the sword hanging over me by a single hair. At sunset we reached our station. The landlady was pouring tea when we took our seats, and I expected a treat, but when I tasted it, it was sassafras tea, the very odor of which sickens me. There was a general surprise when I asked to exchange it for a glass of water; everyone was drinking it as if it were nectar. This morning we drove out here.

My friend's little nest is calm in contrast to the tumult not far off. Yet the trials of war are here too. Having no matches, they keep fire, carefully covering it at night, for Mr. G. has no powder, and cannot flash the gun into combustibles as some do. One day they had to go with the children to the village, and the servant let the fire go out. When they returned at nightfall, wet and hungry, there was neither fire nor food. Mr. G. had to saddle the tired mule and ride three miles for a pan of coals, and blow them, all the way back, to keep them alight. Crockery has gradually been broken and tin cups rusted out, and a visitor told me they had made tumblers out of clear glass bottles by cutting them smooth with a heated wire, and that they had nothing else to drink from.

Sunday, Sept. 7 (Vicksburg, Washington Hotel.) H. did not return for three weeks. An epidemic disease broke out in his uncle's family and two children died. He stayed to assist them in their

trouble. Tuesday evening he returned for me, and we reached
Vicksburg yesterday. It was my first sight of the "Gibraltar of the
South." Looking at it from a slight elevation suggests the idea
that the fragments left from world-building had tumbled into a
confused mass of hills, hollows, hillocks, banks, ditches and
ravines, and that the houses had rained down afterward. Over
all there was dust impossible to conceive. The bombardment
has done little injury. People have returned and resumed business. A gentleman asked H. if he knew of a nice girl for sale. I
asked if he did not think it impolitic to buy slaves now.

"Oh, not young ones. Old ones might run off when the enemy's lines approach ours, but with young ones there is no
danger."

We had not been many hours in town before a position was
offered to H. which seemed providential. The chief of a certain
department was in ill health and wanted a deputy. It secures
him from conscription, requires no oath, and pays a good salary.
A mountain seemed lifted off my heart.

Oak Haven, Oct. 31. Mr. W. said last night the farmers felt uneasy
about the "Emancipation Proclamation" to take effect in December. The slaves have found it out, though it had been carefully
kept from them.

"Do yours know it?" I asked.

"Oh, yes. Finding it to be known elsewhere, I told it to mine
with fair warning what to expect if they tried to run away. The
hounds are not far off."

The need of clothing for their armies is worrying them too.
I never saw Mrs. W. so excited as on last evening. She said the
provost-marshal at the next town had ordered the women to knit
so many pairs of socks.

"Just let him try to enforce it and they will cowhide him.
He'll get none from me. I'll take care of my own friends without
an order from him."

"Well," said Mr. W., "if the South is defeated and the slaves
are set free, the Southern people will all become atheists; for
the Bible justifies slavery and says it shall be perpetual."

"You mean if the Lord does not agree with you, you'll re-pudiate him."

"Well, we'll feel it's no use to believe in anything."

At night the large sitting-room makes a striking picture. Mr. W., spare, erect, gray-headed, patriarchal, sits in his big chair by the odorous fire of pine logs and knots roaring up the vast fireplace. His driver brings to him the report of the day's picking and a basket of snowy cotton for the spinning. The hunter brings in the game. I sit on the other side to read. The great spinning wheels stand at the other end of the room, and Mrs. W. and her black satellites, the elderly women with their heads in bright bandanas, are hard at work. Slender and auburn-haired, she steps back and forth out of shadow into shine fol-lowing the thread with graceful movements. Some card the cot-ton, some reel it into hanks. Over all the firelight dances, now touching the golden curls of little John toddling about, now the brown heads of the girls stooping over their books, now the shadowy figure of little Jule, the girl whose duty it is to supply the fire with rich pine to keep up the vivid light. If they would only let the child sit down! But that is not allowed, and she gets sleepy and stumbles and knocks her head against the wall and then straightens up again. When that happens often it drives me off. Sometimes while I read the bright room fades and a vision rises of figures clad in gray and blue lying pale and stiff on the blood sprinkled ground.

Nov. 15. Yesterday a letter was handed me from H. Grant's army was moving, he wrote, steadily down the Mississippi Central, and might cut the road at Jackson. He has a house (in Vicksburg) and will meet me in Jackson tomorrow.

Vicksburg, April 28, 1863. I never understood before the full force of those questions—What shall we eat? what shall we drink? and wherewithal shall we be clothed? We have no prophet of the Lord at whose prayer the meal and oil will not waste. Such minute attention must be given the wardrobe to preserve it that I have learned to darn like an artist. Making shoes is now an-

other accomplishment. Mine were in tatters. H. came across a
moth-eaten pair that he bought me, giving ten dollars, I think,
and they fell into rags when I tried to wear them; but the soles
are good, and that has helped me to shoes. A pair of old coat
sleeves saved—nothing is thrown away now—was in my trunk.
I cut an exact pattern from my old shoes, laid it on the sleeves,
and cut out thus good uppers and sewed them carefully; then
soaked the soles and sewed the cloth to them. I am so proud of
these home-made shoes, think I'll put them in a glass case when
the war is over, as an heirloom. H. says he has come to have an
abiding faith that everything he needs to wear will come out of
that trunk while the war lasts. It is like a fairy casket. I have but
a dozen pins remaining, so many I gave away. Every time these
are used they are straightened and kept from rust. All these
curious labors are performed while the shells are leisurely
screaming through the air; but as long as we are out of range we
don't worry. For many nights we have had but little sleep, because the Federal gunboats have been running past the batteries.
The uproar when this is happening is phenomenal. The first
night the thundering artillery burst the bars of sleep, we thought
it an attack by the river. To get into garments and rush up stairs
was the work of a moment. From the upper gallery we have a
fine view of the river, and soon a red glare lit up the scene and
showed a small boat, towing two large barges gliding by. The
Confederates had set fire to a house near the bank. Another
night, eight boats ran by, throwing a shower of shot, and two
burning houses made the river clear as day. One of the batteries
has a remarkable gun they call "Whistling Dick," because of the
screeching, whistling sound it gives, and certainly it does sound
like a tortured thing. Added to all this is the indescribable Confederate yell, which is a soul-harrowing sound to hear. I have
gained respect for the mechanism of the human ear, which
stands it all without injury. The streets are seldom quiet at night;
even the dragging about of cannon makes a din in these echoing
gullies. The other night we were on the gallery till the last of
the eight boats got by. Next day a friend said to H., "It was a
wonder you didn't have your heads taken off last night. I passed
and saw them stretched over the gallery, and grape-shot were
whizzing up the street just on a level with you." The double roar

of batteries and boats was so great, we never noticed the whizzing. Yesterday the *Cincinnati* attempted to go by in daylight but was disabled and sunk. It was a pitiful sight; we could not see the finale, though we saw her rendered helpless.

Friday, June 5. In the cellar: Wednesday evening H. said he must take a little walk, and went while the shelling had stopped. He never leaves me alone for long, and when an hour had passed without his return I grew anxious; and when two hours, and the shelling had grown terrific, I momentarily expected to see his mangled body. All sorts of horrors fill the mind now, and I am so desolate here; not a friend. When he came he said that, passing a cave where there were no others near, he heard groans, and found a shell had struck above and caused the cave to fall in on the man within. He could not extricate him alone, and had to get help and dig him out. He was badly hurt, but not mortally, and I felt fairly sick from the suspense.

Yesterday morning a note was brought H. from a bachelor uncle out in the trenches, saying he had been taken ill with fever, and could we receive him if he came? H. sent to tell him to come, and I arranged one of the parlors as a dressing room for him, and laid a pallet that he could move back and forth to the cellar. He did not arrive, however. It is our custom in the evening to sit in the front room a little while in the dark, with matches and candle held ready in hand, and watch the shells, whose course at night is shown by the fuse. H. was at the window and suddenly sprang up, crying, "Run!"—"Where?"—"*Back!*"

I started through the back room, H. after me. I was just within the door when the crash came that threw me to the floor. It was the most appalling sensation I'd ever known—worse than an earthquake, which I've also experienced. Shaken and deafened, I picked myself up; H. had struck a light to find me. I lighted mine, and the smoke guided us to the parlor I had fixed for Uncle J. The candles were useless in the dense smoke, and it was many minutes before we could see. Then we found the entire side of the room torn out. The soldiers who had rushed in said, "This is an eighty pound Parrott." It had entered through

the front, burst on the pallet-bed, which was in tatters; the toilet
service and everything else in the room smashed. The soldiers
assisted H. to board up the break with planks to keep out prow-
lers, and we went to bed in the cellar as usual. This morning
the yard is partially plowed by a couple that fell there in the
night. I think this house, so large and prominent from the river,
is perhaps taken for headquarters and specially shelled. As we
descended at night to the lower regions, I think of the evening
hymn that grandmother taught me when a child:

> Lord, keep us safe this night,
> Secure from all our fears;
> May angels guard us while we sleep,
> Till morning light appears.

Surely, if there are heavenly guardians, we need them now.

Mr. and Mrs. H. L. survived the siege of Vicksburg, and the diary
was continued until August 1863. Mrs. L. was forced to discon-
tinue her entries when she ran out of writing material.

Domestic Life in War-torn Dixie

General Sherman's scorched earth policy as he marched to the sea included tearing up farm fields, and railroads. He destroyed homes, furniture, and personal possessions as his troops descended like locusts. He burned woodlands and silos; butchered livestock. All this activity sorely tested the mettle of the women and children, the elderly and the crippled, who had remained at home. American money had been turned in for Confederate dollars and Confederate bonds that was almost worthless. There were some rebels who had hoarded silver and gold, but they were little better off. There was just nothing to buy at any price. Food and clothes were in very short supply.

Pride was the powerful ally of the women of the Confederacy. They managed to exhibit super strength, fight the pangs of hunger, and make do because in their own minds, they, too, were soldiers fighting for their new country.

A young woman tells the story of her deprivation and hunger, and how she managed to survive. This "delicate flower" of the South proved that she had a will of iron, and the determination of tempered steel—but she always managed to be "a lady." This chapter is taken from *Life in Dixie During the War 1861–1865* by Mary A. H. Gay (The Foote & Davis Co., 1894).

"What is it, Ma? Has anything happened?"

"No, only Maggie Benedict has been here crying as if her

heart would break, and saying that her children are begging for bread, and she has none to give them. Give me a little of the meal or hominy that you have, that we may not starve until we can get something else to eat, and then take the remainder to her that she may cook it as quickly as possible for her suffering children."

We had spent the preceding day in picking out grains of corn from cracks and crevices in bureau drawers, and other improvised troughs for Federal horses, as well as gathering up what was scattered upon the ground. In this way by diligent and persevering work, about a half bushel was obtained from the now deserted camping ground of Garrard's cavalry, and this corn was thoroughly washed and dried, and carried by me and Telitha to a poor little mill (which had escaped conflagration, because too humble to attract attention), and ground into coarse meal. Returning from this mill and carrying, myself, a portion of the meal, I saw in the distance my mother coming to meet me. Apprehensive of evil, I ran to meet her and asked:

"What is it, Ma? Has anything happened?"

With flushed face and tear-toned voice she replied as already stated. My heart was touched and a division was soon made. Before starting on this errand, I thought of the probable delay that inexperience and perhaps the want of cooking utensils and fuel might occasion, and suggested that it would hasten the relief to the children to cook some bread and mush and carry it to them already for use. A boiling pot, left on the camping ground, was soon on the fire ready to receive the well-prepared batter, which was to be converted into nutritious mush or porridge. Nor was the bread forgotten. While the mush was cooking the hoecakes were baking in good old plantation style. These were arranged one upon another, and tied up in a snow white cloth; and a tin bucket, also a trophy from the company, was filled with hot mush. I took the bread, and Telith the bucket, and walked rapidly to Doctor Holmes' residence, where Maggie Benedict, whose husband was away in the Confederate army, had rooms for herself and her children. The Rev. Doctor and his wife had refugeed, leaving this young mother and her children alone and unprotected.

The scene which I witnessed will never be obliterated from

my memory. On the doorsteps sat the young mother, beautiful in desolation, with a baby in her arms, and on either side of her a little one, piteously crying for something to eat. "Oh, mama, I want something to eat, so bad." "Oh, mama, I am so hungry—give me something to eat." Thus the children were begging for what the mother had not to give. She could only give them soothing words. But relief was at hand. Have you ever enjoyed the satisfaction of appeasing the hunger of children who had been without food until on the verge of starvation? If not, one of the keenest enjoyments of life has been denied you. O, the thankfulness of such a privilege! And oh, the joy, melancholy though it be, of hearing blessings invoked upon you and yours by the mother of these children!

While this needful food was being eaten with a zest known only to the hungry, I was taking in the situation, and devising in my own mind means by which to render more enduring relief. The meal we had on hand would soon be exhausted, and, though more might be procured in the same way, it would be hazardous to depend upon that way only. "God helps those who help themselves," is a good old reliable proverb that cannot be too deeply impressed upon the mind of every child. To leave this young mother in a state of absolute helplessness, and her innocent little ones dependent upon the precarious support which might be gleaned from a devastated country would be cruel indeed; but how to obviate this state of affairs was a serious question.

The railroad having been torn up in every direction communicating with Decatur, there seemed to be but one alternative—to walk—and that was not practicable with several small children.

"Maggie, this state of affairs cannot be kept up; have you no friend to whom you can go?"

"Yes," she replied, "Mr. Benedict has a sister near Madison, who has wanted me and the children to go and stay with her ever since he has been in the army, but I was too independent to do it."

"Absurd! Well, the time has come that you must go. Get the children ready, and I will call for you soon," and without any positive or defined plan of procedure, I took leave of Maggie and her children. I was working by faith, and the Lord directed my footsteps. On my way home I hunted up "Uncle Mack," a faithful old negro man, who preferred freedom in the midst of privation with his own white people, to following the Federal army around on "Uncle Sam's" payroll and got from him a promise that he would construct a wagon out of the odds and ends left upon the streets of Decatur. The next thing to be done was to provide a horse, and not being a magician, nor possessed of Aladdin's lamp, this undertaking must have seemed chimerical to those who had known how often and how singularly these scarcely formulated plans had developed into success. This day had been one of constant and active service, and was only one of many that furnished from sixteen to eighteen working hours. No wonder, then, that exhausted nature succumbed to sleep that knew no waking until the dawn of another day.

Next morning, before the sun rose, accompanied by the Morton girls, I was on my way to "the cane brakes." I had seen many horses, whose places had been taken by others captured from farmers, abandoned and sent out to the cane-brakes to recuperate or to die, the latter being the more probable. Without any definite knowledge of the locality, but guided by an overruling providence, I went direct to the cane-bake, and there soon made a selection of a horse, which, from the assortment at hand, could not have been improved upon. By a dexterious throw of a lasso, constructed and managed by the young friends already mentioned, he was soon captured and on his way to Decatur to enter "rebel" service. His most conspicuous feature was a pair of as fine eyes as ever illuminated a horse's head, large, brown and lustrous. There were other conspicuous things about him, too; for instance, branded upon each of his sides were the telltale letters, "U.S.," and on his back was an immense sore which also told tales. By twelve o'clock, noon, Uncle Mack appeared upon the scene, pulling something that he had improvised which baffled description, and which, for the sake of the faithful service I obtained from it, I will not attempt to describe, though it might provoke the risibilities of the readers. Suffice it to say that as it carried living freight in safety over many a bridge, in honor of this I will call it a wagon. Uncle Mack soon had the horse secured to this vehicle by ropes and pieces of crocus sack, for harness was as scarce a commodity as wagons and horses. I surveyed the equipage from center to circumference, with emotions pathetic and amusing. It was awfully suggestive. And as I viewed it in all its grotesqueness my imagination pictured a collapse, and my return home from no very distant point upon all-fours, with one of the fours dragging after me in a dilapidated condition. I distinctly heard the derisive gibberish and laughter of old Momus, and thought I should explode in the effort to keep from joining in his mirthfulness. As I turned my head to take a sly glance at my mother, our eyes met, and all restraint was removed. With both of us laughter and sobs contended for the mastery, and merriment and tears, literally blended. Thus equipped, and with a benediction from my mother, expressed more by looks and acts than by words, I gathered the ropes and started like Bayard Taylor to take "Views Afoot," and at the same time accomplish an errand of mercy which would lead me, as I lead the horse, over a portion of country that in dreariness and utter desolation baffles description—enough to know that Sherman's foraging trains had been over it. Leading the horse which was already christened "Yankee" to Dr. Holmes' door, I called Maggie to come on with her children.'

"I can't bring my things out, Miss Mary. Somebody must come to carry them and put them in the wagon."

"I can," I said, and suiting the action to the word, ran into the house, where to my amazement three large trunks confronted me. What to be done? If they could be got into the wagon, what guarantee was there that poor Yankee could haul them in that tumblesome vehicle? However, I went for Uncle Mack to put the trunks in the wagon, and in front of them, in close proximity to the horse's heels was placed a chair in which Maggie seated herself and took her baby in her lap, the other children nestling on rugs at her feet.

Poor Yankee seemed to feel the importance of his mission, and jogged along at a pretty fair speed, and I, who walked by his side and held the ropes, found myself more than once obliged to strike a trot in order to maintain control of him. Paradoxical as it may seem, I enjoyed this new phase in my service to the Confederacy—none but a patriot could render it, and the whole thing seemed invested with the glamour of romance, the sequel of which would be redemption from all connection with a peo-

ple who could thus afflict another people of equal rights. While
Maggie hummed a sweet little lullaby to her children, I contemplated the devastation and ruin on every side. Not a vestige of
anything remained to mark the sites of the pretty homes which
had dotted this fair country before the destroyer came, except,
perhaps, a standing chimney now and then. And all this struck
me as the willing sacrifice of a peerless people for a great principle, and looking through the dark vista I saw light ahead—I
saw white robed peace proclaiming that the end of carnage had
come. Even then, as I jogged along, at a snail's pace (for be it
known Yankee was not uniform in his gait, and as his mistress
had relaxed the tension of the ropes, he had relaxed the speed
of his steps), up a pretty little hill from whose summit I had
often gazed with rapturous admiration upon the beautiful
mountain of granite near by, I had so completely materialized
the Queen of Peace that I saw her on the mountain's crest, scat-
tering with lavish hand, blessings and treasures as a recompense
for the destruction so wantonly inflicted. Thus my hopeful tem-
perament furnished consolation to me, even under darkest circumstances.

Maggie and the children became restive in their pen-up
limits, and the latter clamored for something to eat, but there
was nothing to give them. Night was upon us, and we had come
only about eight miles, and not an animate thing had we seen
since we left Decatur, not even a bird, and the silence was un-
broken save by the sound of the horse's feet as he trod upon the
rocks, and the soft, sweet humming of the young mother to her
dear little ones. Step by step we seemed to descend into the
caverns of darkness and my brave heart began to falter. The
children, awe-struck, had ceased their appeal for bread and nes-
tled closer to their mother, and that they might all the more feel
her protecting presence, she kept up a constant crooning sound,
pathetic and sad. Step by step we penetrated the blackness of
night—a night without a moon, starless and murky. The uner-
ring instinct of an animal was all we had to guide us in the
beaten road, which had ceased to be visible to human ken.

A faint glimmer of light, at apparently no very great distance, gave hope that our day's journey was almost ended. Yankee also caught the inspiration and walked a little faster. Though

the time seemed long, the cabin, for such it proved to be, was finally reached, and I dropped the ropes, and guided by the glimmer of light through the cracks, went to the door and knocked, at the same time announcing my name. The door was quickly opened. Imagine my surprise when recognized and cordially welcomed by a sweet friend, whose most humble plantation cabin was a pretty residence in comparison with the one she now occupied. Maggie, too, as the daughter of a well-known physician, received cordial welcome for herself and children. And thus a kind Providence provided a safe lodging place for the night.

Nature again asserted itself, and the children asked for something to eat. The good lady of the house kissed them, and told them that supper would soon be ready. The larger one of her little sons drew from a bed of ashes, which had been covered by glowing coals, so large yam potatoes which he took to a table and peeled. He then went outside the cabin and drew from a keg of earthen-ware pitcher full of sparkling persimmon beer, which he dispensed to us in cups, and then handed around the potatoes. And how much this repast was enjoyed! Good sweet yams thoroughly cooked, and the zestful persimmon beer! And I thought of the lonely mother at a desolated home, whose only supper had been made of coarse meal, ground from corn which her own hands helped to pick from crevices and cracks in improvised troughs, where Garrard's cavalry had fed their horses. After awhile the sweet womanly spirit that presided over this little group, got a quilt and a shawl or two, and made a pallet for the children. The boys put more wood upon the fire, and some in the jambs of the fireplace, to be used during the night; and they they went behind us and lay down upon the floor, with seed cotton for pillows, and the roof for covering. Our kind hostess placed additional wraps over the shoulders of Maggie and myself, and we three sat up in our chairs and slept until the dawn.

Accustomed to looking after outdoor interests, I went to see how Yankee was coming on, and found him none the worse for the preceding day's toil. Everything indicated that he had fared as sumptuously as we had—a partly eaten pumpkin, corn, whole ears yet in the trough, and fodder near by, plainly showed the

generosity of the noble little family that took us in and gave us
the best they had. After breakfast we bade adieu to the good
mother and her children, and went on our way, if not rejoicing,
at least feeling better for having seen and been with such good
people. There was a strong tie between us all. The husband and
father was off in the army, like our loved ones. The generous
feeding given to our steed had so braced him up that he began
to walk faster, and was keenly appreciative of every kind word;
and I and he formed a friendship for each other that continued
to his dying day. The road was very rough and hilly, and more
than once he showed signs of fatigue; but a word of encouragement seemed to renew his strength and he walked bravely on.
Maggie would perhaps, have lightened his load by walking, now
and then, but the jolting of the wagon kept the trunks in perpetual motion, and the lives of the children would thereby have
been jeopardized.

Nothing of special interest transpired this second day of
our journey. The same fiend of destruction had laid his ruthless
hand upon everything within his reach. The woods had been
robbed of their beauty and the fields of their products; not even
a bird was left to sing a requiem over the scene of desolation,
or an animal to suggest where once had been a habitation. Once,
crouching near a standing chimney, there was a solitary dog who
kept at bay every attempt to approach—no kind word would
conciliate or put him off his guard. Poor, lonely sentinel! Did
he remember that around the once cheerful hearthstone he had
been admitted to a place with the family group? Was he awaiting
his master's return? Ah, who can know the emotions, or the dim
reasonings of that faithful brute?

Night again came on and I discovered that we were approaching the hospitable mansion of Mr. Montgomery, an excellent, courtly country gentleman, who was at home under
circumstances not now remembered. He and his interesting family gladly welcomed me and my little charge and entertained us
most hospitably. The raiders had been here and helped themselves bountifully, but they had spared the house for another
time, and that other time came soon, and nothing was left on
the site of this beautiful home but ubiquitous chimneys.

An early start the next day enabled Yankee to carry Maggie

and her children and the trunks to Social Circle in time to take the noon train for Madison. So far as Maggie and her children were concerned I now felt that I had done all that I could, and that I must hasten back to my lonely mother at Decatur; but Maggie's tearful entreaties not to be left among strangers prevailed with me, and I got aboard the train with her, and never left until until I had placed her and her children in the care of good Mr. Thrasher at Madison, to be conveyed by him to the home of Mrs. Reeves, her husband's sister.

In Madison, I too, had dear friends and relatives, with whom I spent the night, and the morning's train bore me back to Social Circle, then the terminus of the Georgia Railroad—the war fiend having destroyed every rail between there and Atlanta. Arriving there, imagine my surprise and indignation when I learned that Mr. R——, whom I had paid in advance to care for Yankee while I was gone to Madison, had sent him out to his sorghum mill and put him to grinding cane; and it was with much difficulty and delay that I got him in time to start my homeward journey that afternoon. Instead of being rested, he was literally broken down, and my pity for him constrained me to walk every step of the way back to Decatur. While waiting for the horse I purchased such articles of food as I could find. For instance, a sack of flour, for which I paid a hundred dollars; a bushel of potatoes, several gallons of sorghum; a few pounds of butter, and a few pounds of meat. Even this was a heavy load for the poor jaded horse. Starting so late I could only get to the hospitable home of Mr. Crew, distant only about three miles from "The Circle."

Before leaving Mr. Crew's, the next morning, I learned that an immense Yankee raid had come out from Atlanta, and had burned the bridge which I had crossed only two days ago. This information caused me to take another route to Decatur, and my heart lost much of its hope, and my step its alacrity. Yet the Lord sustained me in the discharge of duty. I never wavered when there was a principle to be guarded, or a duty to be performed. Those were praying days with me, and now I fervently invoked God's aid and protection in my perilous undertaking, and I believed that He would grant aid and protection.

That I might give much needed encouragement to Yankee,

I walked by his side with my hand upon his shoulder much of the time, an act of endearment which he greatly appreciated, and proved that he did so by the expression of his large brown eyes. One of my idiosyncrasies through life has been that of counting everything, and as I journeyed homeward, I found myself counting my steps from one to a thousand and one. As there is luck in odd numbers, says Rory O'Moore, I always ended with the traditional odd number, and by telling Yankee how much nearer home we were. And I told him many things, among them, *sotto voce,* that I did not believe he was a Yankee but a captured rebel. If a tuft of grass appeared on the road side, he was permitted to crop it; or if a muscadine vine with its tempting grapes was discovered, he cropped the leaves off the low shrubbery, while I gathered the grapes for my mother at home with nothing to eat save the one article of diet, of which I have told before.

A minute description of this portion of the war-stricken country would fill a volume; but only the leading incidents and events of the journey are admissible in a reminiscence of war times. In the early part of the day, during this solidary drive, I came to a cottage by the wayside that was a perfect gem—an oasis, an everything that could thrill the heart by its loveliness. Flowers of every hue beautified the grounds and sweetened the air, and peace and plenty seemed to hold undisputed sway. The fiend of Destruction had not yet reached this little Eden. Two gentlemen were in the yard conversing. I perceived at a glance that they were of the clerical order, and would fain have spoken to them; but not wishing to disturb them, or attract attention to myself, I was passing by as unobtrusively as possible, when I was espied and recognized by one of them, who proved to be that saintly man, Rev. Walter Branham. He introduced me to his friend, Professor Shaw of Oxford. Their sympathy for me was plainly expressed, and they gave me much needed instruction regarding the route, and suggested that I would about get to Rev. Henry Clark's to put up for the night. With a hearty shake of the hand, and "God bless you, noble woman," I pursued my lonely way and they went theirs. No other adventure enlivened the day, and poor patient Yankee did the best he could, and so did I. It was obvious that he had done about all he could. Grinding sorghum under a hard taskmaster, with an empty stomach had told on him, and he could no longer quicken his pace at the sound of a friendly voice.

At length we came in sight of "Uncle Henry Clark's" place. I stood amazed and bewildered. I felt as if I would sink to the ground, yea, through it. I was riveted to the spot on which I stood. I could not move. At length I cried—cried like a woman in despair. Poor Yankee must have cried too (for water ran out of his eyes), and in some measure I was quieted, for misery loves company, and I began to take in the situation more calmly. Elegant rosewood and mahogany furniture, broken into a thousand fragments, covered the face of the ground as far as I could see; and china and glass looked as if it had been sown. And the house, what of that? Alas! it too had been scattered to the four winds of heaven in the form of smoke and ashes. Not even a chimney stood to mark its site. Near by stood a row of negro cabins, intact, showing that while the conflagration was going on they had been sedulously guarded. And these cabins were occupied by the slaves of the plantation. Men, women and children stalked about in restless uncertainty, and in surly indifference. They had been led to believe that the country would be apportioned to them, but they had sense enough to know that a mighty revolution involved trouble and delay, and they were supinely waiting developments. Neither man, woman nor child approached me. There was mutual distrust and mutual avoidance.

It took less time to take in this situation than it has to describe it. The sun was almost down, and as he turned his large red face upon me, I fancied he fain would have stopped in his course to see me out of this dilemma. What was I to do? The next nearest place that I could remember that would perhaps give protection for the night, was Mr. Fowler's and this was my only hope. With one hand upon Yankee's shoulder, and the ropes in the other, I moved on, and not until my expiring breath will I forget the pleading look which that poor dumb animal turned upon me when I started. Utterly helpless, and in my hands, he wondered how I could thus exact more of him. I wondered myself. But what was I to do but to move on? More than once the poor horse turned that look, beseeching and pathetic upon me. It frightened me. I did not understand it, and still moved on. At last the hope of making himself understood forsook him, and he deliberately laid himself down in the road. I knelt by his side and told him the true state of affairs, and implored him not to desert me in this terrible crisis. I told him how cruel it would be to do so, and used many arguments of like character; but they availed nothing. He did not move, and his large, lustrous brown eyes seemed to say for him: "I have done all I can, and can do no more." And the sun could bear it no longer, and hid his crimson face behind a great black cloud.

What could I do but rise from my imploring attitude and face my perilous situation? "Lord, have mercy upon me," was my oft-repeated invocation. The first thing which greeted my vision when I rose to my feet was a very distant but evidently an advancing object. I watched it with bated breath, and soon had the satisfaction of seeing a man on mule-back. I ran to meet him, saying: "O, sir, I know the good Lord has sent you here." And then I recounted my trouble, and received most cordial sympathy from one who had been a Confederate soldier, but who was now at home in consequence of wounds that incapacitated him for further service. When he heard all, he said:

"I would take you home with me, but I have to cross a swimming creek before getting there, and I am afraid to undertake to carry you. Wait here until I see these negroes. They are a good set, and whatever they promise, they will, I think, carry out faithfully.

The time seemed interminable before he came back, and night, black night, had set in; and yet a quiet resignation sustained me.

When my benefactor returned, two negro men came with him, one of whom brought a lantern, bright and cheery. "I have arranged for you to be cared for here," said he. "Several of the old house servants of Mrs. Clark know you, and they will prove themselves worthy of the trust we repose in them." I accepted the arrangement made by this good man and entrusted myself to the care of the negroes for the night. This I did with great trepidation, but as soon as I entered the cabin an assurance of safety filled my mind with peace, and reconciled me to my surroundings. The "mammy" that presided over it, met me with a cordial welcome and assured me that no trouble would befall me under her roof. An easy chair was placed for me in one corner in comfortable proximity to a large plantation fire. In a few minutes the men came in bringing my flour, potatoes, syrup, bacon, etc. This sight gave me real satisfaction, as I thought of my poor patient mother at home and hoped that in some way I should yet be able to convey to her this much needed freight. I soon espied a table on which was piled many books and magazines; "Uncle Henry Clark's" theological books were well represented. I proposed reading to the women, if they would like to hear me, and soon had their undivided attention, as well as that of several of the men, who sat on the doorsteps. In this way several hours passed, and then "mammy" said, "You must be getting sleepy." "Oh, no," I replied, "I frequently sit up all night reading." But this did not satisfy her: she had devised in her own mind somthing more hospitable for her guest, and she wanted to see it carried out. Calling into requisition the assistance of the men, she had two large cedar chests placed side by side and out of these chests were taken nice clean quilts, and snow white counterpanes, and sheets, and pillows—Mrs. Clark's beautiful bed clothing—and upon these chests was made a pallet upon which a queen might have reposed with comfort. It was so tempting in its cleanliness that I consented to lie down. The sole occupants of that room that night were myself and my hostess—the aforesaid black "mammy." Rest, not sleep, came to my relief. The tramping of feet, and now and then the muffled sound of human voices, kept me in a listening attitude, and it must be confessed in a state of painful apprehension. Thus the night passed.

With the dawn of day, I was up, and ready to meet the day's requirements. "Mammy's" first greeting was, "What's your hurry?" "I am accustomed to early rising. May I open the door?" The first thing I saw was Yankee, and he was standing eating; but he was evidently too weak to attempt the task of getting the cumbersome vehicle and its freight to Decatur. So I arranged with one of the men to put a steer to the wagon and carry them home. This he was to do for the sum of one hundred dollars. After an appetizing breakfast, I started homeward, leading Yankee in the rear of this turnout. Be it remembered, I did not leave without making ample compensation for my night's entertainment.

No event of particular interest occurred on the way to Decatur. Yankee walked surprisingly well, and the little steer acquitted himself nobly. In due time Decatur appeared in sight, and then there ensued a scene which for pathos defies description. Matron and maiden, mother and child, each with a tin can picked up off the enemy's camping ground, ran after me and begged for just a little something to eat—just enough to keep them from starving. Not an applicant was refused, and by the time the poor, rickety, cumbersome wagon reach its destination, its contents had been greatly diminished. But there was yet enough left to last for some time the patient, loving mother, the faithful Telitha, and myself.

A summary of the trip developed these facts: To the faithfulness of Uncle Mack was due the holding together of the most grotesque vehicle ever dignified by the name of wagon; over all that rough road it remained intact, and returned as good as when it started. And but for the sorghum grinding, poor Yankee would have acted his part unfalteringly. As for myself, I labored under the hallucination that I was a Confederate soldier, and deemed no task too great for me to essay, if it served either directly or indirectly those who were fighting my battles.

After mingling renewed vows of allegiance to our cause, and expressions of a willing submission to the consequences of defeat—privations and evil dire, it need be—with my morning orison; yet I could not be oblivious to the fact that I was hungry, very hungry. And there was another, whose footsteps were becoming more and more feeble day by day, and whose voice when heard at all, was full of the pathos of despair, who needed nourishsment that could not be obtained, and consolation, which it seemed a mockery to offer.

In vain did I look round for relief. There was nothing left in the country to eat. Yea, a crow flying over it would have failed to discover a morsel with which to appease its hunger; for a Sheridan by another name had been there with his minions of destruction, and had ruthlessly destroyed every vestige of food and every means of support. Every larder was empty, and those with thousands and tens of thousands of dollars, were as poor as the poorest, and as hungry, too. Packing trunks, in every house to which refugees had returned contained large amount of Confederate money. We had invested all we possessed except our home, and land and negroes, in Confederate bonds, and these were now inefficient for purchasing purposes. Gold and silver we had none. A more favored few had a little of those desirable mediums of purchase, and sent a great distance for supplies; but they offered no relief to those who had stayed at home and borne the brunt of battle, and saved their property from the destroyers' touch.

What was I to do? Sit down and wait for the inevitable starvation? No; I was not made of such stuff. I had heard that there had been a provision store opened in Atlanta for the purpose of bartering provisions for munitions of war—anything that could be utilized in warfare. Minnie balls were particularly desirable. I therefore took Telitha by the apron, and had a little talk with her, and when I was through she understood that something was up that would bring relief to certain organs that had become quite troublesome in their demands, and she was anxious to take part in the performance, whatever that might be. I went also to my mother, and imparted to her my plans of operation, and she took that pathetic little backward step peculiar to herself on occasions which tried her soul, and with quivering lip she assented in approving, though almost inaudible words.

With a basket in either hand, and accompanied by Telitha, who carried one that would hold about a peck, and two old dull case knives, I started to the battlefields around Atlanta to pick up the former missiles of death to exchange for food to keep us from starving.

It was a cold day. The wind was very sharp, and over the ground denuded of forest trees and undergrowth, the wind was blowing a miniature gale. Our wraps were inadequate, and how chilled we became in that rude November blast! Mark you, it was the 30th of November, 1864. But the colder we were, the faster we walked, and in an incredibly short time we were upon the battlefields, searching for lead.

I made it a point to keep very near the road in the direction
of Atlanta, and soon found myself on the very spot where the
Confederate magazine stood, the blowing up of which by Confederate orders, shook the very earth, and was distinctly heard
thirty-five or forty miles distant. An exclamation of glad surprise from Telitha carried me to her. She had found a bonanza,
and was rapidly filling her basket with that which was more
valuable to us than gold. In a marshy place, encrusted with ice,
innumerable bullets, minnie balls, and pieces of lead seemed to
have been left by the irony of fate to supply sustenance to hungry ones, and employment to the poor, as all the winter those
without money to send to more favored and distant points
found sure returns from this lead mine. It was so cold! our feet
were almost frozen and our hands had commenced to bleed,
and handling cold, rough lead cramped them so badly that I
feared we would have to desist from our work before filling the
baskets.

Lead! Blood! Tears! O how suggestive! Lead, blood and
tears, mingled and commingled. In vain did I try to dash the
tears away. They would assert themselves and fall upon lead
stained with blood. "God of mercy, if this by Thy holy will,
give me fortitude to bear it uncomplainingly," was the heart-felt
invocation that went up to the throne of grace from over lead,
blood and tears that fearful day. For relief, tears did not suffice.
I wanted to cry aloud; nature would not be satisfied with less,
and I cried like a baby, long and loud. Telitha caught the spirit
of grief, and cried too. This ebullition of feeling on her part
brought me to a realization of my duty to her, as well as to my
poor patient mother to whom the day must seem very long, and
I tried to stifle my sobs and lamentations. I wondered if she had
the forebodings of coming bereavement that were lacerating my
own heart. I did not doubt but that she had, and I cried in
sympathy for her.

At length our baskets were filled, and we took up our line
of march to the desolated city. There were no labyrinths to
tread, nor streets to follow, and an occasional question secured
information that enabled us to find the "commissary" without
delay. Telitha was very ambitious that I should appear a lady,
and wanted to to deposit my load of lead behind some place of

concealment, while we went on to deliver hers, and then let her go back for mine. But I was too much a Confederate soldier for that, and walked bravely in with my heavy, precious load.

A courteous gentleman in a faded grey uniform, evidently discharged because of wounds received in battle, approached and asked what he could do for me. "I have heard that you give provisions for lead," I replied, "and I have brought some to exchange." What seemed an interminable silence ensued, and I felt without seeing that I was undergoing a sympathetic scrutiny, and that I was recognized as a lady "to the manor born."

"What would you like in exchange," he asked. "If you have sugar, and coffee, and meal, a little of each if you please," I timidly said. "I left nothing to eat at home." The baskets of lead were removed to the rear and weighed, and in due time returned to me filled to the brim with sugar, coffee, flour, meal, lard, and the nicest meat I had seen in a long time.

"O, sir," I said, "I did not expect so much."

"You have not yet received what is due you," this good man replied, and handed me a certificate which he assured me would secure as much more on presentation.

Joy had gone out of my life, and I felt no thrill of that kind; but I can never describe the satisfaction I experienced as I lifted two of those baskets, and saw Telitha grasp the other one, and turned my face homeward.

A Union Lady's View
of the New York Draft Riots

The Federal government adopted a compulsory draft system and set July 11, 1863 as the date for drawing names. The draft act contained a provision that allowed a man to hire a substitute for three hundred dollars. This was a substantial sum at the time, and a system which so blatantly favored the rich caused considerable resentment.

The names of those selected to serve in the armed forces were printed in the Sunday, July 12 newspapers. Monday morning saw mobs gathered in front of the draft headquarters on 46th Street and Third Avenue. Thus began four days of looting, burning and rioting that necessitated the use of one thousand troops to restore law and order. It is estimated that between 850 and 1,200 people lost their lives in the street fighting. There were pitched battles on Broadway and 42nd Street and on 29th Street in Grammercy Park. As a result of the rioting, the draft was postponed until August, when it resumed without incident.

This account is taken from the diary of Mrs. Maria Lydig Daly, published as *Diary of a Union Lady 1861–1865,* ed. Harold Earl Hammond (Funk & Wagnalls, Inc., 1962). Reprinted by permission of Harper & Row, Publishers, Inc.

July 14, 1863

The draft began on Saturday, the eleventh, very foolishly ordered by the government, who supposed that these Union victories would make the people willing to submit. By giving them Sunday to think it over, by Monday morning there were large crowds assembled to resist the draft. All day yesterday there were dreadful scenes enacted in the city. The police were successfully opposed; many were killed, many houses were gutted and burned: the colored asylum was burned and all the furniture was carried off by *women*: Negroes were hung in the streets! All last night the fire-bells rang, but at last, in God's good mercy, the rain came down in torrents and scattered the crowds, giving the city authorities time to organize. Today bodies of police and military patrolled the city to prevent any assembly of rioters. A Virginian, last evening, harangued the crowd. Fearful that they might attack a Negro tenement house some blocks below us, as they had attacked others, I ordered the doors to be shut and no gas to be lighted in front of the house. I was afraid people would come to visit Judge Daly, ask questions, etc. I did not wonder at the spirit in which the poor resented the three hundred dollar clause.

The news from the army is most encouraging. It is thought that Lee will not be able to escape. It would seem as though the war might now be brought to an end, but this news of the riots here will give the rebels encouragement. The principal cause of discontent was the provision that by paying three hundred dollars any man could avoid serving if drafted, thus obliging all who could not beg, borrow, or steal this sum to go to the war. This is exceedingly unjust. The laboring classes say that they are sold for three hundred dollars, whilst they pay one thousand dollars for Negroes.

Things seem quiet this morning. People are returning to their homes, though the tops of the stages are crowded with workingmen and boys.

Mr. Leslie at Long Branch told me that he was in disgrace with Mrs. Lincoln for having published in his paper a likeness of her taken at Springfield by a skillful photographist sent there for the purpose just after Lincoln's election. At the time she was entirely satisfied with the likeness, but after she had been dressed by city mantua-makers and milliners, she considered it a libel. It was certainly the likeness of a very common looking country body, whilst now she looks like a vulgar, shoddy, contractor's wife who does not know what to do with her money. Mr. Leslie likewise told me that the clerk at Tiffany and Young's had told him that their present largest buyers were the common people, that a common-looking woman came into the store a few weeks since and asked for diamonds. She picked out a necklace, earrings, brooch, and bracelet and ordered them sent to her house. The clerk did not like to do so and asked her name (which he did not know). Then he said that it was against the rules of the store to send things out of such value without payment.

"Oh, my old man will pay for them," said she.

"Then," said the clerk, "will you write something to that effect?"

"Write what you please; I will sign it," said she, and she made a cross. "He'll know that . . ."

July 23, 1863

At last the riot is quelled, but we had four days of great anxiety. Fighting went on constantly in the streets between the military and police and the mob, which was partially armed. The greatest atrocities have been perpetrated. Colonel O'Brian was murdered by the mob in such a brutal manner that nothing in the French Revolution exceeded it. Three or four Negroes were hung and burned; the women assisted and acted like furies by stimulating the men to greater ferocity. Father came into the city on Friday, being warned about his house, and found fifteen Negroes secreted in it by Rachel. They came from York Street, which the mob had attacked, with all their goods and chattels. Father had to order them out. We feared for our own block on account of the Negro tenements below MacDougal Street, where the Negroes were on the roof, singing psalms and having fire-arms.

One night, seeing a fire before the house, I thought the time had come, but it proved to be only a bonfire. The Judge sallied out with his pistol, telling me that if he were not at home in five minutes to call up the servants. This mob seems to have a curious sense of justice. They attacked and destroyed many disreputable houses and did not always spare secessionists. On Saturday (the sixth day) we went up to see Judge Hilton, who thought me very courageous, but I felt sorry for Mrs. Hilton upon hearing that she had been so terribly frightened. She gave me such details that I came home too nervous to sleep. In Lexington Avenue, houses were destroyed. One lady before whose house the mob paused with the intention of sacking it, saved her house by raising the window, smiling, and waving her handkerchief. Mr. Bosie's brother was seized by a rioter who asked him if he had $300.

"No," said he.

"Then come along with us," said the rioter, and they kept him two hours. Mrs. Hilton said she never saw such creatures, such gaunt-looking savage men and women and even little children armed with brickbats, stones, pokers, shovels and tongs, coal-scuttles, and even tin pans and bits of iron. They passed her house about four o'clock on Monday morning and continued on in a constant stream until nine o'clock. They looked to her, she said, like Germans, and her first thought was that it was some German festival. Whilst we sat there, we heard occasional pistol shots, and I was very glad that I had ordered a carriage to take us home. The carriage, it seems, was very unwillingly sent since the livery-stable keeper was so much afraid.

Every evening the Judge *would* go out near eleven o'clock, to my great distress. But he threatened to send me into the country if I objected (which I dreaded still more), so I kept quiet. (James) Leonard, the Superintendent of Police in our neighborhood, said the draft could not be enforced; the firemen are against it, as well as all the working classes.

Among those killed or wounded have been found men with delicate hands and feet, and under their outward laborers' clothes were fine cambric shirts and costly underclothing. A dressmaker says she saw from her window a gentleman whom she knows and has seen with young ladies, but whose name she could not remember, disguised in this way in the mob on Sixth Avenue.

On Sunday we went to see Mrs. (Nathaniel) Jarvis and Mr. James T. Brady, who had just arrived from Washington. I saw Susanna Brady, who talked in the most violent manner against the Irish and in favor of the blacks. I feel quite differently, although very sorry and much outraged at the cruelties inflicted.

I hope it will give the Negroes a lesson, for since the war commenced, they have been so insolent as to be unbearable. I cannot
endure free blacks. They are immoral, with all their piety.

The principal actors in this mob were boys, and I think they
were Americans. Catherine, my seamstress, tells me that the
plundering was done by the people in the neighborhood who
were looking on and who, as the mob broke the houses open,
went in to steal. The police this morning found beds, bedding,
and furniture in the house of a Scotch Presbyterian who was
well off and owned two cows and two horses. The Catholic
priests have done their duty as Christian ministers in denounc-
ing these riotous proceedings. One of them remonstrated with
a woman in the crowd who wanted to cut off the ears of a Negro
(who) was hung. The priest told her that Negroes had souls,
"Sure, your reverence," said she, "I thought they only had giz-
zards."

On Sunday evening, Mr. Dykes came in. He had seen Judge
Pierrepont, who had gone to Washington with others to see what
can be done. Mr. Dykes thinks that New York, being a Demo-
cratic city, may expect little indulgence from the Administration. The Judge went up to see General Dix, now in command
here, who says that the government is determined to carry the
draft measure through at all costs. Yesterday we went to the
wedding of Lydia Watson in Westchester County. Mr. (James)
Adie told the Judge that there was a secessionist plot to burn all
the houses in the neighborhood on Thursday night, that he had
heard that his had been exempted by vote, and the principal
instigator and mover in it was one of the richest and most in-
fluential men in the neighborhood. The purpose of the plot was
to intimidate the government and prevent conscription. Mrs.
Harry Morris, who I hear has been very violent in her invectives
against the North, wished to know if the soldiers could be relied
upon. I told her entirely so, that they declared they would rather
fight these traitors at home who made this fire in their rear
whilst they were risking their life to preserve order and the laws
than the rebels. For her comfort, I told her that the mob had
destroyed the houses of secessionists. I frightened her, I think,
not a little.

A Virginia Girl and the Romance of War

Patriotic fanaticism is contagious. It gets tossed back and forth between people who are exposed to it like a bad cold. It is infectious, uncurable, and unlike any other disease, no one searches for a remedy.

Whether the men infected the women with the spirit of the Confederacy, or the other way round, the verve and the dash of the revolution ran high. The romanticism that captured the hearts of the southern belles made them willing to say goodbye to their loved ones—husband, lover, father, brother—with suppressed tears and quivering lips. It was their way of showing bravery under "fire."

Being in love with love and war is exemplified by the young woman who relates her story. Her fascination with the uniform, the dashing soldiers, her environment of elaborate dinners, high fashion dress, and mingling with the grand society in time of war proves to be a heady experience. It is almost unreal, a dream to be lived over and over again. There is a certain satisfaction that seems to last a life time in kissing a picture of a man who died in the fight for "his country."

This account is taken from *A Virginia Girl in the Civil War 1861–1865* by Myrta Lockett Avery (D. Appleton & Co., 1903).

It was while I was at Mr. Bradford's that one of the most stirring events in Confederate history occurred. This was the

trampling down of John Minor Bott's corn. Very good corn it
was, dropped and hilled by Southern negroes and growing on
a large fine plantation next to Mr. Bradford's; and a very nice
gentleman Mr. Botts was, too; but a field of corn, however good,
and a private citizen, however estimable, are scarcely matters of
national or international importance. The trouble was that John
Minor Botts was on the Northern side and the corn was on the
Southern side, and that Stuart held a grand review on the Southern side and the corn got trampled down. The fame of that corn
went abroad into all the land. Northern and Southern papers
vied with each other in editorials and special articles, families
who had been friends for generations stopped speaking and do
not speak to this day because of it, more than one hard blow
was exchanged for and against it, and it brought down vituper-
ation upon Stuart's head. And yet I was present at that naughty
grand review—which left sorrowful memory on many hearts
because of the battle following fast upon it—and I can testify
that General Stuart went there to review the troops, not to tram-
ple down the corn.

Afterward John Minor Botts came over to see General Stuart
and to quarrel about that corn. All that I can remember of how
the general took Mr. Botts's visit and effort to quarrel was that
Stuart wouldn't quarrel—whatever it was he said to Mr. Botts
he got to laughing when he said it. Our colored Abigail told us
with bated breath that "Mr. Botts ripped and rarred and snorted,
but Genrul Stuart warn't put out none at all."

There had been many reviews that week, all of them merely
by way of preparation and practise for that famous grand review
before the battle of Brandy or Fleetwood, but it is only of this
particular grand review I have many lively memories. Aunt Sally
was away, and we attended it in state. Mr. Bradford had out the
ancient and honorable family carriage and two shadowy horses,
relics of days when corn was in plenty and wheat not merely a
dream of the past, and we went in it to the review along with
many other carriages and horses, whose title to respect lay, alas!
solely in the past.

That was a day to remember! Lee's whole army was in Culpeper. Pennsylvania and Gettysburg were before it, and the army
was making ready for invasion. On a knoll where a Confederate

flag was planted and surrounded by his staff sat General Lee on
horseback; before him, with a rebel yell, dashed Stuart and his
eight thousand cavalry. There was a sham battle. Charging and
countercharging went on, rebels yelled and artillery thundered.
Every time the cannons were fired we would pile out of our
carriage, and as soon as the cannonading ceased we would pile
back again. General Stuart happened to ride up once just as we
were getting out.

"Why don't you ladies sit still and enjoy the fun?" he asked
in amazement.

"We are afraid the horses might take fright and run away,"
we answered.

I shall never forget his ringing laugh. Our lean and spiritless
steeds had too little life in them to run for anything—they hardly
pricked up their ears when the guns went off.

How well I remember Stuart as he looked that day! He wore
a fine new uniform, brilliant with gold lace, buff gauntlets reaching to his elbows, and a canary-colored silk sash with tassled
ends. His hat, a soft, broad brimmed felt, was caught up at the
side with a gold star and carried a sweeping plume; his high,
patent-leather cavalry boots were trimmed with gold. He wore
spurs of solid gold, the gift of some Maryland ladies—he was
very proud of those spurs—and his horse was coal black and
glossy as silk. And how happy he was—how full of faith in the
Confederacy and himself!

My own cavalry officer was there, resplendent in his new
uniform—I had it made up for him in Richmond. Dan was very
proud of the way I got that uniform. He was almost ready to
credit himself with having put me up to running the blockade!
He told General Stuart its history, and that is how a greatness
not always easy to sustain had been thrust upon me. General
Stuart thought me very brave—or said he thought so. The ma-
neuvers of Dan's command were on such a distant part of the
field that I could not see him well with the naked eye, and
General Stuart lent me his field glasses. The next morning, just
as gray dawn was breaking, some one called under my window,
and gravel rattled the pane. I got up and looked out sleepily. My
first thought was that it might be Dan. There was not enough
light for me to see very well what was happening on the lawn,

but I could make out that the cavalry were mounted and moving, and under my window I saw a figure on horseback.

"Is that Mrs. Grey?"

"Yes. What is the matter?"

"General Stuart sent me for his field glasses. I am sorry to disturb you, but it couldn't be helped."

I tied a string around the glasses and lowered them.

"What's the matter? Where is the cavalry going?"

"To Brandy Station. Reckon we'll have some hot fighting soon," and the orderly wheeled and rode away.

I stayed up and dressed, and thought of Dan, and wished I could know if he was to be in the coming engagement, and that I could see him first. But I didn't see him all day.

In forty-eight hours we knew that the surmise of the orderly was correct—there was enough fighting. The first cannon-ball which tore through the air at Brandy was only too grave assurance of the fact. All day men were hurrying past the house, deserters from both armies getting away from the scene of bloodshed and thunder as quickly as possible. Then came the procession of the dead and wounded, some in ambulances, some in carts, some on the shoulders of friends.

In the afternoon we began to hear rumors giving names of the killed and wounded. I listened with my heart in my throat for Dan's name, but I did not hear it. I heard no news whatever of him all day—all day I could only hope that no news was good news, and all day the ghastly procession dragged heavily by. Among names of the killed I heard that of Colonel Sol Williams. A day or two before the battle of Brandy he had returned from a furlough to Petersburg, where he had gone to marry a lovely woman, a friend of mine. The day before he was killed he had sat at table with me, chatting pleasantly of mutual friends at home from whom he had brought messages, brimful of happiness, and of the charming wife he had won! As the day waned I sat in my room, wretched and miserable, thinking of my friend who was at once a bride and a widow, and fearing for myself, whose husband even at that moment might be falling under his death wound. I was aroused by hearing the voices of men, subdued but excited, on the stairway leading to my room. I ran out and saw several men of rank and Mr. Bradford on the stairway talking excitedly, and I heard my name spoken.

"What's the matter, gentlemen?" I asked with forced calmness.

They looked up at me in a stupid, masculine sort of way, as if they had something disagreeable to say and didn't want to say it. I could shake those men now, when I think of how stupid they were! They were listening to Mr. Bradford, and I don't think they really caught my question, nor did my manner betray to them how fast my heart was beating, but they were stupid, nevertheless. I could hardly get the next words out:

"Is Dan hurt?"

This time my voice was so low that they did not hear it at all.

"For God's sake, gentlemen," I cried out, "tell me if my husband is wounded or dead."

"Neither, madam!" several voices answered instantly, and the officer nearest me, thinking I was going to fall, sprang quickly to my side. I gathered myself together, and they told me their business, and I saw why my presence had embarrassed them—they wanted my room for the wounded. A funny thing had happened, incongruous as it was, in their telling me that my fears for Dan were groundless. When I asked, "Is Dan hurt?" one of them had answered, "No, ma'am, it's General Rooney Lee." and I said, "Thank God!" I can't describe the look of horror with which they heard me.

"These gentlemen," began Mr. Bradford, who was always afraid to speak his mind, "wanted to bring General Lee here, and I didn't have a place to put him, and I was telling 'em that I thought that—maybe—you would give him your room. I could fix up a lounge for you somewhere."

"Of course I will! I shall be delighted to give up my room or do anything else I can for General Lee."

I busied myself getting my room ready for General "Rooney" but he was not brought to Mr. Bradford's, after all; his men were afraid that he might be captured too easily at Mr. Bradford's. As night came on the yard filled up with soldiers. In the lawn, the road, the backyard, the porches, the outhouses, everywhere, there were soldiers. You could not set your foot down without putting it on a soldier; if you thrust your hand out of a window you touched a soldier's back or shoulder, his carbine or his musket. The place was crowded not only with cavalry, but with infantry and artillery, and still they kept on coming. I had not heard from Dan. It was late supper-time. I had no heart for supper, and I felt almost too shaken to present myself at the table, but as I passed the dining room in my restless rovings I saw General Stuart's back, and went in and sat by him.

"General," I said, "can you tell me anything of Dan?"

"He is neither killed nor wounded. I know that much. Is not that enough?"

"Yes, thank God!"

"Oh, general! I wish this war was over!" I said again.

"I, too, my child!" He spoke with more than Stuart's sadness and gravity, then, remembering himself, he added quickly in his own cheery fashion, "But we've got to whip these Yankees first!"

He finished his cup of coffee (the kind in common use, made of corn which had been roasted, parched, and ground), and then went on telling me about Dan.

"He has borne himself gallantly, as he always does, and as you know without my telling you. I don't know where he is, but he will be along presently."

And at that moment Dan walked in, without a coat, and with the rest of that new uniform a perfect fright. He was covered with dust and ashes and gunpowder, and he looked haggard and jaded. He sat down between General Stuart and me, too tired to talk; but after eating some supper, he felt better, and began discussing the battle and relating some incidents. He took a card out of his pocket and handed it to General Stuart.

"A Federal officer who is about done for, poor fellow, handed me that just now. I don't know the name. He couldn't talk."

"I do!" General Stuart exclaimed, with quick, strong interest. "Where did you see him? This is the name of one of my classmates at West Point."

"I saw him on the roadside as I came on to supper. While riding along I heard a strange sound, something like a groan, yet different from any groan I ever heard—the strangest, most uncanny sound imaginable. I dismounted and began to look around for it, and I found a Yankee soldier lying in a ditch by the roadside. I couldn't see that any legs or arms were broken, nor that he was wounded at all. I felt him all over, and asked what was the matter. He didn't speak, and I saw that he had been trying to direct my attention to his face. He tried very hard to speak, but only succeeded in emitting the strange sound I had heard before; and on examining his face closely, and moving the whiskers aside, I found that he was shot through both jaws. He made the same noise again, put his hand in his pocket, and gave me this card, with another pitiful effort to speak. I put my coat under his head, laid some brush across the ditch to hide him, and promised to go back for him in an ambulance."

"Thank you, in my own behalf!" General Stuart said warmly.

"Perhaps, poor fellow," said Dan, "he took chances on that card's reaching you. Seeing my uniform of major of cavalry, he may not have considered it impossible that you should hear of his condition through me."

"When you have finished your supper, major, we will go after him."

Tired as they both were, they went out and attended personally to the relief of the poor fellow by the roadside. General Stuart had everything done for him that was possible, smoothed his last moments, and grieved over him as deeply as if his classmate had not been his enemy.

Another sad thing among the sorrows of that supper was when Colonel Sol William's brother-in-law, John Pegram, came in, and sat down in our midst. General Stuart went up to him, and wrung his hand in a silence that even the dauntless Stuart's lips were too tremulous at once to break. When he could speak, he said:

"I grieve for myself as for you, lieutenant, but it was a death that any one of us might be proud to die."

Even then the shadow and glory of his own death was not far from him.

Colonel Williams had been Lieutenant Pegram's superior officer as well as brother-in-law. It had been his sorrowful lot to

take the body of his colonel on his horse in front of him, and
carry it to a house where it could be reverently cared for until
he could send it home to bride and kindred. He had cut a lock
of hair from the dead, and when the troops went off to Pennsylvania, he gave it to me for his sister. I shall never forget that
supper hour, or how the unhappy young fellow looked when he
came in among us after his ride with the dead, and I shall never
forget how I felt about the poor young Federal soldier who was
wounded in the jaws and couldn't speak, and how I felt about
the women who loved him far away; I began to feel that war was
an utterly unjustifiable thing, and that the virtues of valor, loyalty, devotion which it brings out had better be brought out some
other way. If General Rooney Lee didn't take my room, I gave it
up all the same. Two wounded men were put into it. There were
a number of wounded men in the house and, of course, everybody gave way to their comfort. All but my two were removed
in a day or two, but here these two were, and here they were
when Aunt Sally came home. Her homecoming was after a fashion that turned our mourning into righteous and wholesome
wrath. We were sitting on the porch one afternoon, free and
easy in our minds and believing Aunt Sally away in distant
Washington, when we noted a small object far off down the road.
As it crawled nearer and nearer we perceived that it was an ox-
cart; we saw the driver, and behind him somebody else sitting
on a trunk.

"Good gracious! That's Aunt Sally!" cried Mr. Bradford in
consternation.

We were all dreadfully sorry, but it couldn't be helped.

She climbed off the cart at the gate, and called for some
negro to come get her trunk. Mr. Bradford had already found
one, and was running to the rescue. In fact he had been running
in a half dozen different directions ever since he had spied Aunt
Sally. He looked as if his wits had left him and as if he were
racing around in a circle.

"You orter been on hand to he'p me off o' that kyart," she
told him. "It do look like when a man's wife's been away this
long time he might be on hand to he'p her off the kyart."

As she came up the walk she said the yard looked awful
torn and "trompled down"; and she was afraid she would find

it so soon as she heard that the place had been camping ground for the whole army and her away and nobody there to manage the army as she could have done. She greeted me and her niece, and in the same breath told her niece that there was some mud on the steps which ought to be washed off. Then she went into the house, taking off her things and remarking on "things that ought to be done." Presently there was a great stir in the house; she had found out the wounded men. She commented on their presence in such a loud voice that we heard it on the porch, and the men themselves must have heard it.

"Just like Mr. Bradford! If I had been here it wouldn't have happened. The idea! Turning the house into a hospital! I wont have it! Nobody knows who they are. I can't have 'em on my best beds, and between my best sheets and blankets. Dirty, common soldiers! I never heard of such a thing!"

And she got them out before supper.

There was an office in the yard and she had them taken to this. They had to be carried past us, and I can see them now, poor, mortified, shame-faced fellows! I was afraid of Aunt Sally as of a rattlesnake, but I think I could have shaken her then!

Little it was that I saw of Dan or any of my army friends after the battle of Brandy. The Cavalry was too busy watching Hooker's, while our infantry was pushing on toward Pennsylvania, so to spare any time to lighter matters. Every day the boys in gray marched by on their way North.

I watched from the porch and windows if by any means I might catch sight of Dan. But his way did not lie by Bradford's. One morning, however, I saw General Stuart riding by at the head of a large command. I thought they were going to stop and camp at Mr. Bradford's, perhaps, but I was mistaken. As soon as I saw that they were going by without stopping, I ran to the fence and beckoned to General Stuart. He had seen me on the porch, and rode up to the fence at once.

"Aren't you going to stop at all?" I asked.

"Not to-day. In fact we're off for some time now."

"Is Dan going?"

"Yes. He's ahead now with General Chambliss."

"Am I not to see him at all, General Stuart?" I said, trying hard to keep my lip from quivering—I had a reputation to keep up with him.

But he saw the quiver.

"You can go on with the army if you want to," he said in quick sympathy. "I will give you an ambulance. You can carry your own maid along, have your own tent, and have your husband with you. I will do anything I can for your comfort. You would nurse our poor fellows when they get hurt, and be no end of good to us. But it would be awfully hard on you."

"I wouldn't mind the hardships," I answered, "but you know Dan won't let me go. I have begged him several times to let me live in camp with him. I could nurse the sick and wounded, and take care of him if he was shot, and I wouldn't be a bit of trouble; and I could patch for the soldiers. Oh, I'd love to do it! If you come up with him, General Stuart, ask him to let me go, and if he says yes, send the ambulance."

"I'll promise him what I promised you," he said, smiling kindly. "Good-by now. I'll ride on and send him back to say good-by to you, if I can manage it. Then you can talk him into letting you come with us."

I climbed up on the fence to shake hands with him and to say good-by, and I had another word for him. Beneath my dress and next my skin was a little Catholic medal which had been blessed by my confessor. It hung around my neck by a slender chain. I unclasped the chain, drew forth the medal and gave it to him, my eyes brimming with tears.

"It has been blessed by Father Mulvey," I said. "Wear it about your neck. Maybe it will bring you back safe."

I was leaning upon the horse's neck, crying as if my heart would break. General Stuart's own eyes were dim.

"Good-by," I said, "and if you can send Dan back I thank you for us both—I thank you anyway for thinking of it; but— the South and his duty first. Good-by, and God bless you, General Stuart!"

That was the last time I ever saw him, the last time that knightly hand clasped mine. Before he rode away he said some cheerful, hopeful words, and looked back at me with the glint of merry mischief in his eyes, threatening to tell Dan Grey that I was losing my good repute for bravery. Dan did not come back

to say good-by. I had a little note which he contrived to send me
in some way. It was only a hasty scrawl, full of good-bys and
God bless yous.

After saying good-by to General Stuart I returned to the
house. Esten Cooke sat at a table writing. He was preparing some
official papers for General Stuart, I think, and had been left
behind for that purpose. I understood him to answer one of my
questions to the effect that he was going to follow the cavalry
presently.

"Colonel Cooke," I asked humbly enough, for I was ready
then to take information and advice from anybody, "how long
do you think it will be before the army comes back?"

"Can't say, madam."

"Would you advise me to wait here until its return?"

"Can't say, madam."

"Would you advise me to go to Richmond?"

"Madam, I would advise you to go to Richmond."

"You think then it will be some time before the army returns?"

"I can't say, madam."

I felt like shaking him and asking: "What can you say?" He
may have been a brave soldier and written nice books and all
that, but I think John Esten Cooke was a very dull, disagreeable
man.

I waited several days, but as I got nothing further from Dan
than the little note—which was bare of advice because, perhaps,
he didn't have time to write more, and because he may not have
known how to advise me—I took John Esten Cooke's advice and
went to Richmond. I stopped there only a very short time, and
then went on to Petersburg, where mother was. Reunion with
her was compensation for many troubles, and then, too, she
needed me. She had not heard from Milicent since my departure
for Culpeper. Then a letter had reached us through the agency
of Mr. Cridland, in which Milicent had stated her purpose of
coming to us as soon as she could get a pass—a thing it was
every day becoming more difficult to secure—for she was determined upon reaching us before the cold weather came again.
Since that letter there had been absolute silence.

Then came upon us that awful July of 1863, and the battle

of Gettysburg, the beginning of the end. Virginians fell by hundreds in that fight, and Pickett's charge goes down in history along with Balaklava and Thermopylae. There were more vacant chairs in Virginia, already desolate—there were more broken hearts for which Heaven alone held balm. "When Italy's made, for what good is it done if we have not a son?" Again the angel of death had passed me by. But my heart bled for my friends who were dead on that red field far away—for my friends who mourned and could not be comforted.

One of our wounded, whose father brought him home to be nursed, bore to me a letter from my husband and a package from General Stuart. The package contained a photograph of himself that he had promised me, and a note, bright, genial, merry, like himself. That picture is hanging on my wall now. On the back is written by a hand long crumbled into dust, "To her who in being a devoted wife did not forget to be a true patriot." The eyes smile down upon us as I lift my little granddaughter up to kiss my gallant cavalier's lips, and as she lisps his name my heart leaps to the memory of his dauntless life and death.

He was shot one beautiful May morning in 1864 while trying to prevent Sheridan's approach to Richmond. It was at Yellow Tavern—a dismantled old tavern not many miles from the Confederate capital—that he fell, and Colonel Venable, who was serving with him at the time and near him when he fell, helped, if I remember aright, to shroud him. When he told me what he could of General Stuart's last hours, he said:

"There was a little Catholic medal around his neck, Nell. Did you give him that? We left it on him."

And so passes from this poor history my beloved and loyal friend, my cavalry hero and good comrade. Virginia holds his dust sacred, and in history he sits at the Round Table of all true-souled and gentle knights.

draft riots: in New York, 18, 220–24

Dragon, the (naval vessel), 158, 168

Duenkel (prisoner of war), 106

Eighteenth Mississippi regiment, 53, 57, 59, 60

Eighteenth Wisconsin infantry, 36

Emancipation Proclamation, 72, 77, 198

Ericcson, John, captain, 138, 146, 149, 154, 159–60, 163

Evans, Nathan G., colonel, 10

Fair Oaks, battle of, 53

Famous Adventures and Prison Escapes of the Civil War, 79, 181

Fetterman massacre, 51

Fifteenth Massachusetts Volunteers, 5, 9

Fiftieth Illinois regiment, 38

Finley, Jim (Confederate soldier), 55

First Colorado Cavalry, 45

First Minnesota Volunteers, 5

Fislar, J.C., lieutenant, 95n, 99

Fitzsimmons, George H., major, 90, 95n

Fleetwood, battle of, 226

Fort Anderson, 129, 132

Fort Dodge, 50

Fort Fisher: fall of, 113–135

Fort Hatteras, 150

Fort Laramie, 46, 49, 50

Fort Lyon, 45

Fort McKinstry, 48, 50

Fort Pickens, 186

Fort Sheridan, 50

Fort Steele, 50

Fort Strong, 132

Fort Sumter, 4, 136, 185

Fortress Monroe, 120, 140, 145–47, 154, 173, 174, 175, 176

Foster, colonel, 25–26

Fourth Vermont regiment, 23

Fox, Gustavus V., assistant secretary of the navy, 117, 159–61, 173–74, 177

France: role of in Civil War, 72, 183

Freeman, Uncle (slave), 54–55

Fugitive Slave Law, 73

Gains' Mill, battle of, 56–57

Galena, the (naval vessel), 138

Garrard, Kenner (cavalry officer), 204, 209

Gay, Mary A. H., 203

Gettysburg, MD, battle of, ix, 55, 226, 235–36

Goldsborough, Louis M., commodore, 160

Gorman, Willis A., general, 5, 7, 11

Grant, Ulysses S., 63, 66, 199
role of in Battle of Shiloh, 35
role of in fall of Fort Fisher, 113, 115, 121, 126
role of in Indian campaigns, 46, 49

Great Britain: role of in Civil War, 68–69, 72

Green, Dana, lieutenant, 160–61, 170, 172, 173, 177

Grey, Dan (Confederate officer), 227–31, 233, 234–35

Greyhound, the (army vessel), 117–20

Griffin, colonel, 54

Griffith, Richard, general, 53, 57

10/8/87 · HANK